Private Eyes

What Private Investigators Really Do

by Sam Brown
and Gini Graham Scott, Ph.D., J.D.

A Citadel Press Book
Published by Carol Publishing Group

Copyright © 1991 by Sam Brown and Gini Graham Scott

A Citadel Press Book
Published by Carol Publishing Group

Editorial Offices
600 Madison Avenue
New York, NY 10022

Sales & Distribution Offices
120 Enterprise Avenue
Secaucus, NJ 07094

In Canada: Musson Book Company
A division of General Publishing Co. Limited
Don Mills, Ontario

Manufactured in the United States of America

10 9 8 7 6 5 4 3 2 1

Carol Publishing Group books are available at special discounts for bulk purchases,
for sales promotions, premiums, fund raising, or educational use. Special editions
can also be created to specifications. For details contact: Special Sales Department,
120 Enterprise Avenue, Secaucus, NJ 07094

Library of Congress Cataloging-in-Publication Data

Brown, Sam.
    Private eyes : what private investigators really do / Sam Brown
and Gini Graham Scott.
        p.   cm.
    "A Citadel Press Book."
    ISBN 0-8065-1182-6 :
    1. Private investigators—United States.   1. Scott, Gini Graham.
II. Title
HV8088.B76   1991   90-26395
363.2'89'0973—dc20   CIP

Contents

DEDICATION

SAM BROWN: To my daughters Katrina and Felicia, and to their two grandmothers, Grace and Asuncion, who helped them develop their charming, whimsical natures.

GINI GRAHAM SCOTT: To the spirit of adventure, excitement, innovation, creativity, curiosity, and exploration—the inspiration for moving from one project to another, ever searching for something new, in fascination with the world's constant variety and change.

Preface

The revitalization of the P.I. (private investigative) business is taking hold beyond the expectations of many in the field.

The stigma through the last half-dozen decades of the P.I. image has been that of an aloof, alcoholic, uneducated ex-cop who followed errant wives and husbands. Today's private investigation business is a whole other ball game. State regulatory agencies plus continuing education plus professional associations have made the P.I. a respected member of the community. New steps are consistently taken in the industry to increase ethical standards and commitment to excellence.

The business has come a long way from social misfits breaking down doors to gather information. The industry portrayed in the following chapters is as real as the law and confidentiality will allow. The book depicts the various P.I.s as hard-working, diligent individuals whose job is to get the evidence, not make judgments. The trends toward information and technical support have opened a spectrum of on-line database sources that have allowed easy access with the help of a personal computer. And the P.I. has been trained or has trained himself to understand the elements of collecting, assembling and developing information. And information is very much the core of the business.

The chapters in the book reflect a diversity of investigative specialists who are obviously very private about themselves. The investigators speak frankly about their clients and their cases . . . but the clients remain nameless.

Perhaps there is a touch of Sam Spade in the modern P.I.

1

Discovering the World
of the Private Investigator

The American public has long been fascinated by the work of private investigators. Hundreds of films, teleplays and novels attest to this. Yet they also contribute to a romanticized mystique held by the public about what private eyes are thought to do.

For example, the typical private eye in these accounts is tough and burly. He—and almost always it is a he—lives dangerously and carries a gun. He trails people through dark alleys and forsaken warehouses, engages in wild car chases through city streets or country highways. And when not pounding the grubby, crime-infested streets, he is commonly surrounded by beautiful or sophisticated women, jet-setting clients and luxurious surroundings where the wine pours free. It's an image of what might be called the modern-day cowboy—freewheeling, independent, dedicated to the pursuit of truth and justice. And, of course, the private eye invariably solves the case.

While there may be a germ of truth in this, much of it is not true. In fact, a growing number of private eyes are women; most of the work isn't dangerous; private eyes normally aren't even allowed to carry a gun, unless they have previously been law enforcement officers; and the wild and crazy adventures are only a tiny part of the business. It's like the work of cops and lawyers—also full of mystery and romance in the eyes of the public, though other than the occasional high points of drama and excitement, much of it involves quiet, detailed and often routine investigation behind the scenes. And often it can be just this unheralded, behind-the-scenes work that solves or wins the case.

For example, much of private investigation work involves becoming a real whiz at dealing with records in order to find assets and people. In addition, in this high-tech age, many private investigators are becoming computer and communication experts able to work with some of the most sophisticated gadgets for picking up information. Sure, they still do the more dramatic surveillance and undercover work, but this is just part of the story. Today, the world of the investigator involves so much more—everything from the everyday domestic trail-the-spouse kind of cases to investigations to learn about product liability, workmen's compensation injuries, the protection of corporate trade secrets, employee theft, unsolved murder cases—almost any time there is a need for information, a private investigator can be involved.

In any case, I have long been fascinated by both the mystique and the reality. What do private eyes really do?

I think my fascination goes back to when I was seven and started reading Nancy Drew mysteries and working on jigsaw puzzles. There was something intriguing about thinking about how all the clues fit together, like a jigsaw, and there was also that exhilarating mystery of searching for and discovering all these clues.

And then, for a time, I put it away. After all, being an investigator was the stuff of books and movies; it was something that other people did—these shady gumshoe and CIA types that I read about. But then, I came from a very protected middle-class world. So it was not the kind of career to even think about. Just settle down, go to college, my parents said.

However, when I went to school, for a brief exciting time I had a chance to dabble in it. I was at the University of California, at Berkeley, in the early 1960s, and these were wild and crazy times, when anything went, and so, in this try-anything spirit, I called a detective who had an ad in the phone book, and after a little persuasion—I had taken a college course with a noted investigator—he agreed to try me on a few cases.

And yes, it was exciting, though with little training and supervision I managed to do almost everything wrong, and that led me to put my fascination back on the shelf for a while.

The first case I was assigned to went successfully enough. My employer, whom I'll call Norm, assigned me to buy some goods in a bakery, where the owner thought that one of his salespeople was not ringing up everything on the register and was pocketing the difference. I was supposed to watch her, note how much I spent, and collect the register tape. When I came back with the goods—a half dozen jelly donuts, I remember even now—my boss was ecstatic. The tape showed about a dollar less than what I spent, so on my first case, I had actually nailed this employee. And I even had some jelly donuts to eat.

But my next case was a model of what not to do. Encouraged by my initial shining performance, Norm this time sent me out on my first surveillance, and he sent one of his experienced people with me. This was a domestic case, where a man was supposedly cheating on his wife. He was supposed to be having a drink with this woman after work and then driving with her to her place. Soon after I parked my car in position to observe, we saw them go into a restaurant, and then the experienced investigator jumped out to observe them in the bar. "I'll come out when they leave, and then we can follow them," he said.

So my job was simply to sit there and wait until the man came out so we could follow the couple. The only problem was that when the couple went to their car in the next-door parking lot, my companion didn't come out. So what should I do? Wait for him and surely lose them? Or leave and try to follow them?

I opted for the latter, which under the circumstances was probably the only thing to do. However, at this point, I hadn't been trained in following anyone. I was so afraid of losing them, that I stuck very close—so close in fact, just a few car lengths behind them on a street with very little traffic, that they suddenly stopped in the middle of the street, most certainly because they were sure that they were being followed. And then, what did I do? I stopped right behind them, so there we were, two cars parked in the middle of the street. Then, after a few seconds of waiting, the other car suddenly roared off. I did manage to follow them to the woman's house, though obviously at this point, they knew they were being followed. And when they arrived, they promptly pulled the shades and looked out several times while I was staked out across the street. I couldn't have been more obvious if I had put up a sign.

The next day, my boss informed me that the man had gone back to his wife, which was not at all what she wanted, for her goal was to get evidence for a divorce at a time when evidence of fault was still useful in getting more money. She didn't want the guy back.

However, since I was new, my boss was willing to try again, and this time he gave me an undercover assignment. I was sent to San Jose to get to know the daughter of a woman who was suspected of engaging in an insurance fraud with her boyfriend. Supposedly, they had staged an accident in which he rammed her car and then she feigned a neck injury and wore a brace in order to collect the insurance. My job was to get close to the daughter and get her to talk about this, so the insurance company could nail the mother.

At the time, I was just nineteen, a junior at college, and so I decided to take the role of a student at the local university. One morning, I presented myself at the daughter's home claiming to be a staff member of the student paper doing interviews on what was then a hot subject: "How did they feel about integration of blacks into society and what should be done about this?" Amazingly, they bought my ruse, and as I listened attentively and took notes, first the daughter and then the mother offered their opinions. Afterward, since the live-in boyfriend wasn't around, they invited me back.

The upshot of all this is that I soon did become friendly with the daughter, who was about my age, and we started hanging out together. I even had dinner with the family a few times. However, the only problem was that the more friendly I became with the daughter, the more uncomfortable I felt about my undercover role and about trying to find out what the daughter knew about her mother's accident. Soon I just stopped asking questions about the accident, and since that was my whole purpose for being friends with the girl, I was quickly off the case. I had accomplished the first part of the job—getting friendly—with flying colors. But now I wasn't coming up with anything, though, of course, I couldn't tell my boss why.

As a result of that experience and my previous disastrous following episode, I put the thoughts of being a private detective back on the shelf. It was exciting to read about, to see in the movies, but it was something for other people to do.

Yet I think the fascination with the mystique still bubbled under the surface, so that when I saw a small ad in a local free university publication which read: "Learn How to Become a Private Investigator," I knew I had to sign up. I had to get in touch again with what had been a childhood fantasy and a teenage adventure. I had to discover what this being a private detective was all about for real.

And that's how I met Sam Brown, the private investigator who was teaching the course.

As I walked into the small hotel room where the class was held that January of 1988, the image he presented of a private eye couldn't have been more perfect. Sam looked like everyone's preset image of the private eye—tall, husky, in his mid-thirties, a mixture of James Bond, Burt Reynolds, Jack Webb, Dashiell Hammett, and the hard-boiled Mickey Spillane type all rolled into one. Even his name was perfect—Sam Brown, close to the archetypal Sam Spade. And when he eyed me suspiciously for walking in late and wanted to know in crisp tones why I was taking the class, the image seemed even more complete.

Then, when Sam started talking about what private eyes really do, and pointed out, in contrast to that old image, how investigation has become a big business, not just the traditional lone gumshoe, cloak-and-dagger stuff, I was even more intrigued. It was like the blending of my long held fantasies of the private eye mystique and present-day reality, and it was at that moment I decided I wanted to do this book, and Sam was the person I wanted to do it with. I decided I really wanted to learn this business—I wanted to get out in the field and do it right this time. I wanted to learn what to do.

And so gradually, over about two years, this book took shape. Since I was plodding through a fairly heavy schedule in my first years of law school, the project went on hold for a while. But I kept in touch, letting Sam know I wanted to work for him and keeping him posted on my plans for the book. Then, finally, in early 1989, things started to come together. I had a freer schedule, and now Sam had some criminal defense cases that I could work on by interviewing witnesses and checking public records. And so the process started. I began to learn what it's really like to be a private eye. In fact, I actually wrote a book about my early experiences—*Behind the Walls of Justice.*

Meanwhile, Sam began to talk to fellow private eyes about the plan for this book—a look at what they really do and how they feel about their work—and to find investigators who wanted to participate in the project. It took some time to find them since they would be revealing some pretty confidential things abut their techniques and their cases. Though we of course would be changing names, dates, places, and other identifying information to make sure any confidences were protected.

The following chapters are their stories, beginning with Sam's own experiences as a private eye. All of these investigators have been in the field for at least a half dozen years, are licensed investigators (which requires at least three years of work plus a successful exam), and many have specialized in certain areas within the profession or work as general practitioners with a few key specialties. For variety, the investigators were selected with different areas of expertise, or if they were general practitioners, the interviews focused on the areas which were especially interesting to them and which were not already topics discussed with others in the field.

What especially intrigued me about these interviews was not only the great variety of people in investigative work, but also some of the major differences I found from the classic stereotype. For example, in contrast to the tough-talking, action-oriented, fast-on-the-trigger dick frequently presented in books and novels, most of the people I met were quite thoughtful, sensitive, very aware and curious people, who got much of their information from being empathetic and understanding listeners, not by forcing or tricking people into speaking. Some were even very philosophical about what they did as they talked seriously about such issues as truth, justice, and the meaning of their work.

But perhaps most of all, they impressed me as very individualistic and independent, a unique group with pride in their profession, all of them very different. While some of the investigators had come into the field as former law-enforcement officers, others had come into it from less obvious backgrounds. Some were former academics; a few I met had been journalists; one had been a musician; another was a secretary. And some had been bartenders, writers, poets, lawyers, actors, photographers. It almost seemed like investigators might come from just about any profession. And what seemed to attract them to the field was its constant variety, challenge, and opportunity to work in a relatively free-form environment, where they could work pretty much on their own to exercise their curiosity and explore. In a way, the role made me think that the modern investigator was a little bit like the traditional cowboy, the hero of the frontier, who represented a kind of moral individualism—always fighting the good fight, helping the person in trouble, and doing it alone. Or maybe this is just another mystique in a field that has long intrigued with its image of excitement and romance.

In any case, here are their stories. Besides Sam Brown, you'll meet eight other investigators, and I'll describe at the end my own experiences and impressions of the field. Then you can judge for yourself what's fantasy and mystique and what's really true. What do private eyes really do?

—GINI GRAHAM SCOTT

2

Sam Brown:
The Investigation Business

For Sam Brown, today's private eye may still share a little of that traditional mystique and glamour. The image of the lone operator searching for truth and justice may still draw some into the field. But for him, investigation is also a business, much like any other, except that the private eye is in the business of gathering and selling information. Increasingly, he is using high tech tools in which to get it, in addition to the old-fashioned record-checking and plodding the streets.

Primarily, he sees himself as a general practitioner—one who can offer the client a range of information-gathering services. Increasingly he has gotten involved in managing investigations, working alone or with a team of associates and employees he has hired or trained.

Thus, this initial interview with Sam is designed to provide an overview of sorts of the world of the private eye in which the investigator does just about anything—as long as it's legal, as Sam cautioned me. While the traditional image often shows the dick, the shamus, the P.I. solving the case, because as a freewheeling operator, he has been able to go beyond or behind the law, today private eyes operate in a highly regulated environment and most scrupulously pay attention to the law, or they could lose their license. Almost any kind of case can walk in the door; and the investigator can call on all sorts of techniques to help discover the desired information. Amazingly, the average citizen can use most of these techniques too—generally, the private investigator can't do anything the average citizen can't do. But the difference mainly is that the practicing investigator knows what to do and how to do it; he knows the tricks of the trade to get the information missed by others— including sometimes the F.B.I. and the police.

So what are these tricks? Besides interviewing Sam about the private eye business, I wanted to know about some of these techniques.

Sam's a San Francisco native going back five generations. Now thirty-six, he started into the field fourteen years ago with a criminal justice background. He came from a lower-income environment where his father was a taxi driver and his mother was a housewife because there were a lot of children to raise. "So it was a difficult time," Sam remembers, though he came out of the experience with a strong drive for success, and as the oldest son, a strong sense of responsibility too. After three years in the Navy, including a stint in Vietnam in the Tonkin Gulf for eight months, he enrolled in City College of San Francisco to major in criminology with a minor in psychology. His goal was to get into law enforcement, because, as Sam told me, "I like to help people, and I had a strong social welfare interest. So law enforcement attracted me. I had a strong desire inside to save or rescue someone."

After transferring to San Francisco State University, where he studied sociology for two years, he got a certificate in security management from Golden Gate University. Also, he spent some time working with the adult probation department, and attended the San Francisco Police Academy as a reserve officer. This enabled him to attend the Department of Justice Academy to train in becoming a special investigator for the Northern California Criminal Justice Training Center.

About fourteen years ago, Sam started working for a private investigator in San Francisco in the field of retail security, and he also helped with background investigations and trial preparations for attorneys. Then, about seven years ago, when he was twenty-eight, he started his own business, Sam Brown and Associates, using a small room in the back of his house to set up his phones, computer, database linkup, and other technical equipment. At first it was a struggle—"My first year I didn't have any cases," Sam told me—but gradually the business expanded, until now he has an office manager and a few part-time employees and operatives out in the field. In addition, Sam is affiliated with just about every major organization in the business, which include: CALI, the California Association of Licensed Investigators; WAD, the World Association of Detectives; ION, the Investigators On-Line Network; and ASIS, the American Society of Industrial Security. He is also the governing director for the San Francisco chapter of CALI.

So how typical is Sam's background, I wondered?

"I think it's typical in that the majority of investigators do have a law enforcement background, though you'll increasingly find people in the field from other backgrounds. But I think what's different is I have a more entrepreneurial spirit, which helps me to see being a detective in the context of running a business. And for that you have to have an understanding of business and marketing concepts which is the key to success in a business. You can be the best detective there is; you can know just what to do to get the information you need. But if you don't know how to sell your services, it will be difficult to make any money. So I see myself as doing both. Being a private detective as a general practioner, and being in a business, too."

What attracted Sam into the field? What attracts most investigators? The image? The mystique? The adventure? The perceived excitement? Or something else?

"I think it's the diversity," Sam told me. "I know when I first obtained my license seven years ago, there was a certain amount of mystique triggered by the literary and TV/movie image. You know, the image of fast cars, fast women, the debonair James Bond sort of thing. And there were many more men [in the field] compared to women than today, and a lot more law enforcement types, so that could keep up the image.

"But today, that's much less the case. The field is becoming more professionalized, and while many people may be attracted by something they have attained through a television program or a movie, the field is really much more about collecting, assembling and developing information. It's working with insurance companies and attorneys and preparing evidence to be submitted in court. And there's much more gathering information now through databases and on-line information. So many of those attractions of the mystique or image people have of the private eye are unreal.

"But in turn, I think what keeps people interested and it's why I've continued in the profession is because of the diversity. Every case is different. There's something new to do everyday; and there's a kind of emotional excitement you can sometimes feel at being at the center of things; at finding previously unknown or hidden information. It can be a real rush sometimes to discover something new; it's like the eureka experience of the scientist or inventor. And you've found it. You can sometimes feel like a hero for a day.

"However, it's also important to balance this sense of mystique that you may present to others who still hold onto the image or the sense of being the discovering hero with a sense of humility. This is because if an investigator gets a large ego about what he is doing or is attracted to build himself up, he can get into a lot of trouble. The best investigators are the ones who remain silent or humble, because in order to obtain information, it is necessary to be empathetic and understanding, and focus on the other person's needs, so he is willing to contribute to the outcome of the investigation. So generally, you have to learn to ask questions somewhat indirectly and develop rapport so the person answering feels comfortable talking to you. The traditional tough guy approach just doesn't often work, though you still do need to exert your power to control the interview. Thus, it's really a combination of humility and control. And that's one of the things that attracts me too—the challenge of working with people—to help them, to guide them, and work with them to get the information I want."

Now I wanted to know a little bit about the business. Just how many private detectives were there? How big was the typical business? Just how pervasive was this world of the private eye? Sam explained.

"Well, it's definitely growing. Today, there are about 65,000 investigators nationally, about 5,000 in California, with an average of 2.5 people per agency or a total of about 26,000 agencies nationally, 2,000 in California. However, very few of these licensed investigators actually practice on a regular basis. Many of them just work part-time or drift in and out of the field. And then some practice for awhile, but then stop. So though there are more and more investigators and there are rising professional standards, it's still a field where employment can be up and down or hit and miss. But then, perhaps that's because many people are attracted because of the variety and the chance to work independently now and then out in the field and do just part time work. Then, too, many of the people in the field who come in with a law-enforcement background have a pension. Therefore they are not really obligated to work forty hours a week; with a pension, you don't have to work that hard."

Sam also pointed out that the average private detective agency is a small business. There were a few large nationally known firms, with much higher volumes and incomes in the six figures, but in general, according to Sam's observations and an *Entrepreneur Magazine* report in 1988, the average agency grossed about $75,000 to $100,000.

"So it's still typically a mom-and-pop type of business," said Sam, "though the equipment and skills the average investigator must work with are growing more sophisticated every day."

Then Sam described his own business, which showed the kind of mix common for many investigators doing all sorts of P.I. work. About thirty percent of his business dealt with locating people and assets; about twenty percent involved domestic disputes—the typical sort of thing like a husband and wife checking up on each other; perhaps another ten percent was loss prevention—helping companies set up systems to protect against unscrupulous workers and employees; and about five percent was criminal defense work—talking to defendants and witnesses to find out their version of the crime. In addition, his cases included a mix of personal injury, wrongful death, workers' compensation claims, product liability, background investigations, the location of missing persons, and database retrieval. He also occasionally got involved in serving some court papers—maybe two percent of the business, he said.

Like many investigators with their own businesses, Sam started out by doing most of the work himself. But increasingly, his business had grown, so he had to put on employees and associates. Instead, he had gotten more and more into managing investigations through delegating work to others, instructing and training them, meeting with and counseling clients, and keeping track of the results of the investigations through careful reports and files.

"You have to be ready to grow as your business does," Sam told me. "In that way, being an investigator is much like operating any business. So that's what I have done."

My next question to Sam was what kind of people he worked with. Everyday sorts of people who might just have an interest in doing this kind of work? Or did he use people with specialized backgrounds, such as engineering or medicine, for some of his cases?

"Both," Sam explained, "but since there's so much confidentiality in this field, it has to be someone who is committed and serious. It can't be just someone who thinks I'd like to try this. The person has to realize we're often dealing with very private information that affects people's lives. And as for what type of person to hire, a specialist or not, it depends on the complexity of the case. If it's a routine type of surveillance or checking public records, I can train just about anybody with a minimum of effort. But if it's a medical malpractice or products liability case, I may need to get someone with that kind of background—someone who can look at the evidence and come up with an expert opinion. Or sometimes, an expert may be needed just to make sense of the evidence.

"It also helps to have contacts to find these people to work with," Sam added. And then he explained. "For example, I frequently work with independent private investigators, people who don't have their own businesses, but work regularly in the field. And I've met many of these people through the organizations I belong to, such as CALI, the World Association of Detectives, and the American Society of Industrial Security. These contacts are also a source of experts with specialized backgrounds, and then, being a long-term resident of my city—five generations in my case—helps too, because it gives me a lot of contacts. Such contacts are very important in this business, because these people can be a source of information, through their work or their personal contacts. And if they know you and trust you, they may be able to help you by giving you leads or other data. So it makes it much easier to find out what I want to know. By contrast, it's much harder for the person who's new in the field or the city—he just hasn't had the chance to make those contacts."

Sam also noted that his extensive traveling to conferences in the industry helped him in making contacts as well. When I spoke to him, he had recently returned from attending a World Association of Detectives Conference that had lasted for a couple of weeks, and he had a chance to meet other investigators all over the world. "And that can help," Sam observed, "because you may get a case that takes you to another city, even another country, and then you may want to work with someone there, because he knows the area and it's cheaper than taking someone from where you are. Or maybe you may have a request to locate someone who lives somewhere else. By knowing someone who's there, I sometimes just have to pick up the phone and make a call. And then, too, the people from other cities or countries sometimes ask me to help or refer cases to me. So it can really help to be part of this small and closed network of detectives."

Sam gave me some specific examples of how contacts can help the investigator resolve a case.

"Say I have a client who wants to get information from a particular company. Well, maybe through my contacts, I know somebody who works in that company, who may be able to help me look for someone who knows that information, or maybe he can find out what information may be available within the company. A lot of the public contacts or sources of information may be easy to obtain, but the personal and private contacts can take time to develop and are very important. Then, too, a personal contact might give me information which he wouldn't give to someone he doesn't know very well. But then, there's also a price, because every time you ask for a favor, you put yourself in a position where you'll be asked for one and probably two in return. But that's the way this business works. People help each other, and it works two ways. If you want to get help, you've got to be ready to give back help too."

Then, I wanted to know a little about clients. What did he do to find them? What was it like when they first came to see him? How did Sam decide what to do?

"Well, it's much like any business," Sam told me. "Yellow page ads, contacts, networking, that's how they find me. But then, I think there are some keys that are especially important in this business— like honesty and you have to be able to provide a real service. Sometimes, mostly in the past, people have gotten the impression that private eyes can't be trusted. They're sneaky, sleasy, out there for a buck. After all, this is sometimes a spy business when private eyes work undercover. But that all is changing; the business is becoming more professional and codes of ethics are important. You have to convey that integrity to the client, and then that you can provide the service they need. That's number one."

What about the process of assessing a case with a new client and deciding what to do?

"I think the first step is evaluating exactly what they want and thinking how to fill their need if I can. And then, of course, you have to estimate what the services you provide will cost. Today, the typical fee will run about $50 to $75 an hour, though it might range anywhere from $30 to $100. And then you've got to figure in the actual costs and expenses, such as hotels or airline tickets, which can range from the moderate to the low cost or very expensive and first class, if you're trying to present a particular image. Also, if you use a car, travel expenses are billed at about twenty-five to fifty cents a mile.

"Say a person comes into my office who wants to find someone. I'll want to know what information he already has—things like a driver's license number, social security number, address of his last residence, place of his previous job. The more he has, the less I need to do, and if there's not enough identifying information to locate someone well, that makes my job a lot more difficult. So on the average, it might cost about $300 to $500 to locate the typical person. But if there's travel time involved, special complications, that could go into the thousands. And if you're trying to locate someone who doesn't want to be found, then it makes things tougher. And if the person has left the country or has decided to drop out of society, say by becoming a bum or joining a commune—well, you can see how hard that can get. Yet, even so, people leave clues or maybe there are those who know and are protecting them. So even the seemingly impossible case may not be so impossible—but the point is to let the potential client know what the possibilities for success might be, what you have to do, and what it will cost, so he or she can decide whether to do something. It's like being a doctor and giving your diagnosis. Though with private clients you always make sure you get paid up front. That way you're sure you get paid."

And this initial meeting? What if Sam spent a lot of time counseling and advising the client? Did Sam charge for that? And what if the prospective client has a good case, is broke and can't pay?

Sam laughed. "I wish I could charge for every initial meeting or the people I spent a lot of time consulting with. But normally, I don't. Not unless I take the case. It all depends on the private investigator. Some charge for these initial meetings, most don't. It's really a way to assess the case and give the client a way to meet you and size you up. And the amount of time I might be able to give to this initial meeting depends on my caseload. Sometimes I have more time; other times I can be short and abrupt. But in any case, I think these initial meetings are a time for understanding the clients and getting them to focus specifically on what they want. And to evaluate the considerations of what you need to get those things done. So I don't want to charge at first, because I'm really trying to decide whether I can help them or not, and then I want to be really honest about what I can do. Generally, nine times out of ten, I can do something to help them, but then if I can't, I'll suggest some other option—like maybe the person really needs a counselor to help get over a lost relationship, not an investigator to find the person and check him out. Or maybe the client really needs a lawyer to decide if there's any legal grounds for pursuing the case."

And the poor but deserving client, I reminded Sam.

"Well, I do do some pro bono work with certain individuals," he commented. "If they're needy and deserving, yes. I think many other detectives do the same, especially if it's a relatively simple case. Or maybe I might charge less than I usually do, such as happened when one woman on welfare called me. She wanted to get some information to show her ex-boyfriend wasn't able to provide a good environment for their child in a custody case. Since it was just an hour or two to get some photographs and talk to her a little, I took the case and just charged her $25—the cost of the photos and hiring an investigator to go down and take them. Unfortunately, the investigation showed her former boyfriend really did have a good place to raise the kids. He lived in a seedy downtown hotel with a lot of homeless men, which at first made it seem like this wouldn't be a good place. But then it turned out that he was one of the staff members providing therapy to these people, so she really didn't have a good case. But then that's the way it goes. You can only get the information; you can't predict the outcome of the investigation.

"So even in these pro bono or reduced charges cases I try to do what I can. Or if it turns out that the person can't afford the services needed and I really can't take the case, at least I'll make some suggestions on how to pursue it on their own. For example, I might refer them to check some public records, look in the phone book, talk to some former neighbors or a past employer. They may not be as effective as a regular private detective doing this, but at least it's a start."

Sam then described a few recent encounters with prospective clients to show how he evaluated a case and how he decided not to take it. The incidents sounded pretty bizarre to me, but then it was all in a day's work to Sam.

The first case was that of a man who suspected his wife of having an affair with his landlord. The husband wanted to see if Sam could do anything. As Sam explained what happened, it seemed obvious why he had turned the man down.

"He was a Filipino of about forty who had been referred to me by a divorce counselor. And the first thing he did after he got into my office was to pull these napkins out of his pockets and lay them on the table. Then, he asked me to touch them and evaluate them. But of course I didn't, since he said these were evidence, and I didn't know what these were for or where he received them. He explained he had taken them from underneath his bed when he came back from work, because he thought that his landlord upstairs was having sex with his wife and was using these napkins to clean himself off. So what did I think?

"I nearly bust a gut trying to keep from laughing, and I could hear my office manager and another investigator who shares the office trying to control themselves, too. In any case, I knew I wasn't in any position to help him evaluate the evidence; he needed a lab for that. So I simply instructed him to 'Get your napkins off my desk, and stick them back in your pockets,' and I told him to go to a lab.

"Then, I explained that what we could do was install surveillance to see if his landlord was really doing anything with his wife. But he said, 'No, no, that's impossible,' because his landlord lived upstairs, and he didn't think there was anyway we could get a picture of this. There really wasn't much we could do, and so I told him this and he left."

Then, about ten minutes later, Sam got another next-to-impossible case, which also sounded like the stuff of the movies or TV. This was a woman who thought she was being followed by a private detective herself.

"And she wanted us to find the private eye who was following her," Sam told me. "She thinks her brother-in-law hired him, because she filed for divorce two days ago, and the next day, she was out with another man, and she observed somebody on the street taking pictures of her in her car."

So why couldn't Sam find him?

"Look," he said, "there are about 5,000 investigators in this state, and the person taking pictures could be anyone. Without some identifying data to go on, I wouldn't have anywhere to start, and she had no license number, no picture of the man, nothing. So for now, there was nothing to do.

"I told her that if he was still doing this, we could try to grab the license plates from his car or get pictures of him, and maybe I or some other detectives might be able to identify him. But that would be very expensive to just trail her around hoping, so I suggested that she might just be ready to do this herself in the future. Then, too, as I spoke to her, it seemed like what she was really looking for was someone to talk to and listen to her situation, because she really wasn't certain about her decision to file for divorce. There were three children involved and her biggest concern was about them. So she really wanted someone to assist her in her decision—did she really want to get divorced or not. In the end, I finally referred her to a counseling center where she could talk about her problem. It seemed like that was what was really needed, not a private investigator at this point."

But, while such private clients might help to spice up the business, the real meat and potatoes tended to be the larger corporate clients with their need for background investigations on potential employees, workman comp claim investigations, investigations to check for possible employee theft, unfair competition, possible industrial espionage and the like.

And what about official agencies involved with crime, like the police and district attorneys, I wondered.

Sam shook his head. "Sometimes, but not too much. I've worked with district attorneys on domestic relations and fraud. I've worked with state attorney generals on death cases. I've worked with federal agencies, including INS (the Immigration and Naturalization Service), the Post Office, and the FBI. Normally, what happens is they don't hire me; rather, I come in contact with them because I run across some information that would be of use to them or because they have some expertise that I need in working with my own clients.

"But generally they don't hire me and I don't work for them because of the economics. The federal government, for example, pays about $100 a day. But if I'm making from $50 to $100 an hour on my cases, I can't very well contract to the federal government at a $100 a day. Even the criminal cases that come from the public defender's office aren't very lucrative, although I've taken these at times to help out. Basically what happens in these criminal cases is that the public defender's office can't take them on, because it is already handling one accused criminal in the case. So the public defender can't represent both parties legally. What happens is that the judge assigns the case to a private attorney, who then hires the investigator, though the county pays for the investigation costs. However, while these cases can be very interesting, the public defender's office only pays about $25 an hour, and it has ninety days to pay. So we don't get paid until the attorney does, and that can take a long long time, because the bills aren't filed until the case is resolved through a guilty plea, conviction or acquittal, or a transfer to another court. I've had some of these drag on for over six months.

"When it comes to federal cases, the pay on these co-defendant cases is a little better—about $40 or $50 an hour. And when you get capital cases from the county, the fees go up to about $50 to $60 an hour. So I guess you could say in a way that crime pays; the more serious the crime, the more the state or government pays. But then,"—Sam looked a little more serious and thoughtful now—"it really is important to have this representation for criminal defendants, so that they can get their fair hearing in court. Unfortunately, there are usually very limited budgets in these cases, so it can sometimes be hard to do a full investigation and contact all of the supporting witnesses that can help the defendant's version of the case. But you do what you can based on what seem to be the greatest priorities, and you get what you can of that information first. One of the problems is that many people who are arrested do not have the opportunity to pay for their own private attorney and investigators to do this, because they are poor. So they are stuck with this limited budget. And we just do what we can."

I wondered about how it felt to be in this kind of business. What about the stresses, the strains, and the dangers? How much were these a part of the everyday business?

"Well, it's definitely not a nine to five job for most detectives. Oh, sure, you might be able to design it that way if you wanted to just work for another private detective doing things like record searches and workplace interviews. But if you're self-employed or working in most areas of this business, you have to be very flexible and ready to go wherever the case leads. Sometimes you may find you're in demand in the middle of the night to suddenly do things. Or things might go wrong, and you've got to quickly correct them. It helps, as in any business, to use time management, delegating, coordinating, and planning to keep things as orderly as possible. But then you've got to be ready to respond too. So there's a kind of order, but chaos, as well."

Sam also indicated his concerns about safety. Yes, the potential dangers were real, because he was digging up information on people that they often didn't want known. Sometimes the results of his investigation might negatively affect people's lives, like helping put someone in jail. As he told me:

"Sure, there are concerns for my safety and my children's safety. I have two children from my first marriage who live with me, and I know I always have a certain paranoia that something might happen to me or them because of my chosen occupation. I think many detectives feel this. It just goes with the territory, particularly if you do any work on criminal matters. For example, I've put some people in jail and I've gotten a few out on criminal defense cases, so I know I have some people out there who may be mad at me. So to deal with this, I have to be very wary and very careful about what I do to protect me and my children."

Such as what, I asked.

"Well, I think the most important and the easiest thing to do is having a post office box. So I use that instead of my address. Secondly, when I apply for credit anywhere, get a driver's license, or list my address anywhere, I use that. This helps, because this information becomes a matter of public record, and under certain circumstances anyone can reach it. Say if you're in litigation, the other party can contact the DMV for this information or subpoena your credit records. And even if you move, if your old address in on record, it can be used to track you down. For instance, if I have an old address, I can contact the neighbors, and a neighbor might know where you've gone."

Besides keeping his address hidden, Sam also indicated that he took other precautions to protect himself when out on the street.

"I try to be very aware of who's around me, and I make it a point to look in my rearview mirror. Most people don't do this, because they're more concerned with what's in front of them as they drive. But it's important to do this, because you can see who's behind you and maybe avoid a rear-end accident. Also, as I walk down the street I look over my shoulder from time to time. I think that most people in my business develop this same cautiousness. In any case, if I sense that somebody's following me, I take some action to elude him, say by circling back or confront him. If I'm walking, I might slip into a doorway, cross the street back and forth, suddenly stop on the street, get lost in a crowd—it depends on the situation. And if I'm driving, the best thing to do would be to make a U-turn into a driveway and go in another direction. And then I would do it again. The reason for that is there is generally at most a two-person surveillance with two vehicles, and if either one tried to follow you with all this doubling back it would make it really obvious. So they would probably drop the surveillance right then."

But besides having this general paranoia, I wondered, were any of these dangers really real? Had anyone actually tried to do anything against Sam?

"Oh, yes," quite calmly, as if this was to be expected. "Sure. Some people have called and threatened me, told me to get lost, drop their case, that sort of thing. Though it could be anyone, even one of my competitors playing a joke. You learn to live with this. Then, too, I know that people have followed me, though I don't know from which agency, though I think it's probably from a law enforcement agency trying to find out if I'm working on a particular case. And then sometimes I've seen someone trying to check up on the person who has been following me too. Often it can be a crazy world in this line of work. But ultimately, the best protection comes down to being very cautious, very conservative, and not extending your address and telephone numbers to everyone."

"It sounds like this could be a high stress business," I commented, and Sam agreed.

"There's stress involved in dealing with people's problems, and then there's a certain amount of risk. Plus in my case, I have concerns over running the business and raising my kids. So it can be easy to be high stressed in this business. I know I'm the typical type-A high strung personality, and many people in this business are. For example, with all the stress, I have high blood pressure, used to take a lot of medication, and now I smoke a lot, though I try to burn off a lot of tension with exercise. But then there are also many people in the profession who can manage to take it easy, and they're very calm and conservative. So people in this business can respond to the work in a number of ways, though there definitely is a high amount of stress."

So what were Sam's cases like? What types did he prefer? And what were the highlights—the most interesting ones he remembered? What did Sam like the most? He gazed off into space reflectively.

"Well, I guess corporate or white collar crime can be especially interesting. I enjoy it because there's usually a long trail of information on paper, and it's interesting to find out how people conduct their businesses. Sometimes I feel like I'm looking into the guts of the operation, and then, knowing what others do, I won't make the same mistakes on my own.

"Domestic cases can sometimes be fascinating too in that you're dealing with people's fantasies about what is going on in their life and about the role of the private detective in participating in their fantasy. It can be a little like stepping into a soap opera. But at the same time, with lots of long stakeouts, these cases can sometimes become very tedious. Sometimes there can be lots of handholding and emotions, which can be very draining. In fact, I know a lot of private eyes who won't take them because they can involve so much emotion and personal backbiting. Or they feel that the couple shouldn't be using private detectives to spy on each other. They should be using communication to talk to each other and work things out. But usually, they can't communicate, and so that's why someone is seeking a private eye. Anyway, I find it especially interesting in these cases understanding the individual relationship and what brought it up to the point where the person needs a private eye, so I don't make that same mistake myself in my own relationship."

Then, too, Sam found the missing person and lost child cases especially interesting. "When you're trying to locate a family member who hasn't been seen for along time or someone who has disappeared, it's like unraveling a mystery. What happened to him or her? Where did he or she go? And why? Yet while interesting, these cases can also be very serious and dangerous. Take the situation where a child was kidnapped by another parent. That can get very crazy, because you've heard only one side of the story, and you might think the other parent is this monster who has just taken the child to spite the spouse. So you go to the district attorney, get the information you need, get a custody order, and you cross state lines to track down the parent. But then, when you get there, you find the kid and he's very happy living with the other parent. But you've still got this job to do and this custody order, so you go ahead and take the child. You take him back across the state to the parent with custody. Meanwhile, you may have an enraged parent to deal with right there who maybe loves the child very much, so it can be a potentially very dangerous, explosive situation. Though very dramatic, interesting too, because you're dealing with these very basic human emotions."

Finally, Sam especially liked the cases involving travel. "Because I get away from the day-to-day routine. I meet new people. And I can pretend to be anyone I want to be, because when I walk down the street, I won't run into people I know. And I think that's part of the appeal of being a private detective for me and many people—the chance to step into a new persona. For a little while you can be somebody else."

Now the conversation turned to the strategies and techniques Sam or any private eye might use in working different types of cases. We went quickly through the list of the major types of cases he handled, and he described what he did. It was like a crash course in becoming a private eye. Take surveillance, for instance.

"You've got to be sure that the people don't become aware they are being followed. So one key is not to make any eye contact. The easiest way to follow someone is to be across the street. People are not normally looking across the street to see if they are being followed. They're more likely to be looking behind them or in alleys, if they are looking at all.

"Secondly, if you are in a vehicle following someone, it's best to stay to the right of him in the event that he makes a sharp right turn, especially to get onto or off of a freeway.

"Also, the best way to do surveillance is with more than one person. Then one person can get behind the subject and another in front, and one can pick up the trail for awhile and then the other, so the subject you're following doesn't get suspicious. Unfortunately, though, at $50 to $75 an hour, not everyone can afford a two-person surveillance. But generally the norm is that there are two to three people in a surveillance if the client can afford this."

What about finding people who either are hiding or missing or simply dropped from sight?

"One of the first steps is simply to use the white pages of the telephone directory or call 411 to see if there's a listing. It may seem so obvious, but many people fail to do this. So many times, I'll try this first in the areas where the person is thought to be, and often I've been very successful.

"Also, public records are very useful in locating people. They contain addresses; sometimes names of relatives, personal contacts, business associates—all of whom may be leads to where the person is now. For example, there are records when people are married; when they're divorced, when they registered to vote, when they've been sued or have sued people, when they own property. Anyone can get access to these records by just going to the appropriate agency or office where the records are kept, though I'm on line with different databases that allow me to access this information statewide. That makes the process much more efficient. I have access to information on real property, tax liens, foreclosures, notices of default, judgments, et cetera. Then, I can use this information to get the names and addresses of plaintiffs, defendants, cross-plaintiffs, cross-defendants, social security numbers, all sorts of things."

According to Sam, many of these databases were restricted to people who were actually in business, so just anybody couldn't use them. And now, because of privacy considerations, there were going to be even more restrictions in many jurisdictions, such as California.

Then, too, to find people, Sam and other private investigators might draw on their private contacts. "Like who?" I asked, but Sam couldn't tell me. "They're very privileged, so I couldn't very well identify them." He did indicate though that some private detectives might have sources in various government agencies at the local, state and federal level. For instance, a personal friend at the D.A.'s or U.S. Attorney's office might be a source. And lawyer friends might be a source of information too.

Yet, as Sam reminded me, a detective had to be very careful in getting this kind of information, because under certain circumstances, access to it could be illegal. "There's just certain information you're not supposed to know, because of privacy considerations and laws. So getting this information from a private contact in these agencies could well be illegal. It's a real gray area. So without taking the proper and legal steps in order to obtain this information, a private detective could lose his license or be sued."

Then, Sam didn't want to say any more about that topic. "Confidential," he said.

So what about the moral implications of finding someone, I wondered. Did Sam or other private detectives think about that in deciding whether to take a case?

"Well, I think you have to be careful and find out why the person wants to find this other party, and most private eyes will do this too. Say the person comes to me and tells me he wants to locate someone on a personal matter. I would inform him I need to know this information to protect my own interests and that of the person I would locate. Therefore, I would tell this prospective client that I would be willing to locate this person, but I would also want to give the client's phone number to the individual I was seeking. Then, this would allow the person being sought to decide if he really does want to be in touch with the one trying to find him. I think it's important to get all this out in the open and make sure of the individual's motives, because this person who comes as a client could very well have been released from a state hospital or have some harmful intention in mind, and I certainly don't want to be a party to that.

"However, such precautions are usually only necessary when it's a private party who just has personal reasons for finding someone and no legal basis for doing so. It's quite different if an attorney wants me to locate someone so he can serve a judgment or other papers, or if a parent has some documents in a custody dispute. Then, I know I'm acting within the law, and can clearly go ahead.

"On the other hand, if someone clearly wants me to find someone so he can get back at him for revenge purposes, I wouldn't do it, no way. I once had a prospective client who had just gotten out of jail come to me, and he was still pretty mad and wanted to find this law enforcement officer who had put him in. So naturally, in no uncertain terms, I told him no."

But what if people weren't honest in explaining their reasons for finding someone, I questioned.

"Yes, this is very true," Sam acknowledged. "Some people lie. But I try to do as much pre-screening as possible when a new client comes in. Sure it's always possible that someone could fake his or her way through, but I do my best to screen them out. You do what you can do."

Then there's the matter of products liability.

"We get these cases from an attorney handling a client who was hurt by a product, and our job is to help the attorney determine whether the product was up to current safety standards and if anyone involved with the product was negligent. The specifics can sometimes be very complex under product liability law, because whether the product was defective depends on the current state of the art, and negligence depends on whether someone involved in the product from the manufacturer to the distributor to the retailer didn't do something they should have done.

"Suppose you get hurt when you're using a hammer with a piece of machinery. The manufacturer who made the machine could of course be at fault. But the retailer who sold the product could also be involved as a result of selling such merchandise. Also, the liability could extend to the lumber company that made the hammer or the sheet metal company that provided the steel used in the machine. And then the liability might even extend to the company that made the screws used on the machine if maybe something was wrong with them. Maybe the screws couldn't be tightened enough, leading the machine to malfunction due to faulty manufacturing. So the chain of liability can extend quite a bit.

"And that's where the investigator comes in to check out what happened, why, and whether anything like this happened involving this product or manufacturer in the past. It takes a good investigator to track down all these leads and develop the information. But probably the easiest way to start would be to do a computer search for past situations, using a data-base system, and maybe go to a company specializing in such searches to do it. Say the hammer in the case was manufactured by the ABC Ball Pen Hammer Company. One would need to know if articles were written about that company or if that particular type of hammer was involved in other accidents. Then, that could help show that something was wrong with the hammer, and maybe give the attorney some direction in seeking a cause of action against a negligent party in a litigation. On the other hand, if we came back with a clean bill of health regarding past accidents for the product, that could also help the attorney decide what to do."

What types of products were most involved in such investigations, I wondered.

"Just about anything," Sam replied. "From small everyday objects to airplanes. Anytime someone is injured and a product doesn't come up to standards, there's good grounds for a suit. And increasingly today attorneys are pooling their resources to build up collective records of information on products that have caused problems; or several attorneys handling similar cases might hire an investigator as a group. It's a real growing field and the indepth investigation is really important, because if it isn't done completely, many people may not recover as much as they could or at all though they have been victims. They need this information to show a real defect in the product or that someone was at fault in making or selling it."

The whole field sounded really technical and specialized, as I heard Sam talk about the different types of products, machines and vehicles that could be involved in such cases. "Does it help to have an engineering background in these cases?" I asked.

Sam nodded. "Yes, definitely. In fact, sometimes investigators bring in specialists on these cases. For instance, there are investigators who are so specialized in this area that they have an expertise specifically in aviation or fire investigations. So for some of the onsite investigation, of course, you might bring in someone like that. But then, a general investigator could also get involved in checking documents and articles for past accidents. And he might do interviews with the victim or witnesses too to find out more about what happened when the accident occurred, how the person was using the product, what kind of injuries he experienced, that sort of thing. But then, even though some of the information required might be very specialized, the process works much like in any investigation—you figure out the information you need, take into consideration any applicable laws and what your client wants to find out to make his case, and then you decide the best way to go get it."

From products liability it seemed a natural segue into looking at wrongful death cases, possibly caused by defective products. But

Sam pointed out that these cases could be quite a bit more involved. They could involve not only obvious sources of death, but cases of behind-the-scenes cover-up or mistakes in identifying the source of death.

"What sometimes happens here," Sam went on, "is that after a person has died, a family member may be very concerned that there's something more to that person's death than the police reports or coroner's report indicated. For example, everything may seem closed; the presumption is the death was accidental or the person died from natural causes. But there have been cases in which we located other witnesses or reinterviewed people and did a much larger investigation than the law enforcement agency originally involved with the case. And then we have found a different reason or reasons for the death than that first claimed. Or we have been able to identify formerly unknown sources so they could be held responsible through future legal action, such as the manufacturer of a vehicle or boat in a case where a person has died in an accident. Say originally the cause of death might be attributed to the victim's error. But in a careful investigation we might be able to show that something failed in the equipment, so the manufacturer, distributor or retailer had some responsibility for the accident, too.

"And in criminal cases we have also opened up the doors for a person to pursue a rightful claim. For instance, in one case, a law enforcement officer shot someone claiming justifiable homicide; he was just protecting himself. But then, when we reported the case and checked the medical records, we found out the victim had been shot in the back, so there was no self-defense and maybe a justifiable claim for compensation.

"In short, sometimes it can be good to question the accuracy of an official report about a death and check further about what really happened. And then after we collect and review the facts, it may be that the family has some causes for legal action against a particular manufacturer, retailer or even law enforcement official for the family member's death."

In a case of medical malpractice, Sam's job was to find out what really happened; who was really at fault, whether he was working for the attorney, for the patient or for the doctor or hospital.

"It's like solving a medical jigsaw puzzle," Sam explained. "It could be something the doctor, medical staff or hospital did. But then maybe certain conditions of the patient contributed to the death or injury, too. For example, someone dies on the operating table. That doesn't necessarily mean it is a direct cause of negligence in the operating room. It could very well be a number of other variables. Whatever was wrong with the patient could have been misdiagnosed in the first place. But then the question might be, where did that happen? In the X-rays? In the emergency room? Did it happen with the paramedics?

"So that's what the investigator does—tracks down what really happened, using medical records, interviews with staff, maybe learning more about the doctor's or hospital's track record. And in this case, one does need a medical background to help in examining all these possible causes and variables that might contribute to the patient's problem. After all, it might not have been malpractice at all—the patient could have simply died or suffered because he or she was injured or ill in the first place, and there was nothing much anyone could do medically. But the point is to consider what happened in light of the current standard of medical care for a patient with that condition. Then, with the information the investigator provides about what happened, the lawyer can decide whether there's a likely malpractice case."

Now, after this quickie review of the major types of cases Sam and many investigators handled and what they did, I was curious about some of Sam's more special cases. "How about some war stories from the field?" I asked.

The cases all involved travel to find people or to follow them—the classic kind of P.I. job.

The first was Sam's journey through several Western states to track down a person who had run off with someone's truck. His job was to get the truck back.

"This woman had lent it to a friend," Sam told me, "and then he left town with it, and, boy, was she mad. She didn't care about the cost—even if the investigation cost more than her truck—she just wanted it back.

"So, with some leads she gave me, I tracked the truck first to

Tempe, then to Phoenix, and to Tucson, Arizona, and finally to Alamogordo, New Mexico. She had a general idea of where he might go, and that helped. In any case, after about forty-eight hours of traveling by car and by plane, working at $500 a day plus expenses, I finally located the vehicle. It was probably a little crazy given the value of this beaten-up truck, but the woman kept telling me to keep going. She just wanted that truck. I think it was because this guy was a former boyfriend who had run out on her and she just wanted to show him.

"In any case, after I finally caught up with him, I maintained a surveillance of the car, and I saw him loading it full of his equipment and luggage. Apparently he was going to go to a wedding the following day in New Mexico with his new girlfriend. So if I could get the truck, I would be disrupting the proceedings, and I guess that would help my client feel better. It would be like she was telling him: 'See, I've got you, you bastard. How dare you run out on me—with my truck.'

"Anyway, I followed the man and his girlfriend to their hotel which was directly across from mine. Then, as they went in, I parked my rental car at the hotel, and once they were safely inside, I walked across the street, took the truck, and quickly went over to the police station to explain why I had taken it, and showed my authority to do so—the owner's receipt and ownership papers for it. After all, I didn't want to suddenly get busted myself for 'stealing' a truck.

"So the police took the truck, because they said they wanted to inventory it, just to see that everything was in order. Meanwhile, I took my car back to the airport where I had rented it and took a taxi back to the police station so I could pick up the truck. The only problem was when I got back about two or three hours later, there was some question about who owned the truck and what was in it. Then this man I had been following showed up, and he threatened me. 'You S.O.B.—I'd like to break your neck—Tell that bitch what I think of her, too.' That sort of thing.

"Anyway, the police helped to calm him down, and he finally took out his belongings, and I left town in the truck. I then headed back at about midnight, living on coffee to keep me going. I was really tired at this point, and just wanted to get back. But then, around six in the morning, as I pulled into Sentinel, Arizona, I threw a rod in the truck, which cost another $1,500 to fix, plus a $300 tow. The reason for the tow is that after I finally got the truck to a garage to be fixed, I was told it would be a couple of days, so I hitchhiked to Yuma, Arizona, in about 104 degree heat, since there was no bus or other way to get there from this little town in the middle of the Arizona desert. And then I took a plane from there home. Meanwhile, once the truck was fixed, the garage turned it over to a tow company to send back to California.

"So this truck case turned to an even more expensive venture for my client—about twice as much with the thrown rod. But at least she felt she had screwed her former boyfriend, so I guess she was glad she did it. I would probably have chalked up the whole thing to experience and written off the truck if I was her. But then, I'm not the client."

In another case, Sam went off to Hawaii to discover if a husband was seeing another woman.

"According to the wife, her husband claimed he needed to go to Hawaii to reduce his stress. A short restful vacation he told her. But was it just that or was there another woman helping him reduce his stress. She asked me to find out rather than hiring someone in Hawaii because she was here, and she wanted to work with someone local she could meet and trust. Also, if there was any problem with the investigator in Hawaii handling the case, she would have trouble dealing with it from here. And then, if she needed to have any witness to what was going on to back up her claims to her husband about what she discovered he was doing, the investigator would be right here. So her husband couldn't turn around and give her some story and say: 'No, no, I wasn't doing that. You're confused again.'

"So, in any case, I found out what flight her husband was taking, and I had an investigator in San Francisco watch him get on, so he could confirm he was on the flight, determine if he got on alone or with another woman, and describe what they were wearing. Meanwhile, I flew to Hawaii a day early to rent a car, and I arranged to be at the airport there, so I could see if he left the plane with another woman and follow them. I also checked in with my

San Francisco investigator so I knew when to expect them and what to look for.

"Then, when they arrived, I watched them leave the aircraft by the ramp and rent a car. Meanwhile, as they waited for their car, I sat in the parking lot and took pictures, and when they left, I followed them out to their hotel in Waikiki, and shot more pictures of them going into their hotel together.

"The next day, I found out their room number from the hotel clerk, and I was able to watch them leaving and follow them for a few more hours. And it was pretty obvious that they were together, so I had the information the client wanted to know. All in all, it was a fairly routine, easy kind of case, with a trip to Hawaii for a few days thrown in."

And then what happens with this information, I asked. Will she show the pictures to her husband? What do you tell her now that you have confirmed her worst fears?

Sam paused for a moment, then answered thoughtfully. "Well, that's the hard part. I try to break it to her as easily as possible. But then, she's already halfway prepared for this, because she suspected this when she hired me. However, usually, I would recommend that she not show her husband the pictures. They might only make things worse between them if she tries to confront him with this evidence right away. Rather, she should first just explain that she is aware of his activities with this other woman in a calm way, and let him explain. Then, if she has to prove to him she really knows, she can show him the pictures. However, here, for my own protection I would suggest that she tell him she hired a private detective from outside the Bay Area, specifically from Hawaii, who got this information. This way the guy can't find out who I am and come after me. Most wouldn't. But it goes back to being cautious. Reducing my own visibility is a good precaution to take."

So how typical was this kind of surveillance case? And was it usual for an investigation to support a spouse's suspicions?

"Well, they're all so different," Sam reminded me, "though it usually is the wife checking up on her husband, rather than the husband checking up on his wife. Maybe because the husband is usually the one who may be doing the cheating. However, sometimes you don't find anything, because there's nothing to find, and usually this helps to reassure the spouse about the relationship, though again, not always, because there's already some problem in the relationship, and what the spouse really wants is to prove the mate is cheating, so he or she can throw it in their face or use it in court.

"In any case, that's what we found in one investigation, despite having three operatives in the field for three weeks following this guy. It happened in Hong Kong, after a wife contacted me about her husband who was going on a business trip there. Since this business has become increasingly international, I already had some contacts in Hong Kong, and I arranged to meet them there to carry out the surveillance. I arrived a couple of days early to get everything set up, and then, using the wife's information about the husband's flight, we observed him leaving the plane and followed him to the hotel. Then, I managed to get a room right next to his, since my contacts there already had established a good relationship with the hotel clerk, and this made it very easy to monitor his activities. We kept a watch on his door, so we could see him coming and going. We followed him when he went to the restaurant to eat or went on visits with family members, business associates and government officials. And we could observe him around the hotel pool too. But after all that—nothing. There didn't seem to be any obvious infidelity, though he did eat very well. And when I got back, that's what I told the wife. Unfortunately, she was not too happy to hear this news. She had been wanting a divorce, and she thought this might give her a good excuse. But then, after her husband returned, she decided to act as if nothing had happened. And she certainly didn't want him to know about us."

Another area where private investigators sometimes get involved is making an arrest. Though an investigator has no more authority to make an arrest than an ordinary citizen, sometimes a private eye who has seen a crime committed might detain a person under a citizen's arrest until a police officer arrives. Or sometimes a private eye may be called in to help a bail bondsman or a lawyer or party in a court case to help locate, detain and arrest an individual who jumped bail. And in this case, the private eye would be acting under court authority.

"But only if you detain the right person," said Sam, and he

proceeded to tell me about one of his own experiences in trying to track down a bail jumper for a bailsbondman.

"We had a general idea of where this guy might be, since he hung out on the street in a certain town, and we got the word through the grapevine that he might be around staying in a particular hotel. So with that information, I got two other investigators to go with me, and with handcuffs in my pocket, I approached the hotel manager, explained why we were there, and was given the key to the guy's apartment. Of course, since none of us was a police officer, the manager did not have to give me the key; we couldn't order him to do so. But that's one of the things you learn as a private eye—how to use your charm and personality to get people to do the things you want.

"In any case, with the key, we went upstairs, and we opened the door. Inside, there were these two guys without shirts and what appeared to be a woman on the bed, wearing a skimpy dress halfway to her knees, and stockings. But then, as "she" began speaking in a groggy deep voice and looked up at us in a daze, it turned out that "she" was really a drugged up transvestite. Since we had just broken into their party and they were no doubt wondering who we were, I immediately identified myself and my partners as investigators looking for this individual. Then I asked the people on the bed for identification. And at once they just handed us their I.D.s or identified themselves, so that was very easy, and if the guy we were looking for was there, we could have taken him in. But unfortunately, the I.D.'s showed that neither two of the guys was him, and I decided not to detain the third one who didn't have his I.D. with him, because his height, weight and tattoos were a lot different than the identifying data I had. So I didn't want to take a chance on arresting him, because if I wasn't absolutely sure I was correct, I could be risking a charge for false arrest or false imprisonment."

"But what if you thought there was a possibility he was the right person?" I wondered. "Wouldn't you have probable cause to detain him to at least investigate further like a policeman?"

Sam shook his head. "No, there's no difference in my authority from an ordinary citizen, except I'm licensed to conduct lawful investigations, and if I have the proper papers, I can make an arrest. But otherwise, I have no more power than you."

Then, after their lack of success in the hotel, that was pretty much the end of the case. "Unfortunately," said Sam, "the word was out on the street that there were these three guys looking for this particular person, and so he split. So now, he'll probably be pretty hard to find for awhile, since he's on his guard and can blend into the fairly mobile, anonymous, first-name world of the street. But then, this isn't like Hollywood, where the detectives always get their man. Here a lot of them get away, though probably, with this kind of case, this guy will turn up again, when he's arrested for something else. And then the cops will see this outstanding warrant, and book him on that, too. Sure, it would have been nice if we had gotten him; but then, that's life in this business; and eventually, someone will probably bring him in."

One of the issues that continually comes up for the private detective is what's legal and what's not in obtaining private information. How far can the private eye go in using secret personal sources, such as friends and paid informants? And when is it okay or not okay to use a pretext to get information? I asked Sam about this. Just where and how do you draw the line?

"Well, just about everyone in this business uses private sources. These can be friends, business associates, new contacts. And sometimes you ask people for favors and sometimes they give them to you; they know someone or something, or they have a lead. Or sometimes they close up. It all depends—on the circumstances, on who you know, on the possible dangers, on the force of your personality, what they think you can do for them in return. Say you go into a hotel and want to find a room number? Well, what do you do? Do you send flowers over to the bellboy and follow the bellboy up in the elevator? That can work, and I've done that. Or maybe a private eye might lay a little cash on the table, and say: 'Hey, I've got to find this guy? Where is he staying?' That approach can work too, and I know people who have used it."

And what about the pretext of pretending to be someone else, I wondered. At what point might that be illegal?

Sam replied. "If you represent a particular entity or person that's living, that would be illegal—it's called misrepresentation, and it would be even worse if you pretend to be a government official, or even more so if you tried to claim you were with the police. However, if you claim to be someone who doesn't exist, such as a representative of a non-existent company or a made-up person who's a friend, that doesn't violate any name. So if you want, you could invent a company name for yourself. Or you could use another name. And that's fine. For instance, bill collectors, investigators trying to find someone do this all the time."

And then there were the many situations where a private detective might be doing something where the line between legal and illegal wasn't so clear. For instance, something might be technically legal, but it might appear to be against the law, and that could create problems for the investigator, too. Sam gave me an example from his own experience, where he encountered some problems while collecting someone's garbage—now a legal activity, at least in California, since trash is considered to be abandoned property. But even so, it created a touchy, tense situation, as Sam explained.

"The incident occurred when I was hired by a client to conduct a surveillance in a suburb outside of San Francisco. I was there very early in the morning, about 6 A.M., and I noticed it was garbage day, since people had put out their trask for a pick up. Now, according to a 1988 legal decision, any abandoned garbage can be collected by anyone—garbage people, dogs, anyone who wants it, and anything left out on garbage day would be obviously abandoned. So I decided that I could pick up this person's trash, in order to check it for evidence—in this case receipts—to show what this person was believed to have done—possibly stealing from my client's business. However, I didn't want to look through this garbage just then, in the middle of the surveillance. So I decided to just take it, put it in my trunk, drive around the block, and then continue the surveillance.

"The only problem is that when I did this, there was a neighbor who liked to get up early. He saw me and called the police. So a few minutes later, as I'm sitting in my car back on the surveillance, these three police cars with flashing red lights suddenly pulled up behind me. After I identified myself and explained I was on a surveillance, they wanted to know what I was doing looking through people's garbage. Meanwhile, I saw this one police officer eyeing my trunk. Then, I asked if we could move around the corner to discuss this further, and again I explained my purpose in doing the surveillance. 'But why were you looking at or picking up garbage?' the police officer asked again.

" 'Just part of the surveillance,' I said, hoping this would satisfy him, and fortunately it did. Also, fortunately, they didn't ask if I had the garbage in my truck, and I didn't volunteer the information, because they could have very well impounded my car and removed it. Perhaps they might have done so, but at this point, an emergency call came in, and they said they had to leave. They told me to notify them the next time I would be doing a surveillance in the area, which is something I and many private eyes often do—let the police know in advance.

"In any case, after they left, I felt relieved and thought everything would now be fine. I stayed there for a few more hours; then left with the garbage. However, the client's former partner, who was the one under surveillance, saw the police cars and my truck. He called the police, and got my plate number which had been recorded by them, and then ran a check on my number. He told his attorney, who then called my own client's attorney asking why this private detective, Sam Brown, had been arrested, which was wrong of course, since I was merely questioned. And then the attorney commented that if the other attorney's client wanted his garbage, he would be more than happy to dump it on his front lawn.

"Needless to say, though I hadn't done anything illegal, my client was still concerned about the potential for liability in taking his ex-partner's garbage—maybe as a kind of invasion of privacy, though probably that wouldn't hold up in court. And certainly, after this, I couldn't follow the man anymore, nor could anyone else for that matter for awhile, because he was suddenly extra alert and cautious.

"So sometimes as a private eye you can encounter these very gray areas. What's legal or what's illegal? Sometimes it's not totally clear. There are a lot of judgment calls you sometimes have to make, and it can come down to just using good judgment—and then too, hoping for good luck so you don't end up in a situation where doing something legal looks illegal, but can end up causing all sorts of embarrassment."

Since Sam's garbage case had highlighted the privacy issue— what's private, what's not, I asked for his views about privacy generally. Here he was in a business that involved finding out very private information about people and revealing it, at least to his client. How did he feel about this?

"Well, I think you have to look on this as a business," he replied. "I, other private eyes, are in a business to make money, and I think it's important to be guided by the current law. This way you do what's legal and don't step over the line. Wiretapping, for example, is something private investigators do not do; mostly it's just local, state and federal governments. But law enforcement agencies can get a court order to wiretap, and after ninety days the subject is supposed to be notified or indicted. If there's no evidence, the wiretapping might just be stopped without notification. But how often this happens, who knows? And who's going to tell? A privacy invasion? Maybe? But then it's protecting a larger public interest, like protecting against a crime.

"On the other hand, I think some techniques of the investigator can go too far. For example, I think the polygraph is an invasion, and I think taking a person's body fluids in a drug test or for a nicotine test or an alcohol test is an invasion, too. Also, if someone is going to extract blood or urine, I think that is an invasion. I think we sometimes have to balance those invasions with the needs of society, such as we do when we allow the police to make a roadside test for sobriety. Likewise, I believe these tests should be conducted in work places, where there are safety or security concerns involved."

But what about the cases that raised hard moral questions, whether they were legal or not. What did Sam or other private eyes do about them in deciding whether to take a case? What types of cases might they turn down?

"I think sometimes you have to look at the person's motive in these personal types of cases, particularly those involving child custody or marital dispute. You want to be sure that the person isn't going to use the information for illegal or violent purposes, such as what happened in this case where a nut found out the address of an actress and gunned her down. And looking at motives can be especially important in these child custody or kidnapping cases, because I think the best interests of the child should be considered. And it may be that if you think real harm is going to be done to the child, by locating him or her, or kidnapping the child back for a parent with custody, maybe you should turn it down.

"So to some extent, I and other private detectives I know do do some advance checking through pre-investigative inquiries. I might contact a district attorney, say, if there's been a history of domestic violence in a relationship, or maybe I might contact some neighbors to see what they know. Many times, though, you don't have time to do much of this. You have a client telling you: here's the plane ticket; here's your money. So time is of the essence. Or I have orders from the court permitting me to pick up this child. So any moral concerns might really be moot. It's all really up to the courts.

"But then, there are just some cases where you don't know in advance exactly what's going to be involved, so, yes, you might end up doing a case that raises these moral questions, and you wish you weren't doing it. But you're already involved."

Sam gave me an example.

"I've been helping a family who moved here from Asia find out where their daughter is. The girl is twenty-one, and she left home because she wants to be with this guy who she used to work with back there and he followed her all the way here because he wants to marry her. Her family doesn't want this, since he's in his thirties. The daughter split and left a note saying that they're getting married and the family should leave them alone.

"But the family doesn't want to do this, and so they've been trying to track the daughter down. They even managed to find the place where the daughter and her boyfriend used to live. Because the family has a real need to control the children, I got the case. And I've been trying to find the girl and the boyfriend, too. But this started before I was able to find out what the family is really like, and they've been literally driving me crazy. For instance, the mother called me three times today wanting to know whether I found out anything, and five other family members have been phoning me too.

"Well, this is a case where the girl's over eighteen, and according to the law, she should be free to live her own life, and I say, let her live it. Unfortunately, I got deeply involved before I realized the intensity of the family's need to control one of the children, and had I known, I probably wouldn't have accepted the case. Even the police are aware that this family has been trying to track her down, and they don't want anything to do with the case. Leave the girl alone they say. So finding her probably won't have a good outcome for the family anyway, and it'll just bring about a lot of grief for the girl and her boyfriend. And there could be problems for me too, if the couple decides to file a restraining order against the family, saying there's a private detective following the pair around. So it's one of those cases I would have turned down in the first place if I had known, and I wish I had."

And what about the child custody cases, I wondered. Had Sam ever turned down or felt like turning down any of those?

"Again, I think it goes back to having certain ethics and standards that I and many other private detectives adhere to. And since every case is very different, you need to judge it against this. It helps, for example, to look at why the mother or father wants the child back and to consider if there's any possible serious harm. It could be that the parent requesting the child's return may have some ulterior motive, like merly getting back at the spouse. There could be incest involved, and that's why the child was removed from that parent. There could be drugs involved. For in a lot of these cases, the child has become not only a pawn but a victim in this marital dispute. So if I feel like this is happening, I wouldn't take the case.

"Usually, though, where I get involved, there is already a court order that says the child will not be removed from this state. But then the other parent has taken the child away. So this is basically a case where I am returning a child who has been taken out of state, and it's completely legal, bringing him or her back like one would a car. So the law is on my side. Since laws in various states are different, it's important to research the law in each state and check with other detectives there to be sure, so you don't end up getting sued or jailed for child stealing or kidnapping. Usually, the legal authority of the court order in the state from which the child has been taken will apply. But then, there could be special circumstances or even a legal battle over the jurisdiction of the court that issued the order and over the legality of the order. So it's important to check.

"In short, it's important to take into account these moral issues, and be ethical in what you do on the cases, just like you might be in any business. The bottom line is the law. You've got to know it and stay within it. Otherwise you can be sued and put out of business. So it's a big concern in this business—being ethical, moral, and staying within the law. The popular image of the private eye may not suggest this, but for the professional private eye today, this is quite true.

How does being a private eye affect one's social and personal life? Does Sam do anything differently in his relationship with others as a result of being a private eye?

"Yes, very definitely, it has an effect because of the perception people have of the private eye, and because of the time and personal commitment involved in this business. For instance, in a social situation, such as a party, when I meet people, I usually avoid saying: 'Yes, I'm a private detective or a private investigator,' because that can sometimes make them feel very nervous or self-conscious. They might wonder, 'What are you doing here?' or 'What information are you looking for?' I would say something instead like I have an investigative security company. It makes it sound more like an organized business structure, and it gets away from the mystique people have of the private eye."

Sam also pointed out that being in this business often made it difficult to get close to other people.

"I think most people are afraid to get too close to you, because they assume that you may be looking at them like a subject in a cloak and dagger investigation. So they feel anxious, self-conscious. Or they are distrustful, because they feel as if I have some need to find out information about them.

"Usually, though, in social situations with a group of professional people, things go quite smoothly. They are usually fairly confident and sure of themselves to begin with. But sometimes, if I'm with people who aren't respectful of the law, knowing I'm a private eye can make someone very nervous. It's like they're concerned I may be checking up on them—although if I was, I certainly wouldn't introduce myself as a private detective. I'd probably be undercover as something else, if I worked that kind of job."

And what about personal relationships? Did being a private eye make this more difficult too?

"I'd have to say yes," Sam observed. "It's very difficult for anyone to understand my business, because I'm involved in looking behind the everyday facades people show to the world. The unpredictable work schedule makes it difficult, too. Because it's very difficult to maintain a relationship not knowing from one day to the next what may come up. Every week, every day, there's a different type of case, and I never know what hours I'll be working. It's very unpredictable.

"At times, for example, I can slip out of my office at two o'clock in the afternoon, pick up my daughter at school, and call forward my messages or have someone else manage the phones while I'm gone the rest of the day. But there are other times that I'm occupied till eleven or twelve o'clock at night in the office, setting up appointments with clients, catching up on paperwork and files, or just talking to clients, because sometimes people really want you to listen so they can develop a trust in the relationship, and I just have to take the time to do this.

"I know my job affected my former marriage, because I did a lot of work on weekends, doing security investigations mostly, so I wasn't around very much. And then I feel as if I'm married to my business, and it was difficult for my former wife to understand this kind of commitment. Eventually, we got divorced my second year in business, and she's remarried and no longer a part of my life or my children's.

I had one final question. What were the current trends in the field?

"Toward computers. Toward international growth," Sam began. "The big trend today is toward the computer data-base retrieval of information. You see more and more networks and sources of information growing up. Then, too, the field is becoming more and more international, and I think you'll see more of that in the future. Many international companies are diversifying and they're expanding beyond their own country, and as they do, they have a growing need for information, because information is power and money. And that's one thing the U.S. is in a position to export very well— information and technology, so you're seeing a lot of U.S. investigative firms expand into international investigations. This field is becoming more and more professionalized, more and more sophisticated, and in today's information age, it's growing very fast. So I think you're going to see more private investigators, and more and more skilled professional ones. And I think these developments are going to help in improving the image of the private eye, too."

3

Seth Derish:
Finding People and Assets

Sam and I met Seth Derish in his cozy San Francisco office on Nob Hill, where he both lives and runs his business with his wife, Sarah. The place might look like an everyday home, but the office part was bristling with the latest high-tech equipment, the tools of the trade, which Seth uses in doing what are his main specialties in the business—finding people and assets for financial background and personal injury investigations. As we began the interview, I noticed that Seth looks very much the image of the liberal, political reporter-activist, which he once was before getting into this business. And in fact, Seth's political philosophy and ethical ideals influence very much the cases he will take. It's his way of supporting truth and justice by providing information to people espousing the causes or principles he accepts himself. And it's a search that has led Seth to some very intriguing investigations to find people or assets.

Seth got into the business, after graduating from California State University at Chico in 1974 and spending some years as an investigative reporter. From the start, Seth was motivated by exposing injustice and the exploitation of others by those in power, and in 1975, he won *Rolling Stone* magazine's first national award in investigative reporting for exposing a police frame-up of a black activist in Chico, California. As Seth describes it: "The activist was trying to reveal some information about this bully sergeant in the Chico police department, and the police set him up with a gun and got him on felony charges because he had previously been convicted of a felony. So he now had a new charge of felony with a gun. An informant told us how the police had set this whole thing up to frame the guy, and then, when they decided they didn't like their own snitch any more, they threw him in the local jail too. In any event, as I wrote in my article, the wheels of justice didn't work, and the activist still went to Folsom for two years. And he couldn't get the sentence overturned. I tried writing a letter to the judge, but I was just threatened with contempt for interfering with the process of justice. I didn't think there was anything else I could do, at least then, because now I would know what to do differently, such as take the matter to the state attorney general's office or let the D.A. know I have facts contrary to his or her case."

After leaving Chico, Seth lived in Israel for a year and traveled through the Middle East, working as a journalist. Also, he traveled through many other countries as a reporter—Australia, England, British Honduras, Mexico and Spain.

When he returned to San Francisco, he tried for a job on the *Examiner,* but the editor told him to get a few years of seasoning out of town. "He even offered to get me on a Midwest daily for two years, and then when I came back he said he would hire me."

But Seth didn't find this option very inviting, so instead, he answered an ad as a legal secretary in a blue-chip San Francisco law firm. However, soon, after learning to do the things that legal secretaries usually do—typing briefs, pleadings, interrogatories, subpoenas, and discovery motions, Seth found his investigative reporter background turned out to be very useful. "Say I'd be asked to do a discovery motion, interrogatory or subpoena to get information. And I'd tell my boss, look, you don't have to get that information through formal discovery. I can just go and find it out for you. I just have to interview people and check some public records, and then you can get this information without the other side knowing you have it. So that's how my investigative career started. I was still technically a legal secretary, but also doing investigations for this firm. And then, after about six months of this, this young associate I was working for decided to start his own law firm, and I became his chief investigator and then managed the firm. Then, after one year I got my own private investigator's license and hung out a shingle."

His past investigative reporter background turned out to be a real advantage. "A lot of private investigators come into this from law enforcement. But my advantage was that as a reporter, I was already covering government, politics and business fraud. So I already knew the ins and outs of checking records and talking to people about this kind of stuff. And when I switched over into doing these investigations as a detective rather than a reporter, it wasn't that much of a change."

Yet he also had a few mentors who helped him in learning the business, including Michael Douglas, a former stage star in the American Conservatory Theater of San Francisco, who opened up an agency in Los Angeles, and Gene Marshall, who was the chief investigator for twelve years for the well-known San Francisco attorney, Melvin Belli. "They helped to show me the ropes," Seth told us. "For example, Gene Marshall taught me not to fear anyone no matter how important. You can get information from anyone, if you just are confident and know how to ask. And Douglas taught me a lot about human nature and how to use the skills I had as a reporter and interviewer to get people to talk and tell me things. For instance, besides giving me tips on motivation, he showed me how to get information by using certain phrases to be persuasive, and he taught me about things like gags, pretense calls, and pretense meetings, where you create certain scenarios or situations that motivate to people to talk."

And what has kept Seth in the business all these years is the excitement and the diversity. "I just love this business and its diversity. You never know who's going to call. You never know where you might be taking off to do something. And if you do it right, you can make a fair living from it." Though Seth has dreams about going off to Central American to write a novel, for now, he not only investigates some cases himself, but increasingly manages an office with a team of investigators working for him.

What type of cases? Mostly financial background investigations and personal injury investigations, Seth explained, with about 60 percent of the business involving prejudgment and postjudgment asset investigations, and about 30 percent consulting, including due diligence advice to companies contemplating entering into a contract with another company or individual. "We check out the background to make sure its advisable to enter into the contract, purchase the company, go through with the merger, or make the loan." Also, occasionally, Seth might do some trademark work to police whether a company's logo or name was being used illegally, so it could protect itself from having its name connected with knockoffs.

However, as Seth made clear, because of his own political leanings and philosophy, he would handle only certain type of cases. Many private detectives don't do this, but Seth emphasized strong beliefs that guided his practice.

"I guess my approach is fairly unique, but it's my nature. That's why I'm always on the side of the plaintiff and always on the side of the aggressor in these personal injury and financial background cases. That's the kind of person I am. I want to work on the side of the person who's been disenfranchised by the system, even if it's a corporation that's been disenfranchised or taken advantage of by someone else. I like going after the big guys and trying to get something back. Defending is actually where there's a lot more money and steady work, but I do what I choose to do because of my personal commitments."

So what kind of cases did Seth turn down? He gave some examples.

"Well, sometimes I may turn down a corporate job, because I don't feel comfortable with the company's approach, if I don't feel it's ethical. And I don't do any more criminal defense work. I used to handle some criminal cases. I did five capital death penalty cases, and I had a pretty good reputation in that field. But when the attorneys called and they wanted me to do rape defense work, I wouldn't do it. And they would ask me: 'Look, what are you going to do—

selectively pick what work we have?' And so eventually that kind of work dried up.

"Also, I don't do domestic cases anymore. I feel there's a lot of trouble in those kind. You have high emotions. You have invasion of privacy problems. I also feel that maybe these people that I'm supposed to be investigating may have a legitimate right to do what they want with other people. And then, often these clients are having you get the information so they can use it as a tool to get back on somebody, and then they may often turn on you as fast as on their spouse. It can be a pretty messy business. So the only work I do on a divorce case now is on the financial end of it, say if one of the spouses is hiding assets on the other, and my job is just find those assets."

As Seth acknowledged, this pick and choose approach to cases wasn't typical. "Most private eyes will take whatever happens to come to them, which certainly makes good business sense. But I've always wanted to be selective. I just have these strong moral principles, which I've had ever since I was a kid. Maybe it comes from growing up in a family on the Lower East Side of New York, where we were involved in fighting with the unions against management. But, no, most private eyes are not choosy in accepting their cases.

"But then, perhaps this fighting moral attitude does give me an advantage in a lot of ways, because I always challenge authority. And that can often open doors or get me information I wouldn't otherwise get. For example, when someone tells me, 'You can't have this record,' I always find out what my rights are and whether I can have the information or not. Also, this approach has helped me in figuring out what the dynamics of the group or politics are, so I'm better at motivating people to give me information. I've always looked at the way information is shared and the way people in power or in relationships deal with each other. I've tried to understand the corporate mentality or government mentality. Then, I've used this understanding to figure out how to best relate to the person from whom I'm trying to get information. This has been helpful, because you have to look at the person you're talking to and figure out what motivates that person to do things. Then, you can motivate them to do something they normally wouldn't do, such as give out some information."

Yet, while Seth may have a special approach to the business because of personal philosophy and political leanings, it's still a business.

"You have to think of it that way," Seth explains. "Though the one thing I don't like about the business is that as you get more successful you tend to manage cases rather than work them. Why? Because it becomes more expensive to run a really efficient office."

Seth pointed around his office by way of explanation to an array of buttons and dials.

"Today, you really need the access to the high technology data systems to offer the best service possible. So that's why I have the latest computers. I buy all the latest microfiche. I subscribe to all the databases. So I can locate someone or their assets much more quickly and for a fraction of the costs than someone just starting out or without this stuff. But it takes capital to create this system, and there's more money in managing cases with other employees doing the work then working on an hourly rate myself."

For a moment, Seth sound almost wistful for that on-scene excitement as he described some of the everyday realities of the high-tech investigation business—explaining budgets to attorneys, preparing reports, and advising about the limits of the investigation. Indicating, for example, that an overview of a person's real estate holdings is not the same as a title report—"That way," Seth explained, "the client doesn't come back to you and tell you that he tried to take the property, but the guy didn't own it anymore; he sold it the week before. So part of the business is explaining these things—like we're just providing an overview, not date-stamping, so there are no guarantees."

And then, much of the other side of case management involves working with employees out in the field to make sure they know what they are doing and do a good job. To lay the groundwork, Seth would do much of the records investigation work himself, using his computer and database system. Then, he'd send his employees out. As Seth observed:

"The way it works is that when a new case comes in, say for a field investigation, we first take it in-house and develop some background information. If it's a personal injury accident case, we'd look for information on what are the facts in the case, who are the witnesses, where do they live. We also order the police reports. Then, when the field operative goes out, he or she already has a rough idea of what the objectives are and what to look for.

"But more than that, it's important to provide training. You have to direct people to get the right thing and teach them not to miss clues. And then, when they return with their information, I check every file or report for accuracy, and usually, I have to do a summary report too."

So now on a typical day, Seth might have six or seven people out in the field doing interviews, checking records, serving papers.

"I just can't do it myself anymore," Seth commented. "It's hard to do all that by yourself and manage, too."

It seemed a long way from Seth's days as a political activist and investigator to business manager. While there was still plenty of room for the on-the-streets field operative, usually a subcontractor, working at around $15–$20 an hour, or perhaps $25 if they were really experienced, most of the private eyes running a business were increasingly moving into managing cases, like Seth, not working them themselves.

Yet, at the same time, as Seth pointed out, it was becoming an increasingly competitive business—both for employees wanting to work as private eyes and those managing the business.

"I think the field is growing today," Seth commented, "because of TV, the exciting P.I. mystique, and maybe people are bored with their day to day jobs because increasingly, they're just pushing buttons. With computers, things are becoming more and more routine. For example, I've had a lot of lawyers contact me, tell me they wish they could do what I do, because it sounds like fun—something different all the time, and more exciting. And then, several stockbrokers have contacted me, too, wanting to know more about this gumshoe stuff.

"But now increasingly, it's a real hard field to enter. There are so many people out there with licenses. It's become like real estate associates. So for someone entering the field, the best thing is to have some skill that's unique; some way where you have an advantage in getting information compared to someone else. A stockbroker, for example, might be really good in finding out about financial data, such as digging up background data on who does initial public offerings. So that's a special skill he might bring to the field. Or if someone was previously a loan officer, that might help him in getting work doing background financial investigations, because he already knows how the banking and financial systems works. On the other hand, a person with a social worker background might be especially good at getting people to talk. One of my best operatives, whom I met at a pool in Mexico, was a social worker for ten years, and he is really good at dealing with people. They like him and he knows how to get people to talk. So today, a person can't normally just get a P.I. license and hang out a shingle, advertise, and expect to make a living. The field's too competitive. It's become big business. But on the other hand, if a person looks at what he does everyday and is good at, that could be a way of getting in and finding a niche.

"And then, when you're in, it's really a hustle," Seth added. "When you're in business, you've got to fight, you've got to claw, you've got to hustle all the time. You've got to make sure your clients are happy and hang on to them, that nobody's moving in on them. But then, if you do a really good job, they'll always come back."

So increasingly, as Seth described it, the world of the private eye was becoming like a jungle—not only out in the field looking for information, but in the arena of business, too. And yet Seth somehow has been able to move through it while holding onto his philosophy and political ideals. It seemed a strange and unusual mix; yet by following his own philosophy of finding his own niche based on his particular combination of skills (investigative reporting and a strong background in financial and government investigations), Seth was able to make this work.

Financial investigations may not have the adventure-packed drama of a hunt for a notorious criminal or child kidnapper through three continents as described by one private investigator. But it has its own quiet puzzling-it-out fascination, as described by Seth.

"The most usual, standard type [of case] is the postjudgment collection. In other words, our client has a judgment against some people, and needs to collect it, so we get involved in locating bank accounts, real estate, securities, and motor vehicles. Then the client can take his or her judgment, get a writ of execution from the court and levy on that property and sell it if need be.

"The second type of investigation is the prejudgment case. This usually occurs when an attorney is evaluating whether he wants to take the case, and he'll tell you what he feels the estimated value of the case is worth, based on what he thinks the case might bring in damages. I may start by asking the attorney what he judges he can collect. The point is that the case needs to be worth enough to take on or sue on it in the first place. In turn, the amount of assets the other party has could affect what the value in damages might be or whether or not there's anything to collect. So then, what we do in these prejudgment cases is find out what these assets are and where they are. In a way, I'm being hired to be like a loan officer at a bank, and I'm conducting a loan investigation, though without the benefit of the information on an application. And then, like a loan officer, I get involved in evaluating the party's past history. I look at how they've handled themselves and their stability in the community, how much real estate they own, how long they've been registered to vote, and do they pay their bills—that sort of thing. And commonly, these are money claim cases, where the person or company I'm checking hasn't paid some money due, and usually this is because they are in a lot of trouble. So they're trying to protect whatever assets they have. Thus, the big skill in these cases is to determine if they're hiding their assets and how you are going to get those assets.

"Then, thirdly, we do what are called 'due diligence' investigations. These occur when a company or individual is going to enter into a contract with another company or individual or is going to lend money or become involved in some kind of merger, acquisition, franchise or other arrangement. Say a venture capital company is going to lend money to somebody to start in business. Or a franchisor is considering lending money to a franchisee. Our job is to check out the backgrounds of the principals to see what their financial history is. How well have they done in paying off their bills and their assets. We're really acting like a super-sophisticated loan officer in doing the search. In fact, in these big-time Wall Street deals involving stocks and initial public offerings, private investigators are used all the time to check things out."

But if Seth was essentially acting like a loan officer, why didn't the clients just go to their regular bank.

"Because," he explained, "the investigator does a lot more than a bank would do. The bank loan officers just do what they're trained to do, which is to run a credit report and maybe call a couple of the references to companies or employers. But they don't have the time or training to get this other information, such as whether this guy was convicted of embezzlement in Florida twenty-five years ago, or if there's a bankruptcy on file before the credit was given. Then, too, they might not find out that there was some litigation involving these principles in various counties. We just have better sources of information. It's all usually in official records somewhere, but we are better able to get it, and that's where the banks are limited."

Seth gave an example of typical due diligence investigation.

"Let's take securities. Say somebody has a company that's going to sell stock on the stock exchange. Before stock is put up for sale, they have to do what's called an initial public offering which is put together by the investment bankers. So, since the bankers don't do these detailed background checks themselves, they'll come to a private investigation company like us to check out the background of the officers and principals of the company. They want to make sure the people haven't been sued for fraud or bankruptcy or whatever, so we check that out. And the same thing occurs when there are mergers and acquisitions, stock offerings, real estate partnerships, really any kind of deal where someone is going to get involved with somebody else in a business arrangement.

"And it can be really important to do this and then to act on what you find. Otherwise, the client can be heading into a disaster. For instance, I had one case where a client called me and said, 'These guys are going to get a $15 million hotel lease, so check them out.' And I did this, and then I told the client not to do business with these people, because they had a lot of problems. They had a fairly unsavory background involving some litigation and a poor payment record. About a year later, another client called me to do some other kind of investigation and mentioned that he had done business with the same guys I had checked out and warned this other client against. But in this case, they hadn't done a due diligence search before going into business with them, and the client told me: 'Oh, our company got ripped off for $150,000 by these guys.' Well, it was pretty amazing, because as I told him: 'You know, it would have cost you about $1,500 to save $150,000.' So such an advance search can really save a company a lot of grief for a relatively little amount."

Then the conversation turned to the question of finding information about assets and people. Just how and where did Seth look? And what types of assets did he look for, such as in a typical postjudgment collection case?

"Well, it depends on the amount of money involved, how far you want to look. Normally, you start out searching for liquid assets, such as bank accounts, or savings and loan accounts. Maybe you might seek assets through the beneficiary or trustee of a financial plan, pension or estate. It's easier when the assets are liquid, since you have to get involved in selling property, and real property can get quite complicated. So what you go after depends on how much there is in the judgment, and whether the collection costs are worth it. However, if the judgment is in the six figures or even in the five figures category, it [real property] is worth going after."

According to Seth, most of the clients coming to him had at least $50,000 in judgments to collect, though like most private investigators, he handled smaller collection cases too. "Though at some point," he explained, "it's not very cost effective if a client has to spend a lot of money locating assets," typically about $350–$1,500 for an assets report. "For example, if a client is only owed a few thousand dollars, he might want to forget it if the assets aren't immediately available. It just costs too much to make it worthwhile."

So how did Seth go about finding this information? As he explained:

"The computer revolution has really changed things. And then you have to know where to get information. For example, in the old days, if I was checking the type of case which I have now that has four huge volumes of data from court, complicated instructions, lots of money flowing all over, and multiple defendants and plaintiffs, we would have to wade through all that stuff. We'd have to read through the whole thing which could take days. But now, much of the information I'll need will be in computer information bases. Or now by knowing people, I can just call up someone who might have relevant information—say one of the other attorneys on the same side as my client in a multiple plaintiff's case or in another case where they are suing the same defendant—and get a brief case summary about who owes whom, what the major cause of action is, and what the outcome is or is likely to be. And also, I might be able to get some information on where the assets are. So there's this mutual sharing. However, it's also very critical to honor any confidences you get, because if you ever break a confidence and word gets around, then your sources will dry up. Nobody will want to talk to you anymore."

Seth gave an example of how this information sharing goes on. "Well, you start getting to know people. You get inside information. And then you can use those contacts or information to get other information when you need it on a case. I was recently talking to a lawyer, for example, about some high-level corporation guy who owes a lot of money around town, and learned how this person's lawyer appealed a six-figure judgment against his client, and the appeals court sanctioned the lawyer with an $8,000 fine for making a frivolous appeal. Well, this kind of sanction is very rare; you have to do something really bad to get this. And then this lawyer told me some other confidential off-the-record stuff about the other lawyer, which could be useful later on. So there are these understandings about how and when you can share information, and who and what you can tell."

And then, sometimes, this merging of public records, computerized information, and personal contacts can lead to spectacular results—the kind of sleuthing discoveries typically portrayed in movies.

"Today, the amount of information around is just incredible. The problem is not the secrecy of this information; it's all out there in the public records. But it's the sheer quantity that can overwhelm you. For example, Dialog Information Services has over 300 data bases alone, and there are probably several thousand publications in there. So on-line, from just one source, there's probably more data available than in the Library of Congress. The key is not getting the information—it's there, available to anyone. But it's finding your way through it to get what you need to know. And that's where your special knowledge and contacts can come in, so you use what's relevant."

Seth gave an example of how he found someone thousands of miles away this way.

"This guy owed my client one million dollars, and when I was talking to my client, a banker, who lent him the million, the banker happened to mention that the man had a manufacturing business making grocery products in a Latin American country. That's all we knew, and we knew that the man had left the country. So I checked all the databases, and I found some reference to his grocery business in one of them with an international base. But then, even though I had traced the company to one country, I couldn't figure out how to learn any more, because the company was in a country where it's hard to get records; there's no real system. So it seemed like a road-block.

"But then, I used the data base on Dialog that scans about 2,000 newspapers worldwide, and I put in the last name of the guy who had run off with the money. And then, suddenly, his name popped out. What happened is there was a terrorist action in this one country, El Salvador, where we had traced his company, and the guy was a witness to the action. He came running out of his business and he spoke to the police. And that was quoted in the local newspaper. So from that, we figured out what street his company was on and started checking around. Finally, we located the business and found out who owned it—one of those S.A., Society Anonymous, Corporations. And then we had all we needed to begin the collection process.

"But just think of the process. Here's this guy, thinking he's managed to run off with $1 million, and then there's some bombing on the street in El Salvador. And he's sitting in his office on the block having coffee and he comes running out to see what happened and gets quoted in the paper. We find this out, sitting here in San Francisco, and we are able to do a collection. So the key is really being able to ferret out what you need from the maze of information that's out there."

And then, in another case, just asking the right questions, plus using a computer, helped to reveal some startling information about someone who had asked for a huge loan.

"It started when my client, who raises venture capital as a syndi-
cator for real estate limited partnerships, got an application for a
$150 million loan from these guys with a big real estate company.
They wanted to participate in the project, and my client asked me to
check out the principals. Are they solid? For real?

"So I called up their bankers to ask about their financial dealings,
and it turns out that they had about 150 accounts at the bank, with
about $9 million in them. However, about $8 million of that was
secured by Uniform Commercial Code Agreements, which means
that you can't reach that in a collection. And then, just in casual
conversation, the banker happened to mention that one of the principals was on the bank's board of directors. It was amazing. That was
something I didn't know, and the client should have told me.
Because the track record of the bank would then come into question.
Was it solvent, were there inside loans? I learned that the bank had
around $3.7 billion in capitalization and about 3,500 employees. In
any case, after the bank officer told me this, I checked it out on my
computer, and the man's name was right there as a member of the
board of directors and a major stockholder of the bank." As it
turned out, the bank was solvent and the applicant received his loan.

In still another case, Seth was able to discover that some guys
were running a stock fraud business right outside the gates of a
federal prison, where the relative of one was in prison for a commo-
dities fraud.

"They stole $1 million from my client," Seth explained. "And
one reason they were able to do it is that they had managed to put
on this great front where everything seemed on the up and up. Here
they were sucking up millions from people and putting it into phony
stocks, but then those calling up the National Association of Securities Dealers, which is a trade association that oversees these things,
they were told, 'They're in good standing.' When I called up the
guys who were running the stock fraud themselves, they even tried
to get me to invest in some worthless stocks.

"And the reason they could keep going? It takes a long time to do
anything to get any evidence in these complicated money cases. So
our goal was not to try to expose them—just get my client's money
back after my client got a judgment against them. And the big problem was trying to find the money. But finally, we did, by talking to

people, tracing the paper trail of their assets. And finally, we located the money in a vault in New York in the form of physical shares of stock."

So how exactly did Seth do it? In this case, because of confidentiality, he couldn't say. "That's one reason why attorneys hire you in the first place. They don't want to know how you do it, and you don't tell them. You have proprietary sources, confidential ways of finding out what you want to know, special ways of figuring out how to make sense of these data banks. They can't do it, so they come to you."

Seth has also found these same techniques useful in doing some political background investigations on candidates running for federal, state and local office. For example, in one of his biggest cases, he was hired by Lia Belli, then running for the California State Senate on the Democratic ticket, to investigate the private life of her opponent, Milton Marks, the State Senator. "She wanted to see if there was any scandal in Marks's background that might offset the revelations that his campaign had leaked about her own background, showing that she had lied about her past academic achievements, and had falsely claimed some academic awards and distinctions. The revelations were pretty devastating to her campaign, and she hoped we might find something about Marks to counter that."

But unfortunately for his client, in this case there was nothing. In fact, not only was Belli buried in the campaign, but she ended up paying a $75,000 fine for hiding more than $300,000 in contributions, as well as not revealing that she had hired Seth to check up on Marks. However, Seth was quite philosophical about the whole thing.

"If people in office are not abusing their position, there is nothing to bring out, and in this case Marks was clean. But if they are abusing their authority and I find this out, this is perfectly legitimate. In fact, I'm just doing what the media and the Fair Political Practices Commission have failed to do. So then it's like a public service for me to do it. But otherwise, if people are doing what they should in office, this is useful information too. Our job is just to bring out the truth, and when others aren't able to find this out, we have special legitimate techniques to do this, including computers and private sources, and then our know-how on what to look for and where to go for it."

While the computer databases can make or break a case, so can the more personal touch of just persuading someone to talk. "And that can take understanding their underlying motivations, so you know what motivates them and push the buttons," said Seth. And then, sometimes using a pretext—or creating a situation or persona—to give the person a reason to talk to you could help too. Seth described a complex collections case, where he was able to use a bit of creative moxie to solve it.

"It was a case we had about five years ago in Los Angeles County involving a ring of professional white-collar criminals. They were into all kinds of investment fraud, and were then selling shares in a phony cable TV franchise on U.S. military installations.

"We had done all our standard asset investigation techniques trying to find out where the money was—data base searches, checks of public records, but none of it worked. So we decided to try a motivational approach, and we realized it was greed. Using a pretext that we were crooks, too, we called them up at a time that they were running a horse race computerized handicapping system right out of the basement of an aerospace building, and we pretended that we were interested in buying into their deal.

"So they invited us over, and we met them on this military base. It was unbelievable—you'd think they were big shots, squeaky clean. We had to go into this security building past federal guards. Then, after my associate and I talked to them for awhile in their conference room, they told us about how they owned ten racehorses and were selling syndications in them, as well as running the handicapping system. So my partner and I simply pretended to be bigger crooks than they were, and we offered to buy the horses for cash.

"Well, that led their eyes to really light up. They thought they were swindling us, and we were invited into their inner offices and given a real tour of their operations. It was incredible. I found out they were also smuggling computers in from Mexico, and I also discovered that they owned four office buildings under phony names."

So how was Seth able to convince these master scoundrels that he and his associate were also crooks? How could they pull it off?

"Well, it's a lot easier than you think. Some of the biggest crooks are the easiest to swindle, because those who think they are the smartest and best con artists never imagine anybody's going to swindle them. So they are usually the most gullible, because they don't have their guard up.

"And then, when you use a pretense such as we did, passing ourselves off as crooks, the best thing to do is to stick closest to the truth as possible, so you're more convincing. For example, as I did here, I would use my real first name along with a fake last name, and I would be a college-educated professional, say, the accountant for these other guys, because I look like I could be that. I also would have another older investigator with me, to present the image of a more serious, stable, organized business. Also, once you create the image, you let the image speak for you, so you don't have to say things that are untrue. You just let the people you're with build on the image and their assumptions.

"When I was fifteen, for instance, I used to sell fake ivory on the boardwalk in New Jersey. I never actually said it was ivory, but when I showed it to people, they just believed it was ivory because they wanted to. Well, it was like that with these racetrack swindlers. They wanted to believe we were big time crooks with lots of money, but we never said we were. After all, you don't just come out and say: 'I'm a criminal with lots of illegal cash to launder.' Instead, we just let the way we dressed, our expensive car, and the way we talked about wanting to buy their racehorses suggest we had that kind of cash to spend. Then, when they asked to contact us, we just gave them cards with no address and no phone, indicating we were in the investments business. When they asked how they could get in touch with us, we were real cryptic. We just said: 'We'll find you,' and even that mystery helped to add to the image. They thought we were heavy duty mob guys, and after they dropped some big Mafia family names, we made up some ourselves. So I'm sure they thought we had all these connections. It was really wild."

The result of this, of course, is that Seth was able to find all the assets needed, which his client could attach and sell to collect his judgment. But could there be any legal repercussions of passing himself off as someone he wasn't, such as if there was any need to testify in court about any of this?

Seth shook his head. "No, not at all. I would never misrepresent myself in a courtroom or evidentiary situation, and if I did have to testify about anything in court here, I could simply go in and tell the truth—that I went to visit the guy because I said I was interested in the horse race business and racehorses. And besides, in this case, there was already a judgment, so the court case was over. We were just there to find the assets and collect."

Though much investigation may involve finding ways to uncover the truth from people who are hiding something or doing something illegal, other cases simply involve verifying what people say, and here again, it can take some skill in getting the person to talk or even getting through to talk to the person at all.

Seth described a typical case, where a client had an offer from another businessman to buy his company for $15 million. But who was this person? Was the guy legit? Did he really have this much money? Seth's client needed to know to know whether to sell.

"It was incredible. This guy just called up my client out of the blue and said: 'I'd like to buy your company for $15 million.' But my client doesn't know who he is. So he asked me to check him out. And then when I did—running his name on my computer, I found out that he was the president and chairman of the board of the board of one of the greatest aerospace companies in the world, with 30,000 employees. Plus, he's senior vice president of another company, and is in semi-retirement, though he is still running that firm's missile division. So this guy sounds totally legit. Though I still wanted to talk to him, just to be sure.

"However, sometimes it can be very hard to get through to these people, because they have these receptionists, secretaries and assistants who fend off their calls because of the telephone sales people. So even if you say, 'I'm not a telephone sales person,' they think you're lying. So it can be a real problem. However, I've learned that if you can approach people the right way, you can get through, and that when you have the right approach, the people on the top will talk to you too. It's just being confident, fearless, and just pushing ahead to get to the top. It's just an art you develop, though I don't know exactly how its done.

"In any case, after feeling like this guy seemed so legit, I just phoned his office, and after a couple of calls I managed to get through to him, and I used a very straight-forward approach. I just told him there was somebody that was interested in approaching him about a business deal and wanted to learn some more about him before they did it. And he said, 'I understand that. I do that kind of thing all the time.' So he wasn't at all concerned that I was checking him out. For him, that was just a normal, accepted part of doing business, and when I told him that these people were going to contact him, and that he probably already knew who they were, but I couldn't reveal my client, he understood this too. I was just a business consultant asking him some questions, so I could advise my client. I didn't use the term 'private detective' or 'investigator,' since some people have misunderstandings about what that means. They might think they're under investigation for having done something wrong.

"So then I asked him all about his background and history, and I got a whole biography from him. I found that he liked talking about himself. It made him feel important to be asked all these questions about his achievements. Even though he was this really powerful person, there was no need to think this guy is too big to approach. Instead he was receptive to talking with the right approach. And then, when I checked out on the computer what he had told me, that clicked too. So I called my client back and told him: "This guy is as good as gold,' and my client said 'That's fabulous,' and the deal went through.

Then the conversation shifted to Seth's other major area of investigation—personal injury cases. What kind of evidence did he gather here, and how did he gather it? He reminded us that he generally works for the plaintiff, the injured party, and then he began.

"Basically what we're doing is gathering evidence to show that the defendants have some liability for the injuries the plaintiff sustained, and we want to show how much, although the actual percentages of liability are figured out by the experts or decided by the jury in court. Usually, the reason we're involved is that there's a question as to whose fault the accident really is, because otherwise, the case turns on medical records and expert and victim testimony on the extent of damage. In turn, when there is a question of fault, the amount of fault can be really important, because under the current contributory negligence law in California and many other states, that percentage is used to figure out how much the defendant pays, if anything. For example, suppose the damages are figured at $1 million; but if your client is only twenty percent at fault and the defendant is eighty percent at fault, then the defendant will pay $800,000. But if it's the other way around—your client was eighty percent at fault and the defendant only twenty percent at fault, the client will get only $200,000. And then, too, it can be useful for the lawyer to find out how much each defendant has, so he can know what they can pay if they are liable. For example, if one of them has no money and little or no insurance, that can be a problem, and it can affect the strategy in the case."

So what kind of information or evidence did Seth gather to show liability or fault?

"Well, we gather witness statements. We interview a lot of people about what they observed or heard, and we take photographs. Also, we look for information on conditions and other contributing factors. Say it's an auto accident. We would want to look at the condition of the road. Is the road uneven? Is the asphalt defective? And then we would look for contributing factors such as whether somebody parked a pickup truck too far out on the road or whether somebody slipped on some ice.

"Or if it's an industrial accident, we want to look at the equipment too, not just at the events leading up to the accident. We want to see if the equipment is safe, or who actually owns it and who made it. For instance, we've had cases where a guy falls down and breaks his back, and we're trying to find out whose ladder he was on so the lawyer knows who to sue, because someone put up a bad ladder on the job."

Such interviews might sound fairly routine, but in some cases, Seth describes them as frightening and terrifying.

"You don't always do interviews in somebody's office. I've interviewed some people in hard hats who are standing twenty stories up in a high rise and we're hooked up on a safety cable, and I'm scared, shaking in my boots, but these guys think it's perfectly normal."

Seth has also been involved in some especially interesting

personal injury cases, one involving exploding cars; another involving a rape at a bank's automatic teller machine.

In one of the exploding car cases, the local citizens in the community were so incensed, that they themselves even got involved in investigating. As Seth described it:

"It happened in Northern California, around Napa. This car from a well-known manufacturer was traveling at only twenty-two miles an hour when it was rear-ended, and then it suddenly exploded in flames. A couple with two little kids was in there, and the explosion killed the children and burned the couple on eighty percent of their bodies. Well, the local police and the fire department were furious, because these were local citizens, and since they felt there was something wrong with the car, they started cutting up other cars of this type at the local dump. They wanted to go after the automobile manufacturer, because in their view, it had maimed their local people by building an unsafe car. They weren't experts, but they were really concerned, and some of the information they came up with proved useful. So then, when we got involved, we took this information and did our own checking to see who really did what, and it was one of these cases, where the company really ended up paying a lot and paying it quickly. They wanted to settle the case as soon as possible to avoid anymore bad publicity."

And in the ATM rape case, Seth's investigation helped to make the case for a victim who had given up the hope of getting anything, since the rapist was poor. The victim didn't realize she could get any money from the bank. But Seth's investigation showed she could.

"The woman was raped at the ATM at night, and normally, her only recourse for any damages would be against the rapist. However, once we started investigating the case, we found out there were three other rapes at the ATM after hers. And, since hers was the first, it would be hard to prove the bank would be at fault for having inadequate security at the ATM. After all, the bank could argue, how could they know.

"Anyway, we kept investigating. I interviewed the other victims, and two of them had already sued the bank and they were in litigation. And then, when I interviewed the third, it had been almost a year since the rape happened, and she had only about two weeks to go before the statute of limitations on suing the bank would run out, and then, if she didn't act, she couldn't sue. So when I interviewed her, her boyfriend was there, and as she told me the story, she broke down in tears. She had gone to the police, and they never did catch this guy. 'But why didn't you prosecute this thing civilly,' I asked her, and she said that the man was just some poor guy who didn't have any money.

" 'But why not sue the bank?' I asked her. 'The guy just carried out the physical act, but the bank raped you, too,' I said. And then I explained how I had found internal security guidelines the bank had sent to the branches about safeguarding the ATM's because of the previous attacks, but then the branches never implemented them. And then I told her: 'Look, the bank has guys in its security department who are ex-FBI agents. It's a billion dollar corporation. And there are three other women who were raped before you at this location. And the police department told the bank it was unsafe. Yet because of the inconvenience and the bank's profit motive, they left that ATM open in an unsafe place at night, knowing there was some nut who had already raped there before.' So then I took her to a lawyer, the one who was handling the first case, and she sued the bank and got $150,000. And she deserved it too. She was in counseling for a year and mentally scarred for life. She had been a student, and she ended up dropping out of school for awhile. So this incident really screwed up her life. But at least we were able to do something to help her get life back together. Our investigation showed she had a case."

Seth also pointed out that one of the pitfalls of gathering statements was encountering people who were reluctant to talk, and often for good reason. They were afraid of getting involved because there might be repercussions if they were a witness; they might implicate themselves if they were at fault; and some may not want to take the time. So Seth would have to find ways to motivate them, and gave an example of how he did it from a recent personal injury case.

"You have to be able to understand certain things about people to motivate them, and then, even if they are reluctant to say anything, you can persuade them. For in a way, this business is pretty much like war. You want to know something; they don't want you to know it. So you want to know your opposition, and the more you know about your opposition, the more power you have over them. That's why when we call up people to interview them, the more we know about who they are and what their socioeconomic position is, the better we can know their interests and weak spots, and what makes them talk. It's a little like what the salesman does who looks for hot buttons in a prospect to make a sale. And it's not really manipulative, because you're not forcing them to do anything. Rather, you're persuading, convincing, helping them to see why they should share the information they have—you might even use appeals to their higher nature as a responsible citizen. That's what I did in one personal injury case."

Then, Seth explained. "It happened when this guy was in Northern California riding on a motorcycle. He was coming around the turn, and suddenly, he found that the road was uneven, and he couldn't make the turn in his normal lane. Instead, his motorcycle slid into the other lane, and a car ran over him, and as a result, he's a paraplegic now. So, of course, he sues everybody possibly involved—the other driver, the county, the state, anyone who could be possibly responsible for this. Because that's what you normally do—look for whoever has contributed to the negligence that caused this guy a serious injury, and then you sue.

"However, the driver of the other car doesn't understand all of this. He doesn't think he did anything wrong. He was just driving along in his own lane at the normal speed, coming around the turn, and he's just a working guy who makes an hourly wage, so he can't comprehend a suit that's asking for millions of dollars in damages. So his immediate reaction is not to talk to anyone about his case, even though his insurance company is willing to settle the case and pay it, and then release him from any claims. However, we still need his testimony for our client to help his lawyer in arguing what the settlement should be.

"So our job is to persuade him to talk to us, though he's nervous and reluctant about saying a thing. Well, to break through that kind of barrier, you've got to understand who that person is, what he does for a living, and know how to relate to him, so he can understand why he needs to talk and that it's going to be okay for him. And so, that's what I did. When I met with him, I explained how he had nothing to lose, his insurance company was taking care of everything, and we were trying to protect the interests of our client for the rest of his life. Here's a nineteen-year-old boy who's never going to walk again. And so I appealed to this man as a responsible, reasonable family man with kids, because I had learned this about him. And I appealed to him as a citizen who would want to do the right thing. Wouldn't he want some protection for his own kids if something like this happened? Would he want this just as an ordinary citizen concerned about others? And so finally he did talk about what had happened. The appeal to him as a citizen and a father had worked."

Now the conversation turned to some of the issues that come up for everyone in the business—the possibility of danger from Seth's work and how it affects his personal and social life.

In Seth's case, there was a lot less danger than for many private eyes because of his particular specialty in the financial and personal injury cases. "Even though the dollar numbers are more serious, it's a lot less dangerous because we're generally working on already resolved court cases or because there's an insurance company involved. Then, too, we're just really a tool for the attorneys or principles in the case, and the other side won't even know who we are unless they look in the court files. And generally just their attorneys do."

Still, Seth admitted, he had had a couple of threats. But none of them ever amounted to anything, particularly since Seth took the direct approach of inviting the people threatening him to come over and talk to him. As he explained:

"I just told them to come down and make an appointment. But few of them did. And one of the cases was really satisfying—to know that this guy was really mad, because he really deserved it. In this case, the man called to tell me to stay away from a building he once owned after he saw me on TV being interviewed about a kidnapping case. He was calling from the hospital where he was having a nervous breakdown. What had happened was that he had owned his property secretly, and had built several apartment buildings for my client, but had neglected to put in the second floor fire stairs. So one of the tenants opened up the door to go down the stairs and fell two stories. After this happened, and my client got a judgment against him, we found this property and took it away from him, along with most of his other money. And the result was that we ruined him so badly that he ended up having a breakdown. And now he was calling me from there about that. It felt like a real good example of poetic justice to me, and I actually enjoyed this threat."

But apart from these few threats, Seth, compared to other investigators, didn't find there was much effect on either his personal or social life, again because of his relatively low-profile, low-danger specialty. In fact, when he encountered people at social gatherings, he normally didn't even mention he worked as a private investigator or else described his work in such terms that it sounded very boring and uninteresting.

"I usually don't say I'm a private detective at social situations, and if people should find out and ask me to tell them war stories, I usually won't. What I do is simply tell people I'm a financial investigator or I do financial research. Then, they get bored and go on to something else. I'd rather talk about travel or something more exciting."

As for his personal life, Seth was usually able to close off his work when he left the office, even if the office is in his home.

"I guess it would be different if I'm always on call like some investigators involved in surveillance or undercover work. But our line of work is really much more routine. Sure, sometimes, I may take things home and worry about whether I did something right or not, or I may feel concerned because I've got several things all going on at the same time the next day, and I have all these people depending on me. So sometimes it can be hard to sleep. But otherwise, no, I can't see much difference than if I was in any other line of running a business."

And Seth was even able to close off like this despite his wife being involved in the business too. She's his business partner who manages the financial end of the company, after previously working as an accountant and in a bank.

"We just confine our business to the office. As soon as we come in the door, we just do business. But then, when we leave, we don't talk about it that much. We try to keep our business and personal lives distinct."

Then, the conversation shifted to some of the larger issues about privacy. Since Seth was in the information gathering business, how did he feel about personal privacy? How far did he think investigators should be allowed to go in their search for information?

Like many private investigators, and in keeping with his own liberal philosophy, Seth came down strongly in favor of personal privacy protections. Though he recognized that the information business was growing, and that more and more information was becoming available about private citizens, he also felt it important for more and more information to be available about the government too.

"I strongly support the Privacy Act, which protects personal privacy, and the American Civil Liberties Union, which advocates that too. Also, I follow the fair credit laws, which provide for limits on what you can do in collections, so people's privacy is protected too.

"Yet there's also a fine line in this business in how far you should go. When should you get information, and when should you say no. I think ultimately, regardless of how much legislation there is to protect people, it's really up to each individual investigator as to when to say no to a case. And such situations are more likely to occur when one is dealing with the general public, rather than companies and attorneys.

"So that's one reason why I don't like to deal with the public. People call us, and they'll say: 'We want all this stuff on this guy,' and sometimes it may be uncertain as to whether their request is even legitimate. Then, if you find out that there's really no legitimate reason for what they're asking, such as a judgment for money or a personal injury action contemplated, but are really just snooping, well, then, I think, you've got to make the moral decision not to do it."

But how would Seth know before he worked on the case?

"Oh, you just have a feel for it. You know when you look at the case and talk to the person. So I don't do it, because I don't like to do any of that snoopy stuff anyway."

And yet, Seth acknowledged, he, as a member of the investigative industry, was also in the center of competing forces to reveal more or less information about individuals or the workings of companies or government agencies.

"There are really two different forces playing against each other now. On the one hand, there are the suppliers of information, such as the large information companies, who would like to make it possible to more easily get information about the individual. And on the other, you have these people who feel there is a growing invasion of privacy, and they are trying to get more restrictive laws passed. But I feel in the long run the ones who are going to win the war are the guys who are selling the information. They're the ones with more political connections and clout.

"And yet there's a certain irony here in that the ones who are selling it are also interested in restricting the information in some ways too. This is the case because some of these private data-base suppliers have been entering into government contracts, where the government exclusively sells them public records, so they can mark it up several times and resell it at a profit. By contrast, if the public could get it directly from the government, they could get it at low cost or for free. So the companies want to keep their exclusive right. For instance, one agency, Disclosure, Inc., gets information from the Securities and Exchange Commission and resells it, and if a private citizen calls the SEC, he or she will be told to call this company and pay for it.

"So there's this interesting tension now. Companies wanting to restrict the flow of some information, so they can preserve their exclusive right to make a profit from it, at the same time that they want to be freer to collect information generally about the public. And meanwhile, there are people who want to keep their personal privacy at the same time that they can have more access to public records directly from the government, through the Freedom of Information Act. And then there is the interplay of the First Amendment.

"So there's really this fine line. How much are we going to have available to the public? How much are we going to keep secret? And does keeping it private protect or damage the public? So it's hard to say just what should be done. You have to balance these different interests. But I think generally, you have to look at each situation individually, and decide whether the information to be collected or released is about the individual's personal things that shouldn't be obtained or released, or whether it is about government policy or corporate policy that should. I think it's fine to charge fees for the release of information under the Freedom of Information Act, when those seeking this information are corporations trying to find out about competitors to see what the government has on them. In fact, most of those seeking information under this act are such companies, and they're seeking it for economic reasons, so it's fair for them to pay. But then, when journalists are seeking such information to protect the public's right to know, they're exempt from paying. And I think it's important to keep that access to information open too.

"Thus, there are really no black and white answers. In some ways, I'm all for personal privacy, and protecting the individual, which is why I won't take certain types of cases. But in other cases, I'm in favor of the public's right to know, and I think the right to get this information needs to be there. These are questions all private investigators can end up wrestling with, and ultimately I think it boils down to your own personal morality. In what cases do you feel it is right to get information; and when do you think you are being asked to go too far? I personally choose to turn down cases when I think I'm being asked to get information that's illegitimate. But then it's up to each investigator to decide where to draw the line and whether he's going to draw it. And it's not always easy to decide when to draw it. There are all these forces debating these issues, and even they can't always decide."

Finally, we spoke briefly about trends in the industry, and how Seth felt about them.

"Well, it's a funny business. On the one hand, there are these increasingly big companies, like Kroll Associates, which is made up of a lot of ex-federal prosecutors, attorneys and FBI agents, and has created a worldwide network to do financial investigations. In fact, it's the first international company in this field set up along strict corporate lines. So there's this one trend in the industry towards increased size and professionalism.

"But on the other hand, this is still a mom and pop type of business, with a lot of very small companies, even one man-operations. And then there's a great disparity in the industry between the image that many people have of the private detective and what people do. There's also a big range between the professionalism of most investigators and a lot of unprofessionalism in some areas of the business, where investigators may go too far, so that they invade people's privacy, harass them, and overcharge. For instance, if you called up a detective agency out of the blue saying you were trying to locate your long-lost uncle whom you last saw a few years ago in New York, you might get quotes anywhere's from $100 to $2,500 for the same job, and maybe it might cost as little as $2 to do a quick records search of the statewide real estate index or let your fingers do the walking through a telephone book.

"Thus, at times, you can run into a kind of unscrupulous element that will take advantage of people in what it charges, or in how it investigates a case. But increasingly, that's changing. The field is becoming more professionalized, for both big and small agencies, and is increasingly regulated too, by groups like the State Department of Consumer Affairs in California. And then there are professional groups within the field, like the California Association of Licensed Investigators, that are working on increasing the professionalism and ethics in the field.

"And I think this growth of self-regulation is needed, or the person always has a legal recourse against someone who has taken advantage of him, because the state can only do so much and is really ineffective in policing things. And then much of what may seem to be overcharging isn't illegal anyway. For instance, if a client calls up about finding someone and the investigator says it will be $2,500 and does the job, what's illegal about that? And even if that someone isn't found, if the investigator looked through all the records, that would be legal too. The investigator tried and the client agreed to the fee. But whether it's ethical or moral to charge that much if it actually costs much less, that's something else. But then, each case is different. It could cost a few bucks to a few hundred if the person is readily easy to locate but much more if he's not.

"Suppose someone gives me the name of a contractor. I could look in the statewide real estate index, which is available to anybody in the industry. Or I could use microfiche or data base records of other public records, such as voter registration records. And then in about ten minutes, I could get his home address, his wife's name, his real name, his birthdate, where he was born, how long he's owned his house, if he owns any other real estate in California, and his contractor's license as well. But then, that could be just the beginning of the investigation, since I would still have to verify that he still lives there, and if he has an unlisted number, I might call the neighbors to see if they know. And then, if he's still there, I've located him. But sometimes you find people who move around a lot or are trying to hide. So each case is different.

"And ultimately, I think it's up to the individual investigator to make his own choices, though I think the growing professionalism is a good thing too. I know we have always held to a high ethical standard, and I think it is good that others in the profession do too. It will certainly help the image of the private investigator for everyone."

4

Jon Berger and Naomi Thomas: Investigating Murder and Mayhem

When Sam and I arrived to meet Jon Berger and Naomi Thomas, who usually work on cases together out of their offices in the Fillmore district of San Francisco, we were led down a long dark hallway. Subsequently, our entrance seemed fitting. Jon and Naomi were to take us on a long journey that included a look at the very depths of human evil, since one of their specialties is unsolved murder cases. But for the moment, we gathered in a much more prosaic kitchen, where we sat around the table, and Naomi offered us some coffee as I readied our tape recorders.

It was to be an ironic journey, since Jon and Naomi look like the last people to be involved in investigating murders and the other strange cases they described. They seemed a quiet, gentle, typically middle-class couple who might easily fit in at anybody's downtown cocktail party. Jon, tall, thin, silver haired, and speaking very poetically and philosophically at times, appeared more like a college English or philosophy professor, than a private eye; while Naomi, of average height and build, with dirty blonde, casually trimmed hair, looked to be a financial district secretary, which she once was. Yet, in a way, this search into murder and mayhem has been a kind of journey away from the ordinary and routine for them both.

Jon remembers having fantasies about being a private eye, dating back to when he was twelve and read about or watched films on detectives, although he didn't get into the business until he was twenty-eight. He put those fantasies on a shelf and started out living a very ordinary sort of life. He went to the University of San Francisco and the college of Marin, where he was an English major and wrote fiction. Yet there were glimmers of wanting to do something different even then, since, on the side, Jon played jazz and rock for various clubs, composed music, and wrote poetry for many years, although to support himself he took on a series of what he described as very "terrible jobs."

"Usually musicians have to do this to support themselves," he explained, and he described how he toiled in the shipyards, was a janitor, sold records, worked in a boiler-room sales operation selling different things, and otherwise bounced around from one drudge job to another.

But then, after several years of this, he took off for Europe for six months, just to get away, and when he came back, he made the decision that he wanted to have a different kind of life—something more challenging and exciting. Or as Jon put it: "I didn't want to work those horrible jobs anymore. I wanted something interesting. And the only thing I could think of, being otherwise unskilled in anything practical, was to be a detective, since I had had a boyhood fantasy about that anyway."

And what about this boyhood fantasy attached him towards being a private eye? Jon explained:

"Well, I liked the whole idea of ratiocenation. Of reasoning. Of deduction. I thought it was amazing to be able to figure things out—to be able to discover reality from a disparate set of clues, things that seemed unconnected, but in fact were joined. I was fascinated by that idea. And then, it was very important to me to have an eccentric life-style. I liked the idea that one wouldn't be locked into a normal one if one was a detective; or at least that was my impression of the detective's way of life. Living such a life, one could work odd hours. So sometimes you would work during the day, sometimes during the night, sometimes both day and night, and sometimes you wouldn't work at all. I liked the variety and unpredictability of it all. And then, Sherlock Holmes was always a hero of mine, so I thought this would be the perfect life-style for me."

And so, at twenty-eight, Jon started working for various agencies in San Francisco, and that's how he met Naomi and went to work for her agency eleven years ago.

Naomi got into the detective business more by chance than by design, by first working for and then marrying an investigator. She started working as a secretary at various firms in San Francisco, and in 1974, she happened to get a job as a secretary for a former police officer named, coincidentally, Mike Hamer—pronounced the same as but spelled differently from the Mickey Spillane character—who had started his own business as a private eye.

In any event, after a few years of working for Mike as a secretary, they got married and gradually she began working as an investigator, too. Then, as he gradually lost interest in the detective business in the early 1980s, Naomi more and more took over running the business herself, and finally, when she and Mike got divorced, he took over the Irish bar they both owned, and she inherited the business.

Meanwhile, as she increasingly got involved in the business, she began working more and more with Jon, until now they work on most of their cases together, since, as they both observed: "It's more interesting that way."

Jon and Naomi's joint approach to work is unusual, since most private detectives work alone. But for them, the interest and excitement of working together was a big advantage, as was the ability to come up with new ideas and approaches through brainstorming together. In fact, because it made the work more interesting, they frequently worked together, even if it meant less money for them both.

"We do a lot of things together," Jon explained. "Even if I go out
and talk to people in the case, we do a lot of the research and brainstorming, which is very valuable for coming up with ideas. And
then it also helps to fight the boredom factor, which arises in some
areas of the work, such as public record searchers and surveillance.
For example, public record searching is very tedious work, and it's
easier when two people are doing it; it cuts the time in half. And
surveillances can get very dull when there are long hours and nothing is happening. But then, if the work could be done by just one
person, we don't charge for two. So we each would earn less than
we could otherwise, but we'd rather do it this way, because we want
the work to be fun. On the other hand, if the work requires two people, we would charge for that. The point is, for us, we do what we
do because we want to keep things exciting and fun. Otherwise,
some of the work could be very dull and we would hate that."

In fact, Jon indicated that he and Naomi sometimes turn down
many types of cases, because they don't find them interesting or
don't feel comfortable with them. For example, they typically
choose not to do domestic cases and turn down many product liability cases for such reasons.

"We usually don't do domestic cases, such as those where the
man suspects his wife of dating someone else," Jon said. "We don't
feel we have a place in those things. We feel it's between the husband and wife to work things out, and it's inappropriate for us to get
involved. There may be a romantic problem or a marital problem or
a psychological problem, and that should be worked out. But we
don't think it helps for one spouse to have the other one followed to
find out who he or she is sleeping with. So it feels ridiculous for us
to be snooping around like that, and we don't do it.

"And then, I think we'd probably turn down a case involving
defending a large-scale drug dealer. Though we've done these in the
past, it just doesn't feel right now. It would bother us personally.

"And then some cases are just so routine, they're not challenging.
For example, a lot of the product liability and insurance cases can
be very dull, or as some people call them in the trade—they're
'stump grinder' cases. Now if the case involves a complicated piece
of machinery or a horrible injury, it can be interesting because of
the challenge of trying to figure out what happened. But in other

instances, the situation is just so simple, there's no challenge. The machinery, for instance, is intrinsically boring, or the event that happened is."

Boring? So what did Jon mean by that? What kind of machinery? What kind of event?

He went on. "Well, a grating is boring. For example, one client stepped on a grating and snapped both of her ankles. Then she fell down on her nose and broke that as well. So our job was to find out everything we could about gratings. And we did it, because that was our job. But gratings are just not interesting. On another products liability case, though, we had a man who was injured by this new state-of-the-art contraption. And that was an interesting challenge to figure out if it worked properly. It really was."

For Jon and Naomi, no day is really typical, which is the way they like it. As Jon describes it: "Some days we're running around doing surveillance. Sometimes we're doing public records work. Sometimes we're doing a murder investigation. And sometimes we're doing some insurance inquiry. And then there are some days when we just get to stay home and dictate reports or take phone calls. And other times, we take clients out to lunch or make contacts to solicit business."

But perhaps most of all, Jon and Naomi love the murder cases. They're rare—"they come along once in a coon's age," as Jon puts it. But when they come, they offer a special challenge, because they are usually so strange and bizarre that they have previously defied solution by everybody else.

So how do Jon and Naomi end up with these previously insoluble cases? And why aren't the police involved in them?

"Because," explained Jon, "usually we're the court of last resort for the client. The police have invariably worked on it before, but they have come up with nothing, or, as in one case we worked on, the police came up with something, but they came up with the wrong thing, so a man who claims to be innocent ended up being convicted, and now the case is on appeal, and we're trying to find the evidence to prove that this other man did it. Usually, we get the case because nobody knows exactly what happened and the police reached a dead end. And so we're brought in by some interested party, typically a family that wants justice done because someone they loved has been killed or because, as in this one case we mentioned, they want to clear someone's name."

But if the police can't solve it, how can Jon and Naomi? Or more generally, if the police can't solve a case, with their access to crime labs, computerized data banks, the power of the badge, and other technologies available only to them, how can any private detective solve it?

Jon had an easy answer to this often asked question.

"Because in some ways we have a little more latitude in what we do than the police, as strange as it may seem. For instance, the way we talk to people is different. We can talk to them without the coercive pressure of the police. Although it can sometimes help the police to have a badge and a gun and confront the person with an atmosphere of coercion, in a lot of cases it isn't good for them. People freeze up and don't talk, or maybe they lie. But often, especially in a small police department, this approach is tried, and then if it doesn't work, the police don't know what to do next.

"By contrast, since we can't coerce anybody to do anything, and since we have no badge and no gun, we have to use a non-coercive approach. And generally this means we use one which is softer or perhaps a little sneakier than the police are apt to take."

Typically, most cases Jon and Naomi acquired were about a year or two old, making them even more difficult to solve. But why such a long delay? Jon explained people's natural reluctance to give up on the cops and come to them.

"Usually the people are trying to rely on the police to solve the case, which is understandable. And then, when the police don't resolve it, there's a period of time where they don't know what to do. So time passes. Then, too, in some cases, it may take time to get a coroner's inquest going to raise questions about the initial interpretations about the case, and afterwards it can take a while for the family to digest the new information and talk about it. Also, for many people, there's a psychological barrier to not believing the police if the police have messed up on a case. Most people are trusting; they're not skeptical of what the police are doing. So they have to overcome those feelings of resistance before they come to think that a private investigator might be an alternative. And then they have to get the money together too."

And then, when the clients finally do bring these cases to Jon and Naomi, there's still the problem of proof. Sometimes the cases are so difficult, particularly after they have gathered dust for a year or two, that it is hard to find evidence and leads; and even when Jon and Naomi are able to arrive at what they feel certain is the answer to the crime, there isn't the hard evidence to prove it—just circumstantial evidence, incriminating statements from a person, probably the perpetrator, pointing fingers, but not enough to hold up in court. Or maybe the client just runs out of money too soon, so the investigation has to end.

"In the movies, it always seems to easy," Jon said. "In the end, the crime is solved. The detective always has all the evidence in front of him, and it's essentially a drawing room type of murder situation. You've got the blood, you've got the hammer, and you've got the body of Lord Puddingpuss or whoever's lying by the fender. But in real life, you are typically left with ambiguity and gnawing doubt and the feeling that if only I had done something more, I might have been able to solve it. And sometimes, you're left with the feeling that if only the client had more money, you could have done a lot more. Or often you realize there isn't anything else that can be done. You have the facts you have been able to find—but they just don't add up to enough to prove the case."

In fact, as Jon pointed out, the problem of proving these cases was usually par for the course. Unlike the movies, the common result was hitting a dead end. As Jon observed, he or Naomi often came close to eliciting a confession from someone with obvious knowledge of the crime, but the person was apt to couch this discussion in the third person, so what he ended up with were allusions to the crime, *as if* comments, *suppose* statements and the like, making it apparent the person knew what happened or did it himself. But then there was a lack of evidence to confirm what seemed so true.

"Once you get this indirect information, the next thing you have to do is try to corroborate it. And it's very difficult to do," Jon noted. "In the movies, private detectives solve the murder case. But in real life, that's not often the case. What's more often the case is you know who did it, but can't prove it. And that's a very good reason why the police haven't been able to solve the case in the first place. For example, a lot of times, the crime scene isn't known, so the forensic evidence, such as fingerprints or a body, isn't available. And if the forensic evidence isn't available, it's really hard to tie somebody into an act like that circumstantially.

"Furthermore, you don't normally get direct confessions or murderers cooperatively taking you to the scene. I know I've never had anybody sit down and confess to me that he or she killed somebody. Someone may talk knowledgeably about what happened, and in each of these murder cases, I think I know what happened; I know how it happened, and who did it. But it's unprovable.

"And that's one of the things that makes those cases so fascinating. You're in a realm where you are able to know through your impressions, your inferences and your logical conclusions. But the evidence is gone, simply gone; so there's no proof."

Occasionally, Jon observed that an attorney might try to work with such circumstantial evidence in a civil case, if he or she thought it possible to persuade a jury that the preponderance of the evidence showed the defendant did it, such as in a wrongful death action seeking damages. Perhaps here an attorney might chance it, since he would only have to persuade a jury to give the plaintiff the benefit of the doubt if it thought there was a fifty-one percent chance the defendant did it, whereas in a criminal case, the jury must convict beyond a reasonable doubt. But generally, few attorneys would do this, because it would be so expensive to investigate and try a case such as this, and not only would it be chancy to prove, but the defendant probably wouldn't have any money to make the effort worthwhile, since few defendants in murder cases have much money.

"So usually," Jon concluded, "in these cases, beyond finding out what probably happened or who probably did it, there's nothing much these clients can do. There's no legal recourse in most cases. And usually they have run out of money to do anymore."

At least, as Jon pointed out, the clients generally felt a sense of satisfaction that they knew what happened, though they couldn't prove it.

"I think that's true," Jon said, "because the information at least gives people a sense of finality about the case, so they can put it to rest."

Jon gave an example. He and Naomi handled a case in which a young woman was killed in Southern California. She had simply disappeared, and the police wouldn't handle it because there was no body or evidence of foul play. The young woman could just as easily have moved, since she had no roots in the community, but the parents suspected something had happened to her because she called them once a week, and suddenly the calls stopped. Jon and Naomi concluded that the young woman was probably killed in a drug deal.

"They just wanted to know what happened to her, and so that information satisfied them, as upsetting as it was."

And he described other unprovable cases, such as one where a dead man was found wrapped in a blanket.

"The police just thought it was a random murder, which didn't make much sense. But we eventually came to the conclusion that the man was killed by someone with feelings of rage towards him or a self-struggle that led him to murder. Then the man felt a sense of peace."

Yet, as Jon pointed out, though the clients might feel this sense of satisfaction just knowing, he and Naomi were still left with a kind of hollow feeling of frustration. "It's because we know, but we know we can't prove it, and it's beyond our capabilities to affect the case anymore. Or maybe the clients run out of money, and we have to let go. So there's a kind of lack of resolution that can feel unnerving for awhile. Yet we have to let the case go. It's one of those things. You just often get this feeling of being left hanging in these cases, because you know or feel almost there, but they can't be solved."

Jon also spoke of a phenomenon that often occurred in these murder cases when he or Naomi got to this point of knowing as they talked to a person who seemed to be the murderer. He hadn't admitted it, yet they sensed this person's guilt, and their conversation became a kind of collaboration or dance.

"It's really a unique experience, the way these murder cases force you to use your own talents and abilities and even reach further into your perception of what's real," as Jon explained. "And at a certain point, they challenge your own moral equilibrium because you find yourself in a situation where you have to be able to empathize with an evil act in order to talk to the person who has committed it. It's as if you and the murderer have now become engaged in a kind of a dance, and the challenge to the detective is the challenge to any dancer of being able to lead and stay in control. At the same time, as a dancer, you have to be able to collaborate with your partner who happens to be the killer. This requires a lot of balance, as dancing does, as well as a lot of sensitivity and empathy with your partner, in order to get your partner to follow along with you."

So how was the detective "collaborating" or "dancing" with the murderer? Jon went on.

"You're collaborating with the suspect the moment you talk to the suspect, because both of you are aiming at an effort to get to some kind of statement of the truth. You are trying to find out what is real, without any prejudgment, preconceptions, or even any consideration of what the client wants to hear. Just the naked truth. So when you are dealing with a murder case and with a suspect you think may have murdered another human being, you have to collaborate with them in some way to get to a statement of reality. And what is especially interesting about the process is that on some level, the killer also wants that to happen. That's why he or she talks about it at all, even if only in metaphors or obliquely or trying to put it on somebody else. For example, the killer may say something like: 'I think Johnny did it, and this is how I think Johnny did it,' and then he describes exactly how he did it. Well you know, and he knows, that you are both talking about what really happened. It's like he feels this sense of crisis or this horrible shame he has to get out, although he won't come right out and say something like: 'I did it and I'm sorry,' or 'I'm ashamed of myself.' Instead, the murderer will talk about it at an angle. He has to get it out, but he does it tangentially, because it's too hard to talk about it straight on. And you know, and he knows, so there's this kind of shared collaboration or dance, in which you both know that you know, yet you also agree not to let on that you know. So then, in this balance between knowing and not knowing you can both negotiate a vision of the truth that becomes the dance."

Yet this dance could be a difficult one for the detective, in that there was a kind of moral conundrum triggered by this collaboration with a person engaged in evil, even if that collaboration was only to find out the truth.

Jon said, "It's not always to keep your own sense of balance, because this collaboration, this dance can pull you in. For example, you start to see how awful things can be. For you realize you are exposed to real evil, and yet at the same time, you see the banality of the evil as you discuss and talk around the issue. It's like weaving in and out of the cobbles as you dance, trying not to fall. So you see the evil, yet it's also indirect and tamed, and you need to keep this sense of detachment to continue to explore with your partner as you dance. It's hard to explain, but it's a fascinating experience—to have this challenge of facing real evil in all its banality and horror, and at the same time continuing the dance."

Yet, as Jon pointed out, this "dance" with the presumed murderer was a kind of culmination of a more general process that occurred with whomever Jon and Naomi spoke to—getting that person to talk by building rapport, asking the appropriate questions, and overcoming any reluctance to speak with the appropriate strategy and tactics. Initially, Jon and Naomi would start off by being friendly and amenable. But what if people resisted because they didn't want to give themselves away by saying anything incriminating? What would Jon or Naomi do then?

"The tactics you use to get someone to talk to you depend on the situation. For some detectives, the more forceful approach may work at times. Especially for those who have the tough-guy image, such as somebody who is an ex-police officer. They have that air about them anyway, and it comes naturally to them, so for them it works. But I've never had any luck whatsoever trying to be a tough guy, and this approach has never worked for Naomi either. So we don't use it.

"Rather, we usually approach people in a much more friendly, supplicatory way than the police would. Commonly, our approach is to ask them: 'Can you help me out?' Or we'll say something like: 'I'm sort of confused here and I don't really understand what's going on. Perhaps you can explain it to me.' So instead of turning a bright light on them, so to speak, and barking questions at them, we come on very humbly, like we just want some help.

"But sometimes when people resist, there are still a lot of gentle types of persuasion you can use, which work well for us. For instance, you can confuse them or alarm them by suggesting that you have the evidence that shows someone else said what you are trying to get them to admit. Or occasionally you can get around their resistences by talking about something else for a while, and then you slip back into the subject you want to talk about. Or maybe you might get at the subject from a different angle."

Jon gave an example. "Say you're at their house and you sense they feel uncomfortable about a particular topic. You might start talking about a picture on the wall to get them to relax. Or perhaps try children or dogs. Something low-key, non-threatening, is ideal.

"The point is when you see or sense that they're getting uptight or defensive, pull back. And usually, you can tell by people's body language or how they speak when they are getting defensive. For example, people start covering up their body; they get rigid or tense. So that's when it helps to calm them down by talking about something they like. Then, when they feel comfortable, you can bring up what you really want to talk about again, but gently, so you maintain that rapport. Generally, the emphatic approach is the best one to use in talking to anybody."

Yet why would this desire to be understood outweigh the person's desire to protect himself from possible exposure by talking too much? Jon had alluded to this desire for exposure before in talking about the "dance" with the presumed murderer. But now he spoke of each person's very basic desire to confess or reveal his involvement in a significant life-changing event. The person might not be motivated by guilt, but he felt pressured to talk about what had happened, as if this was a way of asserting himself to the world, of saying 'I act!' 'I exist!'

Jon explained this compulsion:

"I think people are willing to talk to us, and perhaps implicate themselves in a crime, even if they don't have to, because people have a compulsion to talk about what they have done. I think that everybody wants to talk about some seminal event in their lives, and if that event is a murder they have committed, they have a compulsion to confess or talk about it.

"Yet, the way they talk about it takes a Byzantine path sometimes. They don't just sit there and say: 'Yeah, I did it.' But in many ways they keep alluding to it or hinting at it or otherwise showing in little ways they want to talk about it. It's as if they want to lead you back through the labyrinth to this subject, if only you know when to lead or follow along?" Jon then described his conversation with a suspected killer who murdered his victim and then dressed him in a suit.

"He just volunteered to talk to us about his theories, when he found out we were investigating the case, and then he spoke about the facts of the case obliquely; he made indirect references, which is the way people who have committed murder or done something terribly wrong usually do. For example, when I asked him: 'What do you think the killer was like?' he started describing the killer in detail. 'I think he was somebody like this and somebody like that.' Well, as it turned out, everything he said fit himself.

"So then, I just let him go on this way, because that's the best way to get someone to talk about a terrible act they have done. It puts too much psychological pressure on them to make them think or talk about it in terms of themselves. But if you ask them to talk about it in the third person, they can often talk about it quite freely, because they're not talking about themselves anymore. They're detached intellectually. So that's what I did with him, and afterwards, I was quite sure he did it, though he never directly said he did."

But why should they do this? Why keep tempting fate by the possibility of exposure this way?

Jon went on. "It's hard to say, but I think in some ways, some people may want to atone for it. On the other hand, most of the people I've met who I think have been involved in murder are not motivated by guilt. They're not really guilt-ridden. So it's not so much that they want to confess, get caught, and have someone punish them. Instead, what seems to be making them want to talk is that the event itself was so horrifying for them or so important to them, that they feel they have to talk about it. So they talk not so much because they want to confess, but because they have a need to release and purge themselves of the horror or the power of the act."

But then, when they do, as Jon reminded us, their talk is indirect.

They talk about it in the third person, so they are giving clues, but trying not to implicate themselves. Or as Jon put it: "They talk about it as if the person who did it was someone else."

And sometimes, such people became active participants in the investigation. They presented themselves as someone who wanted to help.

"The police are quite aware of this phenomena," Jon observed. "The interested helpful party who's really the killer. And often this person will do this as a way to stay involved and reaffirm the significance and power of his act. He gets some pleasure in seeing how much effect his act has had or in his ability to both intrigue and stump the police. Or then again, some people may want to stay in touch to see how much the police know about them, perhaps as a way of protecting themselves, though this curiosity can eventually help to give them away. Their interest arouses the police curiosity, or they may say something that only the killer could know."

Jon described one such case from his own experience. "The man who I believed did it presented himself as a helping hand in the investigation, and he had all sorts of theories about who did it. And it just so happened that all of the theories applied to him, which is what convinced me he had done it. Although it was one of those cases again where there just wasn't the proof. The theories were fine, but there weren't the facts to sufficiently back them up in court."

And then there was another case Jon had recently heard about where a man had come to the police repeatedly with ideas about a murder case where he knew of the victim, ostensibly to help, and then the police finally charged him.

"It's hard to know if he's really guilty or not," said Jon. "But it's understandable that the police thought he did it, because it's a common syndrome—the helpful volunteer who is always hanging around and is always presenting a new theory of the case. It's really unusual for people to do that, unless they have some overriding interest in the case, such as being a family member. But when someone who's not otherwise connected emotionally keeps coming forward, offering theories, or volunteering their help, that's so unusual it evokes suspicion. Because the police buff or fire buff, or whatever, is often the one who has done whatever it is that fascinates him. For example, you frequently find that the arsonist is the person who wants to be a fireman and is always helping out. Like in one case, the hero helped this little old lady out of the burning building, and then he turned out to be the kid who set the fire in the first place. In fact, such hero-criminal types are usually the ones that report it, and they're the ones that help with the investigation, and then they are always on the scene watching it. So that's why it's good to take pictures of a crowd around a fire or serious crime scene, because if you keep seeing the same faces turn up in the photographs or videotapes or similar events, you know you have a suspect."

So why should such individuals keep hanging around, volunteering, or coming up with theories?

Jon went on. "Because, that compulsion to confess is very strong in people. It's not so much that they do it and then blurt out: 'I did it.' But instead, despite their natural sense of self-preservation and self-concealment, they present themselves almost compulsively as a way to stay involved or connected. By coming up with a theory, by saying that I think so and so did it, they are continuing to talk about it and they are getting others to listen. There's also a certain pride in keeping other people tantalized; but then, when the other people aren't quite able to solve it, the real culprits can feel much smarter. Also, they may want to stay connected to find out at what stage the investigation is at, so they can tell how much trouble they are in. It's like playing a game with danger, and there's a certain excitement or thrill in that. But it's a very dicey game to play. They can easily blurt out too much, and suddenly they're snared in their own trap which they have created for themselves.

"It's different if somebody just comes to you as an investigator to find out what you are working on now, because they have a general interest in detective work. Many people might have a general curiosity about that. But if somebody keeps coming to just talk to you about a murder or a particular crime, you wonder why they're doing that. And very often, that's a good indication that they are involved.

Jon and Naomi typically get involved in murder investigations and other crime cases after the police have given up or have come to a dead end, or otherwise have ended up with a result someone disagrees with. We asked to hear about some of these cases. Each one was fascinating, like a mini-TV show unraveling before us, and ironically, each seemed to illustrate a different way in which the police had somehow fouled up. It was no wonder, as Jon explained later, that the police didn't particularly like private investigators. After all, the investigators were in a sense called in on these crime cases because the police had in some way come to a dead end.

The first case Jon described was a robbery and assault. Jon and Naomi were convinced the police had arrested the wrong man.

"It started at a circus," Jon began. "An older man was there, slightly under the influence, and he lost his companions in the throng. Soon this tattooed Samoan man came up to him and asked, 'What's wrong?' He explained: 'I've lost my friends.' The Samoan said, 'I'm with promotion. Come with me and we'll have them paged and we'll find them again.' So in all innocence, the older man followed him. He was taken to a locked hallway on an upper floor. The tattooed Samoan unlocked a storeroom and asked the man to come in. At this point, the older man realized that he was going to be robbed and beaten.

"What led us to get involved was the way the police handled the case. After the older man described what happened, the police weren't able to find the tattooed Samoan he described on the premises. But a few days later, they did pick up a Samoan on a separate robbery charge. The suspect had a prior history of violence. When the police investigator working on the circus robbery heard about this man now in custody, he figured this was a big Samoan on another assault and robbery, so this all fits. Then they charged him with the circus robbery and assault too.

"But the only problem was that none of this really matched up. The suspect's appearance didn't fit the older man's description of a very big, tattooed guy. It didn't even match the police drawing done of the guy's face based on the older man's description. And there was no real connection between this Samoan and the circus. But they charged him with the crime anyway, and based on this, the district attorney took the case all the way to the prelim. But when the police finally took the victim to a lineup and he saw the suspect, he said, 'No, that's not the guy.' At that point, the police dropped the case.

"There was still plenty they could have done at this point to find the right guy, but they had made a series of assumptions about the crime, all of which were wrong. And when none of their assumptions proved right, the police simply dropped the case. They decided that the older man, the victim, was a bad witness because he didn't identify their six-foot-two, 200-pound Samoan as the assailant. In their view, the victim was just flaky and they felt they didn't have enough to go on, so they couldn't pursue the case. But how could the victim be expected to identify this guy as the assailant, when he had said a six-foot-seven, 300-pounder had committed the crime?

"Anyway, after the police dropped the ball, the victim became the plaintiff in a lawsuit against the owners of the facility where he was robbed and assaulted. This time his lawyer picked out another wrong guy, the one we ended up trying to clear. How we got involved as insurance investigators was that there were actually two tattooed Samoan guys at the circus, both of whom had access to the locked hallway and knew where the storeroom was. And the irony of all this is that this crime happened in a locked storeroom which should have tipped off the police from the very beginning that the perpetrator was somebody who was connected with the building. Then, too, he was able to unlock the second floor hallway, and knew exactly where to go, which suggests someone familiar with the premises too, since access to a locked hallway is not always automatic. So certainly, the police could have discovered all this.

"Once we realized that the assailant most probably was someone connected with the building, we went to the managers. We contacted the maintenance company that takes care of the building. We looked through several years of records to come up with a big guy who was at one time or even now working for the building. And in this case, he was pretty easy to find, because the alleged assailant was a tattooed giant. And that's how we found there were two people who fit this description—one a part-time former plumber, and the other an employee of a company that was promoting the circus that night."

So how did the victim's lawyer end up with the wrong guy?

"Well, the lawyer decided that the guy we're representing did it because he was this tattooed 300-pound Samoan who was connected with the company providing promotion that night. Sounds logical, doesn't it? The only problem with their theory is that our client wasn't there that night. He was an employee of that firm. But he was not on the scene that night. They just assumed he was."

When Jon and Naomi investigated, they found the client wasn't on duty or anywhere near the circus. On further investigation, they discovered the tattooed 300-pounder had been a part-time plumber formerly working there.

"So that's how he knew about the locked hallway and the location of the storeroom, and still had keys," Jon said, pointing out how they concluded who really did it, after both the police and the plaintiff's lawyer had ended up accusing the wrong person.

Unfortunately, as Jon noted, this information wouldn't do much to help the victim. The police had already decided that he was a bad witness, that they had no case, and that the actual assailant had no money, so they wouldn't be able to get any damages from him. But at least Jon and Naomi's information helped their client show that he hadn't done it, which meant that the building management wasn't liable for hiring a promotional firm that had an employee who assaulted and robbed the victim.

"And that information was right there for the police to find," Jon commented. "They just had to know where to look."

Then Jon described a case of a murder in a Nevada dry cleaner's where the police made an incorrect assessment of what happened at the scene of the crime based on a coroner's inquest that came to the wrong conclusion.

"The police concluded it was an accidental shooting," Jon explained, "but the family didn't believe the them. They thought the dry cleaner was murdered and they hired us to find out.

"It just didn't make sense to think it was an accident, despite what the coroner said. When we investigated, we discovered that the dry cleaner was shot in the forehead when she was standing behind the counter of her store. And when we looked more closely at the nature of the wound, the evidence showed powder burns, shrapnel and undischarged powder in the wound, making this obviously a close shot. Meanwhile, at the very moment the victim was shot, a man who was allegedly hard of hearing was standing at the other end of the counter. Supposedly, he had his back turned and didn't see what happened.

"The police and the coroner apparently bought his statement in concluding that the death was accidental. But when we looked more closely, we realized that it was ridiculous to think that any kind of shooting, whether murder or suicide, took place without him hearing it. How could he not be aware of it? First of all, the man was not totally deaf. And second, even if he was, a gunshot in a close space is so percussive and concussive that he would at least feel something. He was only about ten feet away. So he was possibly aware of something that he was trying to deny.

"Thus, the case raised a lot of questions about who might have done the shooting, where the perpetrator was, and who might have observed the crime. But the police just relied on the coroner's finding and let it go."

What happened now that Jon and Naomi had come up with this new interpretation and new findings? As in many such cases, the two were just left with the conclusion the man had been murdered, not killed by accident or by suicide, but they couldn't prove it.

"Unfortunately," Jon observed, the witness left the country soon after the shooting. It's just not credible that he wasn't aware of it. And then, when we went to the police and the coroner, they just became annoyed with us. They didn't like the idea that this case was being brought up again, and they really didn't want to deal with it."

So Jon and Naomi were left again with their conclusions and one more technically unsolved case. "But then that's par for this type of case," said Jon.

Still another case got turned over to Jon and Naomi because the police would not become involved. A woman had been reported missing, but there was no evidence of any foul play—no body—although the woman's mother, who lived in another state and who regularly spoke to her each week, was convinced her daughter had been either murdered or kidnapped. Otherwise, she was certain, her daughter would have called, and when the police wouldn't do anything, the mother contacted the private detectives. They eventually concluded that the woman was murdered and Jon explained what happened.

"It started a few days after this woman, about twenty-six, turned up missing. Now this was a woman who called her mother faithfully every Sunday. After the first Sunday went by and the family didn't hear from her, they called the police, who had no record of any crime occurring. The family contacted someone they knew out here, who in turn contacted us."

With little more than the woman's name to go on, Jon and Naomi began their search to find out where she might have been when she disappeared.

"We started off by running her driving record," Jon explained. "And then we discovered that she had been cited a few days before that Sunday in a town in Southern California, so at least she was around down there, which gave us a good place to start. There we checked the local records and found that her car had been towed, because it had been parked in the same spot for days.

"We also learned that the woman had a roommate, who led us to some of her friends. From all these people, we learned that this woman had another life, which her mother didn't know about. It seems she was a call girl who traveled around to various conventions in Las Vegas, New Orleans, Los Angeles and so on. And she had disappeared in this Southern California town which had a large criminal population and was a center of drug dealing."

But at least the police there proved to be very helpful.

"The cops couldn't do very much themselves about this drug problem in town, since the police department consists of just two officers and a chief. But they helped us investigate. They gave us some useful information on the people in town involved in drugs and where they were. Some of them lived way up in the hills, and we wouldn't have found them otherwise. The police also gave us some background on their criminal history.

"With this information, we began talking to different people who knew this woman and discovered that she had had a falling out with these guys who were the suspects. Apparently, they had been involved together in the drug trade. They didn't have a very good relationship in the past, and had threatened the woman before."

Following these leads, Jon eventually found himself face to face with one of the suspects, who, if he didn't do the actual killing, at least knew something about it. What made Jon think so?

"Because he lied," Jon said. "He had driven up to this area with the victim, and then told a story that was absurd. On the surface, the story seemed okay. But once we looked at it more closely, we decided that it was impossible for the man to have observed what he said he did, and that the amount of time he claimed the trip took was all wrong. Basically, his story was that the victim had picked him up and they drove toward the town together. Before they got there, though, the victim let him off. He then saw the victim turn her car around and leave town in the opposite direction without waving at him or giving him any explanation. So unexpectedly, he claims, the victim just took off going north, and that was the last he saw of her.

"But when we checked out his story, going to the stop where he said he saw the victim turning around, we found it was physically impossible to see the freeway from where he said he was. He couldn't have witnessed this from that spot where he said he was standing; or else he couldn't have been there. That made us feel he knew more than he was telling us, because when somebody is so definite with his or her story and it turns out to be impossible, then there's a good chance a lie is being told. Maybe he didn't do any-thing to the victim himself, but it seemed like he probably knew who did and just didn't want to say."

As Jon pointed out, this was a normal practice—to check out someone's story, by actually going to the place where it is said to have happened.

"After all, you want to see if it's true. So you ask the person, 'Tell me what happened.' Then you ask him where he was when he saw it, and he says: 'I'm standing here and this happened.' So then you go to the spot to see if it really could have happened this way. Well, in this case, we discovered there was a wall on this access road where he said he was standing observing the freeway, so it just wasn't possible for him to see what he said."

As is commonly done, Jon went back to confront the individual with his lie. And that led him to who he thought was the real suspect.

Jon observed, "As soon as we confronted him with what I found, his hands started shaking and his voice started quavering, and usu-ally that's a sign of some inner turmoil, unless somebody's freezing to death. So then, while he was shaking like a leaf, he announced that he would have to talk to this other person before he could tell us any more. He just blurted out the name of this guy, because he was so frightened. But when we asked him why he had to talk to this particular person, he just froze up like a clam. He was probably more afraid of that person than he was of us, which is a wise thing, since most likely this other person is the one who killed the victim.

"In any case, from what this guy had said, we knew that the victim had been in town that night she disappeared and that she was going to meet these other guys, including this person she wanted to talk to. And later, from other witnesses in this circle of drug dealers, we learned that the victim had in fact been with these guys we think committed the crime.

"So basically, our evidence seemed to check out and point to this. The woman's car was found abandoned near town; this guy had seen her driving there that night; she was going to meet these drug dealers, and supposedly she did. It all fit together. These facts left us with a theory of what had happened—that she had met with these dealers and there had been a fight and one or more of them did away with her."

We wondered if this theory was correct.

"Well, subsequent events seemed to confirm it. We couldn't locate her ourselves, but a few days later some hunters found the body in the woods. According to the coroner's report, the woman had been beaten to death.

"Unfortunately, we never had enough information to tie these particular guys more directly to the body and the death. And the police didn't think there was enough to go on. And of course the witnesses who knew what happened weren't talking. But at least when we were done, the family felt a sense of peace because the uncertainty was over. It wasn't pleasant to realize that their daughter had been involved in prostitution and the drug trade, and was probably killed because of it. But at least they knew."

Perhaps Jon and Naomi's most fascinating case ended up with them because the police couldn't find the crime scene. In Jon and Naomi's view, the police had the wrong theory. This was the case in which a doctor had been murdered and then discovered in his own home dressed in a suit.

"It was really very puzzling at first," said Jon, "because there was very little blood on the body. He obviously hadn't been killed in his home, since there was no blood, no sign of a struggle there. But there was no clue as to who might have done it or where. The police felt if they could figure out where the crime was committed, they would have found the killer. But they couldn't and they didn't have a good motive to help guide them, so eventually they dropped the case. The doctor's colleagues came to us and asked us to look into it."

Then, Jon described how he and Naomi eventually came around to their theory that the killing was done by one of the victim's patients.

"First we started thinking about who this guy was and how he was killed. It seemed especially significant that he was a doctor, and he was very well-known, a very decent guy, active in the civil rights movement. Now various people thought that maybe the doctor was killed by some right-wing nut who hated what he was doing, and that was possible. But the manner of death suggested something else. As we found out later, by checking the coroner's report, the body had been dressed very carefully *after* the murder.

"Now that act could be simply to keep the body neat. But we thought it was more than that—it was a very gentle act, an act of homage to him, that didn't fit the right-wing profile. Why? Well, look at it this way. Say you are a right-wing lunatic Nazi or Ku Klux Klanner who hates this type of person. So then you murder this guy because he offends everything you find awful in society. Well, it doesn't make sense to think that such a person would turn around after committing a murder, carefully dress the body, and return it home."

Jon went on painting the picture of what might have happened, showing how each piece of the murder puzzle seemed to fit together with a very different conclusion than the one the police had come to.

"Now another important piece of this," Jon continued, "is that this doctor was a big guy. He was about 190 or 200 pounds. So that raises the question of who can carry a dead weight of 200 pounds? It must be a strong man or maybe even two men. But then, it points to just one man, if you think about the way the wounds were on the body, because they were all frontal, indicating the victim was stabbed by just one person who was in front of him; not two, which might have produced wounds on the sides or the back as well.

"Thus, just with this limited information that the police had to start with, the case offers a very different view of things. Initially, it might suggest the redneck, white sheet, or swastika type of hate killing. But now, it suddenly presents a very different portrait of who might have done this, probably a lone killer and a very strong one. And it's somebody who probably knew the doctor and cared about him.

"Plus he had to be someone who could lure the doctor out of his house, because the crime didn't happen there. And as we discovered through investigation, the victim didn't leave the house for just any reason. Rather, it turned out, he was slightly paranoid, so when called on the phone, he had to know who the person was before agreeing to a meeting at night. There was nobody really threatening him, so there was no particular reason for this paranoia. There wasn't anyone in particular who might provide a lead to the killer. But the doctor apparently was very concerned about his personal safety, which suggests that when he went out, it was because he knew whoever this was and felt comfortable with him."

So why would the doctor go out to meet this person? Jon went on with his theory.

"It seems like he left very suddenly, because when the police checked the doctor's house after finding the body, they discovered he had been fixing dinner that evening, and that he left quickly. This seemed apparent, because food was laid out with the wine open, and he probably left in a particular hurry. Obviously, he was interrupted in the middle of things, probably by telephone."

But what kind of interruption? What would be so important about it that the doctor would just up and leave?

"When we spoke to several people who knew him, what seemed to make the most sense was that the doctor was acquainted with this person and was responding to a cry for help. In fact, we asked the people we spoke to just that—why would this doctor leave in such a hurry in the middle of the night and leave all this food on the table? We were told he would leave if he thought a friend was in need of help. As they said to us, this was important to him, to help people.

So that's what we concluded was his motivation—helping someone. That's what would have gotten him out of the house."

The theory was starting to come together. As Jon summarized, the doctor had been lured out by a large man who knew him personally or was a friend of his, was good with a knife, and brought him out to some spot on the pretext of needing help. Then he killed the doctor there and dressed him and brought the body back to his home.

But why now? Why should this killer suddenly decide to act at this particular time?

Jon tried to explain the possibly unexplainable.

"It may not have been any particular event, exactly. There's no way to know if there was a final insult or a final anything that triggered the act. Perhaps the tension just built up and the man was fed up.

"In any event, the man was somebody who knew the doctor well, somebody able to get the doctor to go out suddenly in response to his call for help. Based on that theory, we talked to a number of people, and we think we did meet the one who called the doctor.

"It's really a funny moment, a dangerous moment, when you suddenly encounter somebody who fits the picture just sitting in an armchair talking about the case. After all, you could still be wrong. So you can't assume too much from that fact that something fits. You still have to hold on to that reserve, that analytical part of you which watches and judges. But then, in the course of the interview with the subject, as you talk about the case, you may start to notice things are even more clearly coming together; like the last pieces of the puzzle are fitting too."

What pieces? We were eager to know who Jon thought did it and why.

Jon went on. He spoke generally, but it was clear he also was describing what had happened in his interview with the suspected murderer.

"Well, as you talk, you note the person's emotional responses. Is there something strange, unusual about them? Also, the questions you ask allow him to talk about the third person—the victim—so he can detach and speak freely, he may start coming up with details that suggest he has an intimate knowledge of the case. And so,

gradually, you start to get an intuitive feeling, a kind of inner knowing that, yes, he knows something, he is connected. And that's what
I felt with this person we spoke with—this knowing he was the murderer."

So what about him led to this, to this knowing? Did he seem
especially angry? Nervous? Knowledgeable?

"Well, there was a certain oddness about his reactions," Jon commented. "He didn't seem angry about the doctor's death, and at the
same time, he was also mourning the loss of this person. Now this
mourning would make sense if this man didn't do it, which is possible, since we had no other evidence against him. He could have just
been a devoted follower who was very forgiving in his devotion and
so felt no anger. But if the man did do it, his mourning still made
sense, too, because of the way the body had been dressed—as if to
honor it."

Unfortunately, as in so many other cases, Jon and Naomi weren't
able to get beyond their suspicions to any hard evidence. They just
had a man who might have done it, strangely mourning the doctor,
but he wasn't about to confess. And they had no crime scene.

As Jon explained, "A crime scene can be characterized as either
organized or disorganized. An organized scene reveals an underlying plan, whereas a disorganized one results from a spontaneous act.
For example, a serial or contract killer will usually create an organized crime scene, even though it may be incredibly chaotic and
bloody, because he begins with a plan of action, which involves
going to a place and killing someone and then getting away. Usually
he was a car. Then, if he transports the body from the point of the
murder to some other place to get rid of it, that's part of an organized killing too, even if the culprit should get rid of the victim's
head in one jurisdiction and the rest of the body in another to confuse matters. The point is that the crime scene is organized,
because the killer brings his weapon with him and is in control of
the scene throughout the commission of the crime. It may be a made
thing to do, but it's an organized killing.

By contrast, a disorganized killing might be something like this: a
woman leaves for work in the morning but never gets there, and is
found murdered later that day on the rooftop of her own building,
where she has been sexually assaulted and strangled with her purse

cord or her own nylons. Well, that's a disorganized crime scene, because the murderer used the tools at hand—the victim's own belongings—to kill her. And that means he didn't intend to commit a crime before he saw the victim, and probably lives in the neighborhood, didn't use a car, and didn't transport the body anywhere. He just killed suddenly and split.

"Thus, this kind of analysis of the kind of crime and the kind of crime scene helps to narrow things down, so you see a pattern that tells you a little about the killer. It's like he has left a kind of signature behind, so you know more about him—if you read the signs correctly.

"Now, typically, when a rage-filled crime occurs, it's not just by someone off the street, though many people have this image of the mad, random killer. Normally, most killings of this type occur as a result of a cumulative series of grievances, because the killer perceives that the victim is psychologically oppressing him in some way. For instance, he thinks the victim has insulted him or taken advantage of him in some way. It could be anything, and what the victim has done could be real or not, but the killer just perceives the offense that way. Meanwhile, the victim doesn't know what he's doing or how the other person is feeling about this, and so eventually, the killer's anger keeps rising until it reaches its boiling point. Then with the next action or real or perceived insult, the killer snaps and takes revenge on either the victim or someone important to the victim.

"Once again, it was one of these intriguing but unsolved cases. And that's part of the fascination of it all. To come so close; to think you know, but then to be left dangling. It's like an exquisite mystery that keeps tantalizing for all time."

Changing the topic, we wondered about Jon and Naomi's experience in working with the police or the district attorney in a town where a crime occurred. Since they were dealing with crimes normally the jurisdiction of the police and D.A., did the Jon and Naomi ever work with the authorities when the two did start coming up with theories or suspicions about who did it? Did they ever turn over evidence or leads to these officials, so that now the police could pursue their investigations further and maybe charge someone with the crime? Or did the police or D.A., when stumped, ever come to Jon and Naomi to get their help?

Jon shook his head, emphasizing that the police and D.A. rarely worked with private investigators or vice versa.

"You may see that in television or in the movies, but in real life it's not that way. The police have certainly never come to us. We've never had our help solicited in any jurisdiction, and usually the police are not willing to be too cooperative when we come to them, because they don't like private investigators. Generally, the reason for this is the police resent us investigating at all. They think it's ridiculous; why should a private detective be able to do anything the police haven't done? So it's a little like a turf war. But beyond that, they tend to think that private investigators are amateurs, while they are the professionals."

Yet there were times when Jon and Naomi did find out information that the police hadn't. What if they uncovered information that would help to support a particular theory of a crime? Would the police then become cooperative if Jon and Naomi found evidence that could help them out?

Again Jon shook his head. "No, that doesn't happen. I've never seen it. The police generally want to do the whole case themselves for them to be interested, or they don't want to do anything. They really aren't very good at sharing what they do with outsiders."

And according to Jon, the same was true of the district attorneys they had contacted about various crimes from time to time.

"We tried contacting them for a series of child abductions once. These were the kind of cases where one parent had kidnapped the child from the other, and every time we brought the matter to the attention of various district attorneys, the response was: 'Well, what do you want us to do about it?' They reacted as if the matter wasn't even a crime, although child abduction, even when parents do it, is a felony."

Was it because of their heavy case load, because they just didn't have the time?

"No, not at all," Jon responded. "I don't think they were interested in the crime. They didn't seem to think it was a crime to kidnap your own kid, though in fact it is. So we never got very far with the D.A.'s, either, on any of our cases. It's like the police, district attorneys and private investigators exist in separate worlds. They have their turf and we have ours, and about the only place these seem to meet are in the movies and on TV. But in real life it just isn't that way."

Jon had just finished cataloging a variety of cases where he and Naomi had ended up investigating because for one reason or another the police had not pursued the case, had not been able to find the killer, or had perhaps found the wrong person. We wondered about the responsibility or liability of the police for their actions. For example, if Jon and Naomi were able to find the right killer or, in the course of their investigation, come up with the evidence showing that the police hadn't followed through properly, could the police be liable for negligence? And if they turned up the real killer and the wrong person was prosecuted, could the real killer have liability, too?

Jon answered slowly, thoughtfully. "Well, I think theoretically there would be liability for either or both of them. But in practical terms, I don't think there would be much hope. First, there might not be much point going after the real killer, because in actuality, few have any money. Also, so much time has generally gone by when the real perpetrator is unearthed and the wrongly-accused person vindicated, that it would be hard to make a case. Then, too, when it comes to the police, it can be very difficult to prove if they did or didn't conduct the investigation correctly, knowing what they did or didn't know at the time. What should they have done or not done? That can be hard to say. It's a very thin line, very difficult to prove. Besides, by the time these cases wind up, the people are usually just glad to get the information—to know what happened or didn't, and they just want to be finished with all this. They want to move on."

Jon also pointed out the difficulty of first getting the official cooperation to help them resolve a case the police hadn't and then turning around and suing the police for not having solved it.

"It's a real double bind," he went on. "It would be rather odd to ask the police to help you investigate, and then to sue them for their negligence in not solving the case in the first place. Besides, if we were able to crack the case, we would have to turn our evidence over to the district attorney and then he or she would work with the police to conduct their own investigation based on the information we gave them. So normally you wouldn't try to go after the police. The only time would be if you were convinced that the local authorities were so incompetent or so politically biased that they wouldn't handle the case fairly. Then you would take it to the attorney general of the state, not to the jurisdiction where the crime originally took place. But generally, that sort of thing doesn't happen. Rather, you just have a situation where the police or prosecutors have made a call based on their own interpretation of the facts, or they just haven't pursued the case at all given their own good reasons. But is that really negligence? There's this fine line between being negligent or liable or not, and it's really hard to say."

In any case, as Jon pointed out, he had never been in a situation where any client had sued either the police or the real criminal. "It just doesn't normally happen that way. People don't normally sue," Jon said.

By contrast, a much more common situation that came up in working with clients was getting them, after an investigation, to accept what really happened.

"Sometimes it's just very hard for them to accept the truth," Jon pointed out. "On the one hand, they want to know, although, when it turns out the facts are not what they hoped, they really don't."

Still, as Jon noted, sometimes he and Naomi at least tried to soften the blow in telling their clients upsetting formation. As he pointed out, this kind of need for counseling was more common in the domestic cases they used to handle, such as when a husband wanted a wife followed.

"We had one case where our client was convinced that just about everybody was having an affair with his ex-wife—her tennis instructor, her boss, the bus driver—and he wanted her followed. In fact, she had no outside social life whatsoever. She just didn't want to live with him anymore. But he didn't want to believe this. He felt there had to be another man involved in her leaving him. So when we reported that there was no one, he at first wouldn't believe us, and he kept trying to deny this could be true."

But why, we wondered. Wouldn't it be worse to feel she had left him for another man?

"No," Jon said. "For him, there would be a great psychological comfort in thinking there was someone else, because then he wouldn't have to acknowledge the reality that 'She doesn't love me.' Instead, he could think that she was seduced by Raoul the tango dancer and his gypsy ways or whatever, and if it wasn't for Raoul, she would still be with him. So he doesn't have to face the fact that there was really something wrong with their relationship, which was dysfunctional from the beginning of their marriage, or with him. We're not qualified to get into counseling him in any psychological way about why he's doing what he's doing, even though we might have a good idea of what's going on. But we do try to tell him what's going on. And if he's attempting to deny that, we'll tell him that and try to get him to acknowledge what's really happening. But beyond that, dealing with the psychological effects of this knowledge is really up to him. We try to be as gentle as we can, but our job is to try to help the person see reality."

Next, Jon described how he and Naomi had located a child who had been missing for seven years. It was an international child custody dispute, where the father had spirited the youngster away to Cancún for a while before bringing her back to another state for several more years, and finally ending up in California. But with some careful sleuthing, Jon and Naomi were able to zero in on the child's location, and this time, the case did have a happy ending—mother and child were reunited.

So how did Jon and Naomi do it. Again it was fascinating to hear how they pulled together the various strands to figure out the case.

"It started with this detective from Mexico contacting us. The mother had already gone through several dozen detectives. The father had taken his young daughter from a private school in Rio. Then, after some time in Cancún, the father came back to the States, and for a few years the detectives were trying to track him somewhere in Florida. And then after the mother, living abroad, went to this Mexican detective who specialized in such things, we were contacted, because there was a grandfather in California, and it was thought that maybe the girl ended up here. Or at least the grandfather might know where the two were, since it was logical to assume he was in contact with his own son."

But was he? Jon and Naomi soon discovered that in this case, the police were actually involved in trying to find the man and his daughter, since there were warrants out from several jurisdictions. The police thus far hadn't had much luck, and the grandfather denied having any contact.

Yet, on a hunch, Jon and Naomi didn't believe him. "It just didn't make sense," said Jon, "a father not being in touch with his son for years."

So around the girl's birthday, Jon and Naomi decided to check out the grandfather's garbage, to see if maybe he was in contact with her, and that's when they found their first clue—there was birthday wrapping that read, "To Sally from Grandpa." "So that's how we knew the kid was in town," said Jon.

But where was she?

At first, the two investigators followed the lead on some papers they found in the garbage near the wrapping, thinking maybe the name of the storage facility on them was near the place where the father and child stayed. But it was only a place where the grandfather had boxes stored.

"Then we got the idea of pretending to be a friend of the father's," Jon continued. "I called and said I had worked with the father years ago when we had been in the Army in Germany, and now that I was back in the States, I was hoping to get everyone together for a big reunion. And the grandfather basically fell for it. 'They just moved,' he told me, 'so I don't have their new address written down. But I do have their phone number.' He even told me where his son was working. And that was accurate. So then we put a surveillance on the place of business."

It was the logical thing to do. But unfortunately, it didn't work, because as Jon explained, "The man was using an alias. We tried going to the parking lot and checking all the cars. We ran all the license plates, thinking one would be traced to him, and all we would have to do was follow the car. But as it turned out, he was still very much on guard, even after seven years of running, so not only did he use an alias, but he was parking the car in the lot adjacent to his business and then walking. So there's little chance we could find him this way."

The break came when Jon called the grandfather back to check on the number he had, and found that the man was going to the storage facility on a certain date to move some boxes to his new residence. So again, Jon and Naomi tried a surveillance on the place, and this time they tailed him. Meanwhile, as they continued to keep an eye on him, they called the wife who had contacted them through the foreign detective and she flew in with the appropriate custody papers, so she could get the girl back through the court.

The other big break in the case was discovering the youngster's school.

"We found it the same day as we did the father's residence," Jon exulted. "In the end, we actually didn't need it to find the child, but we did get the mother to come to the States. She had been so frustrated over the years, coming so close to getting the child before, but then finding the ex-husband and kid slipping away. And working with so many investigators, she didn't want to go anywhere until we had this information. She just didn't want to go through this emotional turmoil of almost having her child again, but then nothing."

So how did Jon and Naomi find the school. It was almost too easy.

"Well, once we knew the town where the father was, we called all the schools in the area. We were pretty sure it would be a private school, since the father was wealthy and wouldn't want to put his child in a public school because it wouldn't be good enough for his kid. So we focused on calling private schools. And sure enough, she was there. And what made it so easy was that the father didn't use a totally invented alias, which would have made it impossible to find the child. Instead, he simply reversed the child's first and second names, as a security measure, and when we called the correct school, the woman in the office simply corrected us. 'Oh, no, her name isn't so and so; it's so and so.' And then we had it."

But why didn't the father invent a name for security? After all, he had done so for himself on his car in the parking lot.

Again, Jon had a logical explanation. "Because it was probably too hard for the kid to remember all the time what her name really was, and this was just a young kid, not an adult skilled at ducking the law. So her father just tried to do the next best thing, by reversing the names; though if he was really smart, he would have used an alias."

And so, with the girl and her father located and the mother contacted, the investigation went into its final phase—getting the girl away from the father, arresting the man, and reuniting the youngster with her mother.

The windup started in the early evening, before the father had returned from work but after the girl had come home from school.

"It was amazing," said Jon. "Like you see in the movies. The girl is quietly relaxing at home, watching TV. And meanwhile, there is this veritable army of cops amassing outside. We have our own operative watching the house, communicating with us by walkie-talkie. And just around the corner, there are a half dozen police cars from the town and sheriff's cars from the county, and everyone has warrants for the kid to come to court for this custody hearing. But the cops and sheriffs are just waiting out there, deciding what to do. Nobody wants to serve these documents about the court hearing, because they're all afraid they may get sued by someone in this case. So they're arguing: 'It's not our jurisdiction,' 'It's not our jurisdiction.' And then: 'Let's wait for the sheriff.' And meanwhile, the mother is amazed by this jurisdictional battle going on.

"So then, finally, the sheriff arrives, and after everyone explains the situation to him, he agrees that he can serve the papers. But the only problem is that since it's about 5:00 P.M. Friday, the sheriff says the kid is going to have to spend the weekend in juvenile hall, because the courts are all closed until Monday. And then, when the mother's stateside attorney, who is also there, suggests that everyone come back on Monday, the mother goes absolutely bonkers. To fly all this way, to be so close, to maybe risk losing her kid again, and someone suggests coming back Monday. So what if the kid spends a weekend in jail?

"Thus, the cops agree, we'll go in now. And so the lawyers calm the mother down and everyone goes in. Meanwhile, up and down the street, neighbors are peering out of their windows or standing on their doorsteps wondering what's going on, because there are ten cop cars. Then, one of the cops rings the bell, and the kid answers, and the cop says: 'Your mother's here,' and at once the scene is mindblowing. The kid runs across the lawn onto the street, and in moments, they're embracing, and everybody is crying. The cops are sobbing; we're sobbing; it's like a Hollywood ending. And then, so the kid doesn't have to spend the weekend in juvenile hall, a sheriff's deputy announces that he'll take her. And so everyone's happy. And on Monday, after the hearing, the mother and the kid fly home together."

But what happened to the father?

"Oh, him," Jon commented. "Well, apparently, the father didn't go back to the house, because a girlfriend, brother-in-law, or somebody tipped him off about all those cops out there. But we learned that the deputy who had taken the girl for the weekend and heard her story decided to go after the guy and staked out his girlfriend's place until spotting him. Then with police backup, he ran down the guy in a high speed chase and had him arrested.

"But then, after the hearing, after the kid and the mother are gone, the police release the father, because they don't have the victim anymore, and the mother and kid aren't about to stick around. So they can't press charges. Later, though, the mother sues the father for what she spent trying to locate the kid. It was thousands, and she was less interested in seeing him in jail than getting the money back."

And according to Jon, she finally did, though by then he and Naomi were no longer involved in the case. They had been able to find the kid and that's all they had to do.

We had one last question about the case. Why would the father do this? Since the kid was so glad to return to her mother and related a terrible story of hiding to the sheriff's deputy, it didn't sound like the father really loved and wanted to be with his daughter.

"Unfortunately true," said Jon. "He wanted to screw the wife and make her unhappy. So he took the kid. It was a pure vengeance kind of thing. It wasn't because he loved or was trying to protect his kid or anything like that. But then that's one of the things that often happens in these custody cases. One spouse tries to screw the other, and they use the kid to do it. So the kid becomes a kind of pawn fought over between them. But at least, in this case, there was a happy ending. The mother got the kid back and the father had to pay for all the hurt and damage he caused.

Now, after listening to Jon describe a variety of fairly gruesome, hair-raising and emotionally wrenching cases involving murder, drugs, child-stealing and other crimes, we wondered about the dangers. Had Jon or Naomi felt at all threatened or frightened by all this contact with potentially dangerous criminals and crime? Or suppose they were zeroing in on the details of the crime with the person they suspected of doing a killing? Wasn't there any danger that they could be killed too?

Jon shook his head. "No, never. Neither of us has been pushed around, so we don't have horror stories. I know some investigators have had some hairy run-ins, particularly where they are trying to serve subpoenas, such as in one case, where a guy with a bat came after a process server. But we've never had any problem serving them. Certainly, people don't throw a party for us when we come to the door. But they're always polite and accept service.

"And, as for interviewing possible killers. That was really never any problem. We just tried to be empathetic, to listen and understand, and so there was never any threat. Sure, sometimes we take some precautions, such as meeting people in a public place, which is certainly safer. But there have been a few times where we have had to interview in his home a person we thought was a killer or other criminal. Doing it there was not a good idea classically, but we had to. It was the only way to get the interview, and it worked out."

But what about other precautions, like taking along a gun, just in case?

Again, Jon shook his head. "You can't carry a weapon—at least most private detectives can't. Usually, just retired policemen qualify, unless you live in an especially lenient county. So, popular films and TV to the contrary, the most you can usually do is be as alert and aware as possible.

"And besides," Jon said emphatically, "I wouldn't think that it's necessary to carry a gun in most cases. In fact, even if I could have one, I don't think it's a good idea. When I go to interview someone, I don't intend to or even expect to get into a physical confrontation with that person. What I want to do is have a talk and get him or her to tell me something. So the feeling of what's going on is completely different. Now it's true that people can get so agitated they might want to hurt me, because my questions are upsetting them or frightening them or are getting them to reveal information that may be dangerous to them. But then, when I see that starting to happen, I just back off. I talk about something else. I get them relaxed and start again. So nothing has ever happened.

"So it's really not a good idea to come to an interview with the idea that there's going to be a fight. You still want to be cautious, but you want to be there with the idea that you're just going to elicit information and be as understanding and empathetic as possible. And then you take that risk. But to go to an interview with a gun, baseball bat or any other weapon? No, I wouldn't. That would only be more likely to provoke the confrontation you fear."

Then, since we had been talking mostly about crime cases during the interview, we wondered what Jon thought about the system? Any thoughts about the philosophy of crime or punishment?

Jon had a few. But first he wanted to distinguish between the kinds of intriguing, Hollywood-like cases we had been talking about and the routine, everyday crimes. As he pointed out, these kind of cases, these types of criminals, were somewhat far removed from the everyday sorts of cases most investigators deal with.

"There's really an artistic difference between a murder case like the ones we've been talking about and the run-of-the-mill murder or crime case. That's because most criminals are horribly ignorant and pathetic. They come from the underclass and they have no imagination, no expertise, and they're very bad at committing crimes. They're very good at being prisoners, at being cogs in the system, and they keep coming in and going out on a kind of a treadmill of crime. And while they may be very violent, what they do really isn't very interesting, because most murders or crimes of violence are very pedestrian. For typically what happens is there is some kind of drug deal or other beef on a street corner, and some guy pulls a gun and shoots the other in front of dozens of witnesses. So it's not creative; it's not imaginative. The crime is just stupid, and brutal. And then, what we're supposed to do is just defend the poor guy, and any investigation is usually pretty cut and dried. Unlike these other more exotic, who-done-it or how-it-was-done cases, everything is pretty much known. So the investigation involves basically taking statements of who saw what, and whether the witness could have really seen what he says he did because of where he was or maybe because he was under the influence of a dozen wine coolers. So part of the investigation can be questioning the witness's recollections and attacking his credibility. And then you are often getting character witnesses to support the person, and say that he really is a nice person after all, just got in with a wrong crowd, wouldn't have done it if not for drugs, and that sort of thing. It's pretty much the same story again and again.

"So qualitatively, this kind of routine investigation is really quite different from one in which you are trying to see which one of these otherwise normal-appearing people has committed a monstrous act with horrible consequences for a lot of people. That's the kind of thing which really fascinates everybody in the movies and on TV, and that's what fascinates me—getting to the heart of this human darkness; discovering, understanding it, and making some sense out of it all."

Then, having shared his ideas about crime as art, Jon turned to his thoughts about the role of the investigator and the criminal justice system. As he explained, he didn't normally handle mundane crime cases, because he didn't find these kind of crimes or the people who did them very interesting. He agreed, though, it was important for someone to investigate to help provide the accused with a defense.

"It's really fine line. As a defense investigator, one is trying to find information that will mitigate the guy's sentence, if not get him off. And it's important to do that in an adversary system. After all, the state has the obligation to prove its case against the individual, and it can't be allowed to run amok in accusing people of crimes, which maybe they didn't commit. So the defense system serves as a good counterbalance to that.

"But then, the big problem in the system is that it's so overcrowded that sometimes the prosecution will just plea bargain a case or drop it, because there's no time to handle it. So the prosecution sometimes for no reason lets people walk away from the things that they did, and you get these revolving door defendants. It's like an old morality play that gets acted out again and again, so that everyone finds it so boring."

Then, what did Jon think should be done about all this? In his view, the key was personal responsibility, though as an investigator, there wasn't too much he could do about this—indeed, if he did work as an investigator for the defense, the ideal solution was that he would be, perhaps, providing the attorney with information that could help the client get off or get a lesser sentence. But then, as Jon pointed out earlier, it was still necessary for the defense to be able to do this to counterbalance the accusations of the prosecutor and force him to prove his case.

Jon further elaborated on the ideal of personal responsibility. "Fortunately, I think there's a growing trend to make the individual more responsible for his acts. About fifteen or twenty years ago, everyone wanted to blame society because some guy went out and committed some heinous act, such as robbing a liquor store, getting incredibly drunk, and then perhaps using the knives he had stolen to disembowel a dozen nuns on their way to High Mass, or something like that. People would say that somehow it's society's fault because the criminal did that.

"But now, there's a pendulum swing away from the idea that society is responsible for every horrible act that people commit. Instead, people are more interested in ascribing personal responsibility to individuals for what they do. And I think that's good, because that acceptance of responsibility helps to elevate people. In truth, it's really demeaning to their own humanity when these defendants come through the revolving door of justice time and time again for the same dumb crime, and then protest, 'It's really not my fault. I'm really just a victim of society,' and the probation officers, social workers, judges and others spout this same line. It's demeaning, because it really is their fault, and it's demeaning to them as human beings not to give them responsibility for their acts. And people need to take responsibility for their own acts for society to improve."

It was a fitting kind of philosophical note on which to end a discussion of crime and the investigation of it as a kind of art, and the need for personal responsibility to help stem the growing tide of crime. But we had one last question. Where did Jon think the business of investigating crimes was going?

"Unfortunately, growing," Jon said. "Fortunately, for us and other investigators, there will be more and more criminal defense work because there are more and more crimes. But on the other hand, it's unfortunate for society, because that's the way it is. But then, maybe somehow, there's still a balance because of the adversary system. So you have defense and prosecution evenly matched. Yet if there were less crimes, there would be less need for both. But now the trend is definitely up."

Then, as we got up to leave, Jon pulled out a hefty file. It was still another unsolved case.

5

Terry Finn and Cameron Rolfe: The World of High-Tech Investigation

Sam and I drove out to meet Terry Finn and Cameron Rolfe, who specialize in high-tech and aviation investigations. We got together in a large warehouse of a building, which looked like a huge aircraft hanger. In fact, as we were led on a brief guided tour we saw dozens of battered cars, small planes and other vehicles, some of them covered by weathered tarps. It had the look of an auto wrecking yard.

"Oh, that's all evidence," Terry, an intelligent looking man of about forty with a trim beard explained. "We're one of several such private facilities in the Bay Area, and we keep the evidence here for the cases we and other investigators and attorneys work on. Then, when it's needed for trial, it's here."

Terry led us down a long corridor into a small room piled high with files, odd-looking metallic equipment, black boxes with knobs, and framed certificates and awards on the walls. It felt like we could easily be recorded, videotaped or viewed somewhere, which is perhaps fitting, since, after all, Terry and Cameron specialize in such high-tech surveillance or countersurveillance protective work.

Then, after introducing us to Cameron, a smooth-shaven clean cut engineer type in his late thirties, Terry wondered if we were aware that they could prevent us from tape recording anything. I glanced up surprised, since I was just now setting up our tape recorders, as I did for every interview.

"But how?" I asked, noticing that the tape recorders seemed to go on and off perfectly.

"By just blocking the sound with a high-pitched white noise that you can't hear. But the tape recorder can." He pulled out a small black instrument with a few buttons, called a jammer. "So all you'll end up when you play it back is a light whir."

It seemed an appropriate start to an interview on the art of high-tech investigations.

And then, with a grin, I explained that the only way we could do this interview was if we could tape it, so I could write from the transcripts. Terry relented. However, just to emphasize the importance of doing any high-tech investigation legally—by following the rules designed to protect everyone's privacy—Terry went through a long introductory procedure in which we clearly announced on the tape that this was a fully lawful recording and that everyone agreed to it. The introductory conversation went something like this:

Me: This is going to be an interview with Terry Finn and Cameron Rolfe, and we're going to be talking about different kinds of equipment.
Finn: And who are we talking with?
Me: This is Gini Scott and Sam Brown.
Finn: And what's the date today?
Me: Today is January 8.
Finn: And what time is it?
Me: It is 5:25 P.M.
Finn: And what year is it?

Me: 1990.

Finn: And everyone understands this is a lawful recording?

Me: Yes.

Finn: And we are all aware that we are being tape recorded? Yes, we are. And do we all give our permission to make this tape recording? And do we all understand that a subsequent transcription will be made?

Me: Yes. And subsequently, after the transcript is written, the chapter will be resubmitted back to you for your approval.

Finn: Then, great. Okay. By doing this, we have taken the first important step. Everything is lawful, as it would be if police officers were doing this. Because if we do anything that's not, we could end up in municipal or superior court, and it's not ethical. So what we will be talking about here is running a professional, legal operation. Everything we do with this high tech equipment is perfectly legal.

So, that was the way the interview started. Then, after Sam and I agreed we understood, the regular interview began.

Terry began with a brief run-through of his background. Like many investigators, he happened into the field because he had a specialty in something else—in his case, being a pilot and knowing a great deal about aviation. Then, gradually, from doing aviation investigations, he branched out into the high-tech field and formed "Incognito services," located in Burlingame and San Carlos on the peninsula south of San Francisco.

His experience in the aviation field dates back to 1969, when he was an aircraft mechanic and bush pilot in northern Canada, where he was born. Then, until 1977, he worked as a police officer in Canada, where he got involved in all phases of criminal investigation and enforcement. After this, he went to San Jose State University in San Jose, California, getting his Bachelor of Science Degree in Criminal Justice and Psychology. And afterwards, he even went to law school for two years at Golden Gate University and studied at the police college in Taiwan.

In the process, Terry decided to stay in the United States. As he explained: "I liked it so much here, I stayed. I had the full intention of earning my law degree and going back, but as I became more accustomed to the warm climate of California and the ways of the country, I found myself more and more drawn to staying here. For awhile, I would return to Canada for the summers where I was a bush pilot and would fly helicopters for three months.

"But then, my first year in law school, I was hired by a San Francisco law firm which practiced aviation defense law, and I got the job because they told the law school that they wanted a law clerk with a commercial pilot's license. Then, when I was there for a week, the senior partner came to me and said: 'Boy, you're awfully good at discovery,' which is the legal term for finding things out. 'Can you get a private investigator's license?' So I checked into this, found I would have to take a test, and after I took it, I got my license in about 1981, when I was in my early thirties. So instead of working as a law clerk, I ended up working for the firm as an investigator.

"And then, I found my work as an investigator was expanding so much, that I had to hire another fellow to help me, and pretty soon I had to make a decision. Do I stay in law school, or do I work as an investigator? And after my second year in law school, I decided to put it on the back burner, because I wasn't getting any sleep. I was working as an investigator during the day, going to school at night, and then getting home and reading into the wee hours. So it just got to be too much.

"And so I decided to become a full-time investigator, and to supplement my background in aviation, I went through a variety of programs to gain the necessary certificates. For instance, I went through a program on safety at the Institute of Safety and Systems Management at the University of Southern California, and I also went through an aviation safety certification program there, so I had the certification to qualify as an expert witness, which is what's needed in the industry now to be an aircraft accident investigator and be able to testify. In fact, I was one of the few civilians in the program, since most of those involved in these aircraft investigations are government or military people.

"Meanwhile, I stayed with the law firm until 1983, and then I joined an investigation agency specializing in product liability related to automobile accidents; and I took some more courses in reconstructing these kinds of accidents too. And then, in 1985, I decided to set up my own firm, and since I already had a good background in electronics and technical things, I took some courses in this, including two in electronic countermeasures.

"And so now Incognito specializes in the more technical side of the business—in electronics, aviation, automotive, product liability, and most recently sub-rosa investigations using vans and video equipment to check up on people who might be involved in fraudulent insurance cases. Those are the kinds of cases where people are accepting all this insurance money, but they are in fact working at some other job, because they don't have a serious physical injury, and what we do in sub-rosa work is document that they are in fact healthy and working."

Terry pointed to some of the black boxes and other mechanical equipment with dials and buttons around the room. "Plus we also provide a full range of electronic and technical countermeasure services for our clients, to protect them from eavesdroppers, telephone taps, bugs planted in the room and things like that. And also . . ." he pulled out a catalog showing a variety of these gadgets which were around the room, ". . . we make this equipment available to people who want it too.

"And it's all perfectly legal. Anybody can own and use equipment like this. Most people don't know about all this or where to get it— but it's all quite legal."

It was a theme Terry and his associate Cameron would play up again and again to help counter this underground image of "sneaky" surveillance and spying. In fact, as Terry pointed out, most of their high tech work was done for protection—to get bugs, taps, and other spying devices *out* for their clients, not putting them in, which was illegal.

Then, Terry pointed to all his plaques on the wall to show the various organizations he belonged to. It was like going through a Who's Who of the field of investigation. There were certificates, membership documents, and awards from all sorts of organizations including: the award for Investigator of the Year for 1988 from the California Association of Licensed Investigators; a 1988 Arbitrator of the Year Award from the Better Business Bureau of San Mateo County; a certificate from the Council of International Investigators; several others from the World Association of Detectives, the Helicopter Association International, and International Toastmasters. In addition, Terry was on the board of the American Helicopter Society, Local Chapter and the International Society of Air Safety Investigators, Local Chapter. It was an impressive collection, and we commented on this.

"Well, I think it's important to be involved in all these professional groups, and do some volunteer work as well, because I want to see the field of investigation stay professional. Too many people have this sleazeball investigator image; but the field is really not like that for most investigators, and I want to keep things professional."

Finally, Terry pointed out his amateur "ham radio," operator's license, and he noted that as a hobby, he talked with people around the world. "And I'm into electronic toys. The latest gadgets and I'm also flying as a hobby."

But when it came to his personal life, Terry wouldn't comment. "Let's just say I like to keep a low profile. As a private investigator, I believe in keeping my personal life private," and that's all he would say about this.

Then, Cameron Rolfe described how he ended up in the business, and like Terry and other investigators, he came in through his own area of specialization, which was communications broadcast electronics.

He first got into the field while he was working in the field of broadcasting, while he was getting his B.S. from San Jose State University in broadcasting electronics communication, and a second degree, a B.A. in communication electronics. He started out as a production person doing radio-television production, which led him into engineering, and soon he became licensed in the engineering field as an engineering broadcast radio technician. From television, he began working with two-way radios, and that eventually involved him in police communications and working with other organizations with two-way radios and radio electronics. Ultimately that led him into surveillance electronics.

"At first, I was doing these various things for a private company that would send me out to trouble shoot or repair radios or electronics devices being used for surveillance. Then, gradually, I gained more and more background in this field, and picked up a variety of credentials along the way, including a Federal Communications Commission first class license and general class license; a credential as a technician with the National Association of Broadcast Engineers; a credential from the Society of Communications Electronics; and a ham radio or amateur radio license.

"Then, after a few years of this, about fifteen years ago, I started a business that specializes in two-way radio communications. For example, we worked with companies that might use a radio to dispatch a fleet of trucks, and at the same time, we offered assistance to the police departments when they needed help with their own communications. And soon we were helping the police by supplying the electronics or technical assistance they needed to conduct large scale surveillances. So now I do both law enforcement communications and work with the private sector."

As Cameron explained, he did this as an employee for Terry's company, and also worked independently doing electronics communications for the police through his own company.

"So as you can see, private investigators can be very specialized and fairly well-educated," Cameron concluded. Like Terry, he was concerned with dispelling the popular image of the skulking, low-life private eye so popular in the everyday media.

Terry and Cameron later would get into the specifics of what they did and the state-of-the-art high-tech gadgetry they used. But first they wanted to explain why individuals and companies came to them and to emphasize that everything they did was "perfectly legal," a phrase they repeatedly used as a kind of counterpoint to the potential abuse of the sophisticated technology they demonstrated.

"Sure, we work with bugs and taps and other listening devices," Terry commented. "But our job is not to install them, which is illegal. Our job is to find them and get them out, to protect the individual or company from being spied on by somebody else."

Then, he went on to explain how they usually got involved in a case.

"Typically what happens is the attorney for an individual or a corporation or the company itself will contact us. In many cases, major companies will already have an internal investigation department in charge of internal security. For example, this department will do background investigations of the people who are there or want to join the company, and it will check for any misuses of the phones or the faxes, watch out for breaches of employee communications, and that sort of thing. But then, they may need some extra help.

"It's a little like a physician who attends a seminar to learn about doctoring. He already knows what he is doing, but he wants some information on new state-of-the-art or cutting edge techniques."

Terry gave an example. "Take fax interception. Until recently, many companies didn't realize this was going on. They knew that some of their confidential information must be getting out of the building. Somehow computer programs, plans, documents were getting out. But how? The paper was sitting right there in their office under lock and key. So they came to us to find out where it has gone—trace it. And we showed them how it had gone through the fax machine, since one of the latest trends in information theft is fax interception. And then cellular phone communications are another weak link, too. So that's one of the things we do--help find these weak links or educate clients on the state of the art, so individuals and companies can protect themselves."

Terry also pointed out how he might use a white noise blocker, much like the one he could have used to stop us from tape recording anything, to protect the privacy of the company conference or other conversations within the company.

"But then, that's a relatively expensive procedure, because you have to put these blocking devices all over for protection. And it might be better to root out the basic problem, such as finding the sources of the bugs or the taps."

So typically, for basic or preliminary protection, Terry's company would do a basic electronics sweep, starting initially with the phone system. Then, depending on how much protection the client needed, the sweep would cover the walls and furniture in each room, and there would be a physical investigation too, for optimum protection.

"If a client believes there has been a breach of information, we always suggest taking a look at the phone system first. Say if someone has a house with one phone line. That could be probably done for about $500. But then, if there are a lot of phones, such as one company which had 107 phone lines, that can be pretty expensive. This company wanted each phone instrument system checked manually and electronically, and wanted the complete switchboard done, too. But then, the company had some very valuable plans which it wanted to protect, so the money for protection was worth it."

Terry also explained that the next step beyond checking the phone lines would be doing a sweep for bugs, or small devices planted around the house or office for eavesdropping.

"Usually, for that a team comes out, at least two or three people who have a whole vanful of equipment, and then they go around checking, listening for things like electronic pulses, surges, radio frequencies that shouldn't be there. There may be a manual check, too, which can involve looking into likely hiding places, such as electric wall brackets, since sometimes these bugs can get very sophisticated and can be operated by remote control or by timers. Today, just one investigator with a single device to do an electronic counter-measures sweep just isn't enough. The state of the art in these devices has become so sophisticated that you need a team."

And what would this cost we wondered. "About $1,500 for a regular small house with two bedrooms and a bath," Terry estimated. "And if it's a company, it might be several thousands, maybe more, depending on how large it is and how comprehensive the sweep."

As he pointed out, one of the main reasons a company might need to do this was industrial espionage, where one competitor was trying to get information from another.

"So they plant a bug in the boardroom. Or they get a mole in the company to spirit out plans. Have you ever wondered how it is that so many companies within a few months of each other suddenly come out with the same tremendous breakthrough? Why many competitive products come out on the market about the same time? Such as a major computer company introduces a new model with all sorts of attractive new accessories and options. Then thirty days later, the competition comes out with the same product. Well, that's how they do it. They manage to get some inside information that they shouldn't have.

"So how do they do it? How does someone get in? Very easy in some cases. Salesmen can be a great in. For example, a salesman is working on a half-million dollar bid, and he makes a presentation to someone. On his way out, he leaves a little transmitter behind and then he goes and sits in his car. What happens then is the man who just interviewed him is going to be meeting with other people who are making bids. So, at the end of the day, after hearing the competition, the salesman calls him back and says 'I'd like to resubmit a bid for this amount,' and now he can undercut the others, because he has heard them.

"Or consider this—the salesman who spends a little time chatting with the boss's secretary. In the past, salesmen used to bring flowers and candy to help bribe the secretaries. But now they just leave a disposable device behind. So it can be very easy.

"And the reason, of course, is all the money riding on these deals. So the competition is keenly interested in finding out about its competitor's new multimillion dollar product. And some may use all sorts of techniques to find out—such as salesmen, if that works, or even hiring underworld types to do a black bag job and leave behind some sort of device.

"So sometimes, these bugs just seem to magically appear. And that's where we come in. To try to prevent these competitors and con artists from getting the information; or on plugging the leaks, so they won't get it in the future."

In fact, as Terry pointed out, one major source of danger arose at company and industry conventions, so much of his company's work was done in hotels and casinos to protect the rooms where people would be staying or meeting.

"It's much like what we would do in protecting a company at its headquarters. We look for taps on the telephones. We go into the rooms where people will be meeting looking for transmitters or hard-wire microphones that could be sending information out. What frequently happens is that competitors will go to a convention if they know that there are going to be certain meetings or strategy sessions going on, and try to get a plant in there. Even a so-called salesman just happening by could be a means of dropping off a tap or a bug. So we try to ferret these out.

"Likewise, a lot of this espionage can go on between law firms, when they're going to be in a trial. For example, one firm may go and rent a whole suite of rooms in a hotel and they'll be there for a month or so for the trial. Or maybe they'll rent a temporary suite of small offices. So to protect themselves, the firm may want a complete sweep, and then we'll go in to check that their lines are protected and their rooms are secure. We want to make sure that the lines are clean, that there are no bugs, and that someone hasn't put hard-wired microphones into the meeting rooms, and that sort of thing."

Also, Terry and his company have worked with labor and management in contract negotiations, to assure the confidentiality of their conversations.

"And in this case," Terry commented, "we'll usually just use a white noise device, since the negotiations are taking place in just one place. It can be pretty expensive to keep sweeping the room as people go in and out during the course of the negotiations. So instead, all they have to do is flip a switch before they start talking, and everything will be fine. No one outside the room can hear a thing, even if someone tries to leave a bug, because any conversations within the confines of that room can't be recorded or transmitted. And that's because all the microphones hear this tone, which is louder than the conversation. Yet no one within the room can hear it because it's at a higher frequency than the ear can pick up, though it might drive some dog crazy, I'm sure."

Yet, while an electronics sweep or a white noise device might provide some protection, for total protection, Terry felt a physical inspection was necessary. There were just some things these other techniques couldn't protect against. So what happens in a physical inspection?

"When you do a physical inspection, you literally tear the place apart. You go into all the heating vents, you go into any false ceiling, and you go into every electrical outlet, because that's the easiest place to hide anything, behind a switch or a plug. You can snap the device onto the AC current, and you've got your power, and you don't need a battery which can wear down."

The way Terry described it, the process sounded like literally exploring every possible crevice and cranny, rooting around to the very foundations. He felt this necessary because of all the tricks that those implanting such devices could do.

"The techniques are really very sophisticated now," he explained. "For instance, you could put a hard-wired microphone just about anywhere. You could run it under the carpet, drop it down the side of a ceiling, put it behind a picture. And you don't need very much room for it. A microphone can be as thin as a wire." He held up a small example, about 1½ inches long, which he retrieved on a previous job. "You see. It's hardly noticeable. So someone can just drill a tiny little hole through the wall and put this wire through there. And then that becomes the microphone, and it's hooked on, ready to pick up anything in the room. So unless you did a physical inspection, you wouldn't know because the mike would be just transmitting to a remote location. So an electronic sweeping device might not pick this up."

It seemed mind-boggling to consider the huge expense for an extensive investigation like this. Had these things become so pervasive that such investigations were part of the day to day cost of doing business? Was this type of investigation something that would now be done routinely?

Terry shook his head. "No, generally they would do this because they suspect something, that some information is getting out. Now it could be that they're paranoid. That's a possibility because some people are. But normally, there is a good reason to have a complete sweep or full search done. It's not something that would be routinely done, because it costs thousands and thousands of dollars."

Finally, by way of introduction to the type of work a high-tech investigator does, Terry spoke briefly about the growing need for computer security.

"Basically, what we do is an in-house computer check, both for clients and on our own system. For instance, we use several clean-up programs that eliminate any virus problems. Also, these programs are designed to prevent potential eavesdropping from tuning in when someone tries to access an outside database to get information or communicate with other computers. After all, you don't want someone coming into your system and playing around with your files to see what's there."

As Terry explained it, any kind of security program for computers began with a client interview to determine what kind of hardware and software system is currently being used and what the client thought the problem might be.

"And then our computer man goes over their manuals and to the site to see what might be going on. Usually, the company has some idea of the kind of information that is getting out. So our job is to find out how and where it's going."

Terry gave an example. "We had a case where a big company called up to report that someone had accessed their computer three times during the past week and caused the computer to send money via Western Union to a specific individual at a casino in Las Vegas. 'Now we want to know what's going on and how to control this,' they told us. So our computer guy went out, and after he took a look at the system, he discovered that there were only three people in the company who had the access codes and the knowledge to go into the computer and cause it to generate the money and send it via Western Union. And one of these codes had been broken. Our man simply reprogrammed the system, so that the next time the person came in, accessed the system, and broke the code, we were able to find out where the call was coming from. Then, that indicated who was making the call, and the client turned that information over to the local law enforcement people, who soon moved in. As they discovered, one man in the company was sending the money to his brother in another state, and they thought they were so smart. But they got trapped by their own high-tech methods, when we used the computer to discover the source of the problem and prevent it from happening again."

And was it typical that the solution involved uncovering the offender who had placed the illegal equipment or had illegally removed the information?

Terry shook his head. "Sometimes our information may help the police or other government agencies do that. But we're not in the business of enforcing the law ourselves. At times, like here, the information we provide can help to zero in on the culprit. But many other times, the individual or company spied on will never know. But at least the equipment doing the spying has been removed or they know how to keep their information from leaving the building. Or they feel secure knowing now that nothing's there."

In another case, Terry was able to discover what was going on in a motel room for a wife (who suspected her husband of having an affair) by using an electronic device that picks up sound through a window.

Terry explained, "The husband kept telling the wife that he was doing some extra work, but she didn't believe him. She thought he was involved in some bizarre sexual activity with one of his co-workers. So she asked us to follow him and find out what was going on in these motel rooms he went to, and we followed him for six weekends in a row.

"Since we weren't sure where he would be going, we used a device to follow his vehicle electronically. It's basically a beeper with a radio transmitter and a receiver that lets you know when the vehicle turns left or right and how far away it is, so you don't have to keep the vehicle in sight. And then, once we got to the motel, we used a large microwave dish to pick up the sounds in the room." Terry pointed to a large black device that looked like a small version of a satellite dish receiver. "Essentially, that platelike device on the pole in the center is an amplifier. Or think of it like a bionic ear. And basically what it does is act like an amplifier. So if you point it at a window or at someone seated on a park bench across the street, it amplifies what your ear would hear. And the reason it can pick up through glass is that glass vibrates when there is any noise. So if someone inside is talking, the glass is vibrating, and if you're outside you can pick up what's going on inside."

And was this legal?

"Yes, perfectly legal," Terry assured us. "It's quite different than putting in bugs or taps, where you're invading someone's privacy and trespassing on their property to put something in. In this case, you are simply enhancing what your ear and eye can do. So as long as we're picking up this information while we're on a public spot, such as sitting on the street in a car, that's perfectly fine. It would be different if someone tried to stand up next to the window with their ear on the glass, because they would be standing on private property which is trespassing. Or if someone tried to walk into the motel room of the person under surveillance or drilled a hole through the wall and put a camera in there, that would be illegal, too. That would be invading their privacy or trespassing on private property.

But just listening or observing, and improving your ability to do this from a public place, that's fine."

And so what was the outcome of all this listening and observing?

"Well, that was the odd thing," said Terry. "After all this effort, he wasn't doing anything at all. Just carrying on business as usual. Nothing sexually bizarre."

In another odd case, Terry and his associates not only uncovered telephone taps on a line, but they apparently turned up a federal agency as well. It also had taps on the line, and was perturbed that someone had discovered them.

"An investigator we had worked for before called us to handle a case in another county for a law firm he was working with. 'We need a sweep,' he told us. 'This company is primarily concerned about the telephones in their office. They think that somebody's listening in.'

"So, a few days later, I drove out to their offices with a technician, and after we did a telephone inspection, we discovered these four little wires. Well, normally, one only needs to use the two center wires on the phone, unless there are extra things hooked up to the lines, such as video phones, or a system with clocks or other gadgets. Immediately, we got suspicious, and pretty soon we discovered that these two extra lines were alive, though the people in the company didn't have anything connected to them, so we realized they were tapped. And we also discovered that these lines were on all the time, so the tappers were not only listening to the phone conversations; they were listening to anything from a hidden microphone.

"It's hard to explain exactly what they did without getting too technical, but essentially what they were using was an infinity microphone. They had taken an extra pair of wires and were using it as a microphone to pick up everything going on in the room. An amazingly sophisticated bit of technology, and normally very hard to trace. But we found it and told the investigator, so he could tell the law firm.

"And then, after we packed up, drove out of the parking lot, and were headed down the street, an unmarked car with a flashing red light pulled up beside us and we were pulled over. It was like something out of a CIA spy novel. Then, these two older men in gray suits and ties jumped out of their car and came over to our window flashing their Federal ID cards. 'So who are you? And what are you doing?' they asked, in a very intimidating way.

"Well, we weren't about to be intimidated, since everything we had just done was perfectly legal. So in turn, I got out my own ID, my official State of California Private Investigator's License, and I flashed it at him, and in the same intimidating tone, I said to him: 'Well, *who* are you? And what are *you* doing?'

"They backed down, because it really is hard to intimidate somebody in this business, and they knew I had found their tap and that now I probably knew it was their tap too. It's not that I said I found it, or they told me I had done so. All I said was that we had just found this tap, and I don't know if it's yours or somebody else's. But obviously, it was theirs or they wouldn't be there stopping us. So then, I simply gave them my business card, and said I don't know anything about the case, and I told them they could talk to my client, the private investigator, who was in a car that had stopped down the road behind me. And then I drove off telling them to have a good day."

According to Terry, the federal agents' tap on the line was legal, but they were upset because their cover was probably blown, and that might mean the end of any further surveillance. As Terry explained:

"Almost certainly, they were legally tapping the line. Otherwise, they wouldn't have stopped us. So if they were legally tapping it, that meant they had a warrant from a judge, and that warrant is good for ninety days. Meaning that anything they pick up in conversations during those ninety days can be used against the subject if the subject is charged criminally. But then, on the ninetieth day, if the agency is going to be using it in the prosecution against the subject, they have to tell him or her that they have had the tap and they are going to be doing this.

"However, what sometimes happens is that the law enforcement agency will listen to that line for eighty-nine days, and then they will pull the tap off so they don't have to tell the person. That means they can't use any of that evidence they have heard, against the person directly. But everything they have heard for that eighty-nine days may help them in their ongoing investigation. So I think what happened is we stumbled into that. Now the people they have been investigating will know the feds are onto them and will clean up their act. And the agents have to find another way to get any of the evidence they need. So no wonder they went off angry.

"But meanwhile, our client was quite happy. We found what he wanted to know for his client."

In an even more complex high-tech case, Terry and his company uncovered an off-the-premises phone set up to listen in on some high level strategy conversations at city hall.

"It was incredibly difficult," Terry said. "The client, at one city hall, thought his phone, which was connected to a new AT&T switchboard, was tapped. But finding out where—that was the problem, because this was an incredibly mixed up system, with some old equipment dating back several decades, plus some only a few years old, and then there was a brand new system. So we spent about three days working with the wiring, trying to find the problem, and we came up cold.

"But then, our computer expert started exploring the software in the system to see if maybe it might be possible to program one phone to relay calls to an off-premises extension, and that turned out to be exactly what it was. The phone was programmed that way, and even their in-house computer programmer didn't know it. Somehow, someone had gotten into their system, so that when a call came into this particular phone, it triggered a phone in another office in the building, so the people over there could monitor all the calls this man received. And they didn't have to pick up a receiver to do it, which might have tipped someone off. All they had to do was turn up the volume on a speaker, because they were already wired in."

Terry explained a little bit more about how an off-premises extension worked.

"Just think of how you have phones around your house. You may have a phone in your kitchen, and in the bedroom, and maybe in the living room, too. So then, when you pick up a phone in the bedroom, you can listen to a phone conversation in the kitchen. It's an extension phone, though it's on the same premises.

"Now suppose you want an off-premises phone. Say you open up a word-processing service in the next city, but you want the phone there to ring in your house, too. That's an off-premises extension.

"Well, you can just set that up legally with the phone company, and the phone will ring in both places. But if someone wants, they can do a little behind-the-scenes maneuvering, and they can arrange—though it's quite illegal—an off-the-premises extension for someone else's phone, too."

But how? Terry gave a hypothetical example.

"Suppose someone wanted to listen to his neighbor for some reason, and he already knew his neighbor's number and his name. He could then rent an apartment or a warehouse under a pseudo name and pay cash, so he's already set up a cover for himself. Then he could call the phone company, claiming to be that neighbor, and ask to have an off-premises extension installed at this new address. The phone company then goes out and installs it. Thus the person could be there listening to these calls, or he could set up a tape recorder to record everything on the line. And he might do this for only a week or two, and close up the place and be gone after that. Meanwhile, the person being listened to won't even know that the phone extension is there until he gets his bill next month. And then when he sees this billing for the off-premises extension and complains, the phone company will investigate. But by then, the person who was listening in has already cleared out of that apartment or warehouse and nobody has any idea who he was. So it can be easy for somebody who wants to do something like this, and a lot of this goes on.

"Well, something like this happened in this case. Someone set up an off-premises location from which to monitor this guy's calls. The only difference is they programmed the system internally to send them out, rather than getting the telephone company involved in doing the switching."

And why did he do it, we wondered.

"You might say it was his way of getting an ear at city hall," said Terry whimsically. "Or again, maybe he had a grudge against this person and was trying to get something on him. Since our job is basically just to find the security breach, we don't always know what happens after that. And here, like in so many other cases, we just turned our findings over to the police, and then it's their job to investigate from here."

Now it was Cameron's turn to tell us a little bit about the special technology used in uncovering hidden devices and protecting against technological intrusions.

He began by dialing a number on what looked like a normal office phone receiver, with hold and extension buttons. We could hear the beeps of the number being dialed in the background, and at first it didn't sound like anything was unusual. But then, Cameron explained that as a security feature all of the beep tones on this phone sounded the same, unlike regular rotary and touch-tone phones, where there were distinct tones or numbers of beeps for each number.

"And the reason this phone is like this is it has a special electronic device that makes all beeps sound alike, so no one else can tell who you are calling. Otherwise, if someone could hear these tones, and I was making a confidential call, he could easily determine the number I was dialing, just by knowing which tone is for which number. Or he could even tape record the tones, and figure out the number that way. For example, we have a device that if you tape record the tones and play them back, the numbers dialed are played out on a little screen."

Then, hanging up, Cameron picked up some round plastic devices and wires from the desk, and held them out for us to look at.

"You know what those are? They're bugs and taps." He pointed to the wire with two small alligator clips hanging from it. "Now that's a tap," he said. "A tap is where you take a wire which clamps onto a phone wire, so you can listen in on whatever is going over it. Basically, what happens is the alligator clips draw the energy from the phone line, and then, that energy goes into a small radio transmitter..." He held up a tiny black box to illustrate, "...and then that transmitter retransmits the signal to a radio receiver that picks it up, such as someone stationed in a room or in a van down the street who's either listening or tape recording everything."

"But who?" I started to ask. "And is this legal?"

But Cameron interrupted me. "Now remember, legally, a private party can't do this. Only a law enforcement officer can do this, with a wire tap warrant from a magistrate or judge. To get this, the officer has to tell the judge that he has reasonable and probable grounds to believe that the person who's phone is being tapped is engaged in some criminal activity, and the judge believes that and issues a warrant. And then, the law enforcement agency has to go to the local telephone company with the warrant to make the arrangements to listen to the line, and the phone company lets them do this. But if a private party or private investigator tries to do this and gets caught, they can go to jail or we get sued for thousands of dollars for invasion of privacy. Neither ourselves nor any other legitimate private investigator is involved in putting these things in. Our job is to take them off, and that's where these taps have come from. I do know one guy who tried putting some in one time, but he's in San Quentin now doing a lengthy term. So if you want to know anymore about putting these things in, you'll have to talk to him there."

Then, changing the subject, Cameron pointed to a fax machine behind him.

"Now, not only phones can be tapped, but fax machines too. Sometimes people think they just stick some papers in the machine, press the button, and the document is transmitted. So if no one sees those papers, they are perfectly safe. But someone can tap that line, just like any phone. Because the fax machine is simply a device sending data out on the same phone lines a normal conversation goes on. Then, once that tap is in, all they have to do is take a normal tape recorder, attach it to that line, and then when there's a transmission, they have tape recorded that fax. They just have to play that tape recorder back into another fax machine and, poof, they've got the document.

"And it's amazing. All sorts of information can end up leaving the company that way. Software programs. Advertising programs. Plans for strategies. Faxed across the country into the hands of the competition. For example, one company managed to get another's client list this way, and then, through continued taps, the competitor was able to send sales personnel to those clients. So one way to stop it, of course, is to find the tap. Many companies are spending tens of thousands of dollars to encrypt their faxes, so if the tap picks up anything, it just turns into a mess."

So how could these taps be detected? Cameron reached into a large brown suitcase and pulled out a black metal box, about four inches by six inches in size, and about two inches deep.

"It's a phone tap detection device," he explained. "And it can tell when there's a tap on the line, because the tap is always on and draws power from the line. So the device can detect when this is happening."

Then, after putting away the tap detector, he dropped two small black vinyl objects with coils attached on the desk in front of us.

"Now suppose you found something like that attached with double-sided sticky tape to the bottom of your desk? What do you think this would be? What does it look like to you?"

"A listening device?" I guessed, and Cameron nodded.

"Exactly. That's a bug. It picks up and transmits whatever is going on around it in the room. Any noises; any vibrations; any conversations. And this one . . ." he pointed to the larger of the two objects, which had two small screws at one end of it, ". . . this one enables the person who puts it there to adjust the frequency. That way, he can pick up certain types of sounds, such as conversations, but screen out other extraneous noises.

"Now these things are commonly found taped under desks or up in false ceilings. Or maybe someone puts it behind a picture or into the plumbing."

Again, Cameron emphasized that he and Terry and other legitimate private eyes didn't install such things. "These are illegal, and all of the equipment you see here are things that we have obtained from cases where we have either found them after they were installed or intercepted them before somebody was able to put them in."

So how did they locate these bugs? Was the equipment different than that for locating phone taps?

"Very definitely; much different," Cameron explained, and this time he pulled out a medium-sized black box, about the size of a reel to reel tape recorder, with several knobs and buttons on it. "It's called a bug detector," he continued. "And basically what you do is place it in a room, and it produces a tone which can pick up any form of electronic transmission. So if the bug is transmitting anything, the detector will pick this up.

"Now normally, most of these bugs are what are called active devices which means they are on all the time, so they are always transmitting, whether or not there is any special sound in the room. And the detector can discover this because it can sense even the smallest electronic oscillation or transmission. In fact, a detector can even check for bugs on different transmitting frequencies and indicate the frequency of each.

"But then, sometimes, a bug can be what's called a passive device which is one that turns itself on or off, in response to the noise level in the room or other external control. So to pick up that, the detector also has a tone generator which creates noise, that causes a passive device to come on and start transmitting. And then the detector can pick that up.

"Once the detector indicates there is some sort of transmitter there, we can narrow it down using hand-held equipment to indicate exactly where the bug is." Cameron held up a small black box, about the size of a portable tape recorder with an antenna. "Basically, what happens is the closer we get to the device, the louder the device sounds."

But what if this was a remotely controlled passive transmitter, that only came on when someone signaled it? How could a bug detector detect that?

"Well, that's a very sophisticated piece of equipment when someone outside is controlling it. Now if it's being controlled by phone or by a two way-radio, a physical search for taps would pick that up. But on the other hand, if they are doing something else, such as using a touch-tone pad to send radio signals, the tone generator wouldn't be able to turn it on. So that's why a physical inspection would be necessary too."

Cameron explained the process. "Normally, we'll do the electronic search first, and then we'll do a complete mechanical or physical one. And that involves literally taking the whole place apart. We take off all the wall panels. We dismantle every light switch. We check for false ceilings. We check the plumbing. So it's normally a two or three man job which takes several hours. To find these sophisticated devices, just a quick electronics search isn't enough."

But what if the bugs still remained hidden? What if a complete search is financially unfeasible? Or what if someone was able to sneak in with a bug after a search? Or even had a bug or other listening device with them, such as a concealed tape recorder?

Cameron had still more devices which could provide such protections. This time, he showed us another small metal box, about seven by nine by three inches, with several nodes, and four small black cases about the same size that looked like miniature stereo speakers.

"That's an ultrasonic microphone jammer or white noise device," he explained. "It's too expensive to have these all over the place in every room. But if something important is going to be happening in a limited space, say in a single office or conference room, what that will do is mask any normal conversation, so a tape recorder or bugging device can't pick it up. Basically, these four little boxes go in the corners of the room. The boxes flood the room with a high frequency tone that's above the normal range of hearing. No one in the room will be aware that this is occurring, although the microphone will be sensitive enough to hear it, so that any conversations or other sounds recorded within this cone of silence will not work. And that includes conversations over electronic telephones."

According to Cameron, such a device might be particularly useful to counter someone who tried to secretly record a meeting. "For example, these devices are very popular now in union negotiations, in corporate strategy sessions, or in product introduction meetings. What happens is that someone may try to bring in a concealed tape recorder. Or maybe the person is there with a concealed microphone, which could be small enough to fit in a tie clasp or even mounted on the top of a pen." To illustrate, Cameron pulled out a wireless mike about the size of a fingernail. "So somebody could very easily be in the room and record," he went on. "Thus, to prevent this, this jammer is the perfect device to confidentially jam. The person thinks he's recording; the meeting goes along smoothly; and then when the spy tries to listen to the recording, all he hears is a high pitched noise."

Cameron even had a device which could detect tape recorders. It looked like a small, thin metal antenna, about the size of a pen. "If there's a tape recorder on, it either lights up, or some of these vibrate. Or if someone suddenly puts a tape recorder into the record mode, this will happen. Basically, this occurs because the device detects the erase oscillator on the head that erases the tape when it's recording. And that oscillator signal radiates an electronic bias for a couple of feet, so you can know. This way, someone can do some advance screening before an important meeting if he or she chooses, perhaps instead of, or in addition to using a jammer. Then, as people walk into the boardroom, a security officer or other person doing the checking would have this equipment on his body, taped to an arm or in a pocket, so he can tell if someone has a recording device. Or if the person waits until after the meeting starts to turn the recorder on, he might pick up the conversation then. And then, so there's no need to disrupt the meeting, there's always the jammer, so not a thing will be recorded."

And what about somebody trying to jam the jammer? Cameron hadn't heard of anything like that, though he supposed it was possible. "I imagine anything can be defeated electronically, if you wait long enough or throw enough money into it. Maybe the military even has such a thing. But for now, for all practical purposes, no. The jammer is really the state of the art."

And then, besides jammers, there were also scramblers. Cameron pulled out another small black box to demonstrate.

"Now this little device snaps over the headset of your telephone or on your cellular phone, and it scrambles your voice, and it can only be decoded by someone who has a similar device set to a prearranged code, which you choose. For example, a stockbroker might use this to protect these tips he's giving out to his customers. A reporter might use it to prevent some other reporter from scooping him. In fact, anyone having a private conversation might find these useful, and particularly businesses trying to guard against the competition."

Cameron gave a few key examples.

"These scramblers can be particularly useful when businesses have two-way radio systems in which their dispatchers can communicate with their trucks. Just consider the way a competitor can use this information. Say a sewer clean-up company dispatches a truck by radio, and the driver is asked: 'Can you go to this address?' He radios back and says: 'It will probably take me ninety minutes to get there.' If a competitor is listening in on a standard police-style scanner radio and hears that, he knows the address, and with a criss-cross phone directory, he can quickly look up the number. So the competitor can call the woman needing service on the phone and say: 'You need service? We'll be there in thirty minutes. Just call the other company back and cancel, and we'll respond.'

"So the competitor takes the call. It wasn't lawful, although the competitor was legally able to intercept the transmission, because he was using this information in an unlawful manner. But this kind of thing goes on anyway, and one way to protect against it would be to encrypt the truck radio with a speech encoder or voice scrambler to keep the information confidential.

"And another particularly good use of these devices would be on cellular phones. Many people think such phones are secure, but they're not, because they operate like radios on a particular frequency. So when a stockbroker makes a call at four in the morning, he could be just feeding information to a rival who can then take that information and use it unlawfully with his own customers. But again if the broker's voice is scrambled or encoded, the competitor can't understand it."

Now, as Cameron began to pack away the equipment he had just shown us, we wondered about the various legal issues he had raised about using it or the information gained. At what point this use become illegal? And when illegal devices were located, what might be done to track down the person or company that put them there? And when, if ever, did these cases involve the police?

Terry came in to explain the legalities of the business. "There are a number of laws that define what's illegal or not and they're quite specific. But mostly, what's illegal is a matter of common sense. If you're going to be using the information you intercept from someone else's conversation for profit and gain, it's not lawful. If you're going to use this information to injure someone financially, emotionally, physically, or in any other way, it's unlawful. It's just common sense. For instance, if you get a wireless microphone and plan to use it to sing in a nightclub act, that's perfectly legal. But if you get this wireless microphone to leave it in the boardroom or a major corporation and go out in a truck to listen to it, that's clearly unlawful. You don't need to know the law to realize that."

Then, pulling what looked like a history book from the shelf, Terry gave another example.

"Say I go to a meeting, and I have this book with me, and I leave it on the table. Well, it could be any kind of book, and everybody

looks at it and they think it's interesting, a nice book. But then . . ."
Terry opened up the cover to reveal that this wasn't a real book after
all, but one with a large cavity cut out of its pages in the middle of
it. "Well, that's where the tape recorder goes, and it's recording. Or
there's a wireless microphone there and it's transmitting information
and somebody outside is listening. Well, again, that's illegal, and
that's where a white noise generator could help. But again, there
could also be a very legal use for this book, say to put your jewelry
in it and store it on a bookcase, so no one will find it. So something
can have a legal purpose as well as an illegal one. It depends on
how to use it. It's like using a necktie. You can use it to close your
shirt collar and be fashionable. Or you can use it to suffocate someone. So there's all this equipment out there for people to use, and
it's just a matter of how they use it. Legally or illegally. It's up to
them."

Terry pointed to his own phone. "Now here's another example."
He indicated a small black box alongside the receiver. "This is a
device that's hard wired into this phone, so that all you have to do is
plug in a wire for a tape recorder here, and you can record phone
calls." He inserted a tape jack to illustrate and lifted the receiver.
"Now, if I simply go ahead and record a call without saying anything to the person I'm talking to, that's illegal. But if I'm calling
someone and say I want to record the conversation, so that person's
aware he's being recorded, that's fine.

"For example, say as an investigator I'm calling Joe Blow who
recently was a witness to a traffic accident, and I say, 'Hi, Joe, this
is Terry Finn, and I'd like to spend a few minutes of your time talking to you about that crash that you witnessed the other day, and I'd
like to make a tape recording of this? Is that all right with you?
Okay, great. And I have your permission to tape record this? Okay,
thanks Joe. Now where were you standing, Joe,' and so on. Well,
that's a legal tape recording. But if I didn't tell Joe that I was tape
recording him, and he doesn't know I'm doing this, then that's illegal. I can't do this. And anyone who does this kind of illegal taping
could go to jail if caught. In addition, he could get sued for invasion
of privacy. And worse, any evidence that anyone obtains in this illegal way is not admissible in court. So everything that this witness
tells you is unusuable, and this includes any leads coming from this

information. That's still another reason why it's important to use any of this equipment or information legally. There's just no payoff if you do not."

But what about the people who weren't using it legally, when their illegal devices or intercepts were discovered?

"Well, when we discover an illegal device or interception," said Terry, "we tell the people the device was there. And then we normally call the police. Though we don't try to find out the source of the device or the competitor, because now it's up to the police. It's become a criminal matter. And sometimes, the police may turn the problem over to the federal authorities, too, because some of this involves federal law, and then whichever agency handles it, they have their own skilled, well-trained technical people. But we have nothing to do with law enforcement ourselves, since we deal strictly with the private sector. That's up to them."

Cameron then pulled out some even more sophisticated high-tech equipment. This time he held up what looked like a long zoom lens for a camera. It was of black metal, about one foot long.

"Now this is an especially powerful video-lens," Cameron said. "It's a long telephoto lens which fits onto what looks like a regular 8 millimeter video camera, and it provides a 280-power magnification. But this is quite a bit different than what you see in the stores, because this camera is meant for surveillance, since it is designed to accept a more powerful lens. And it also can accept a night vision lens."

Again, Cameron explained this is quite legal, just not normally available in the usual retail channels, and in this case, Terry had purchased the lens and camera from the manufacturer.

"They have a special security division for such equipment," he commented, and then explained how such a device could be used for security.

"Say a company wants to protect its environment at night from intruders. A night vision lens with high magnification would be the perfect way to do it. For instance, take a place like a recreation park or a casino. The company could set up towers in the parking lot or at the entrance with night vision equipment. Someone monitoring this from inside could see who's going in and out, and if there's some danger, like a mugger lurking around by the cars, the one monitoring could see this too. And this could be especially important at a casino, because people are going in and out with quite a bit of cash, so they are likely targets. But with night vision, a guard could possibly see some potential problem before it occurs, and someone could get out there to escort the would-be victim to his car. So then the possible crime is averted, and the guy goes home with his cash."

How did this night vision work?

"Usually it works through light image intensification. There's always some light—starlight, moonlight, something. So basically, the lens works like a television camera which conveys an image to a monitor located somewhere else. Or if it's very dark and you want to increase the night vision, you can use an infrared camera and lens. There are even devices now using television or VCR remote control techniques which can turn an ordinary night vision lens into infrared." Cameron pointed to a small button on the camera body. "For example, all you have to do is squeeze that button, and an infrared light fills the room. Then the TV monitor or VCR sees a certain pulse light combination which triggers it to respond. Your eye can't see that color of light, but the TV or VCR receiver does, and so it responds accordingly. It works much like your ordinary remote control on a VCR. If you take it into another room or point it in another direction and flash it, the VCR won't work, because it's not receiving that light pulse. But if you should turn around and point the device at a white wall, then the light will bounce back from it and the VCR will pick this up. So that's the way it works."

Cameron picked up a VCR control switch from the desk behind him and pressed the button on it a few times. It seemed like nothing was happening. But as he observed: "See, you can't see this; I can't see this, but there's light coming out of it. An ordinary light image intensification lens can't see this, but an infrared lens can. So if there's total darkness, we just turn on the infrared, and the camera can now pick things up."

According to Cameron, a lot of this high tech equipment, such as the night vision lens, was originally developed by the military.

"And then some of the less powerful devices have been released to the general public. But if not, you can't buy it," he cautioned, adopting that same warning tone he and Terry had used before, each time they told us that something was illegal. "Here, it's especially dangerous to cross over that line," he continued, "because in many cases, possession of military level devices is considered espionage."

What kind of devices?

"Some ultra-secret scrambling equipment to scramble your fax or radio-communications," Cameron commented.

But how do you know what is illegal or not?

"It comes on the market," he said. "And that means the open market, usually the specialty outlets or catalog sources, that sell this kind of thing. They usually keep up with what's legal to own, so they know."

Then, since we had been talking about all this super high-tech stuff, we wondered about the so-called spy devices placed in the newly-built United States Embassy in Moscow which led the U.S. to abandon the building. And was this a technology that spies might use here? Cameron commented briefly on what had happened.

"Basically, what happened there is the Soviets poured in thousands of transistors with their wires cut off, when they were mixing the concrete. These transistors are like little silicon chips, and what happens is that whether these are active or passive devices which are turned on or off, there's an electronic integrated circuit there, and some kinds of detectors used in sweep electronics can pick these up. So though lots or maybe all of these devices are broken, defective, or dead, the existence of the electronic circuit is detected, and there's no way to know whether other real devices are being used. The detection machinery just bounces off the wall. And then it's too expensive or unnerving to keep using white noise generators to overcome every conversation going on in the building; it's like living in a glass house; and so the U.S. planned to tear it down.

"As to other people using such devices, for now probably no. It takes years for this military level equipment to trickle down to the civilian level, and as for detecting and protecting against this kind of thing, it's beyond the scope of most agencies. For now you're dealing with high-level military sorts of devices, so possibly the federal agents or military police might get involved."

Unfortunately, both Terry and Cameron had a gripe with the way some of these specialty sources for this high tech equipment, notably catalog houses, presented the image of the private eye.

"It just contributes to the false mystique which people have of the private eye," Terry commented, "of someone snooping around, doing illegal, clandestine things."

He pulled out a slick looking catalog with a mostly black cover, featuring a Mata Hari type woman, with long dark hair, a sultry come-hither look, a black fedora, a black raincoat, and a walkie-talkie.

"Now, that's what I mean," Terry said. "She looks like the popular image people have, which is also on TV and in a lot of books, of the investigator as someone who goes around skulking in the shadows in trenchcoat and hat."

Inside the catalog were all sorts of legal protective and sleuthing devices, like those we had just been talking about, combined with high powered marketing copy, like: "Record phone conversations anywhere!" and "The desktop scrambler: a small black box that could save a career" and "Want to hear what's going on in your home or office while you're away?"

But what he objected to were the intimations that this equipment might be used for illegal purposes, despite some warnings here and there about the illegality of intercepting oral or wire communications without permission. And then there was that unfortunate image of the sneaky and spying private eye.

"You have to understand that we've been combatting that image for years, much like the police officers have been battling against the usually totally false image of them presented on TV and in the movies. For example, most cops go for years and never draw a weapon. But in these shows and films, not only are the cops frequently drawing their guns, but people are dropping like flies.

"Well, this kind of catalog image just feeds on the same kind of fantasy which we've been fighting ourselves. For example, take Tom Selleck in "Magnum, P.I." He does his surveillances in a red Ferrari. Now what private investigator would do that? The idea is to fade into the landscape, to be discreet, not stand out and announce yourself. And then these films and detective shows make it sound so easy and so glorious—the investigators discover the clues, solve it, and the person is convicted, all within less than two hours. But in fact, it's really hard, often very plodding work, where the investigator spends hours searching through files, making observations, or looking for hidden devices. So in real life, most private investigators are really well educated, professional people who have a background in a specialty or technical area and take their work very seriously. In fact, there are now organizations, such as the California Association of Licensed Investigators, which are trying to present this professional image. But then TV shows and catalogs like these come along, and often projected an image that can be very hard to counteract. It's an exciting, glorified one that people seem to like, even if it isn't true."

Yet, in the long run, Terry and Cameron seemed to think the trend was towards a growing professionalism in the field, as did the other investigators we had interviewed.

"And I think the professional organizations we have now will help to do it. Increasingly, you have licensed, professional, well-educated people in the business, and the sleazeballs and underhanded tactics featured in the movies and on TV will eventually fade away." Terry listed several organizations besides the California Association he had just mentioned—the World Association of Detectives, the Council of International Investigators, and a few others. "So these groups should help in cleaning up the image of the profession. But it'll take time." He threw the offending catalog back on the floor with a shrug.

Still, as both Terry and Cameron acknowledged, there were some major hurdles ahead, mainly because of the excesses of a few disreputable private eyes that had brought down the pressures of the lawmakers and society on the industry as a whole. He referred to the relatively recent case of actress Rebecca Schaffer, in which an investigator in another state had found her home address from a West Coast detective who had obtained the address from driving records. The investigator had given this information to his client, who then had gone to her home and shot her.

"Now that was a real tragedy," he said. "It was a case where information was secured which shouldn't be revealed or is revealed inappropriately. Unfortunately, this person who wanted the information was a nut or deranged fan, and the investigator unethically got it for him, without checking him out. Well, most professional investigators don't do that. Most would question the client first, ask why he wanted this information and perhaps what he was going to do with it, which would help to protect against this kind of thing happening. But in this case, the investigator didn't do it. He just went ahead and used a colleague to obtain this information.

"The result was that the media, the lawmakers and the public have viewed all investigators as the bad guys, and now there have been moves to restrict information access to investigators, which is terrible, because it will make it more difficult for people to get the kind of information they need to protect themselves. And it will even interfere with day to day court procedures, because if it becomes impossible to find out home addresses, even for legitimate reasons, we may not be able to serve people with subpoenas or legal papers.

"So it's important to look at what happened realistically. It doesn't make sense to come down en masse against one profession or one group of individuals and try to close off information to that one group, simply because one of its members made a mistake. Sure there need to be controls, but that's going too far. Because most investigators are serious, reputable professionals, not bad guys, skulking around in the shadows, getting information illegally— though that may be the image which we're trying to combat.

"And besides," Terry emphasized, "most of the information that we get is generally available through public records. The equipment we use is all perfectly legal. We're in fact more like information brokers, and the way we get paid is by simply knowing where to go and how to get this information or equipment, and then how to use this to help the average individual or company protect itself."

And so, with the reminder that the majority of the people in the business were very ethical and honest, not the types frequently described in the media or in films or TV who would do just about anything to get information, the discussion of the world of high-tech investigation ended. "And besides, such people generally don't last very long in the business," Terry said.

Then, Cameron was off for another assignment. But Terry remained to talk about his unique specialty—investigating aircraft disasters. Only a very few investigators in the field were qualified to do this, and after a brief break, we turned on the tape again to talk about this.

It was an appropriate time to talk about airplane disaster investigations, since a big crash in New York had recently been dominating the airwaves. But first Terry wanted to clarify that these weren't the kinds of accidents he was normally involved in. "The Federal Aviation Administration, the National Transportation Safety Board and the airlines have their own investigators who do that. What I get involved in are the cases involving general aviation—basically the smaller, private planes that crash."

Terry explained the basic approach. "Essentially, you investigate a crash from the liability point of view. You're trying to figure out whether it was the person's fault or a failed component in the plane, so the lawyers or insurance companies involved can figure out how to settle the case or argue it in court. And to do that, we essentially do a reconstruction of what happened. We try to figure out what the plane was like before it crashed, how all the parts were working together, and normally, we will call on experts. For example, in one case, we used a metalurgist, who was able to show which part in the plane failed first, what came second, and ultimately what caused a series of components to fail, causing the catastrophic crash."

It sounded a little like putting a jigsaw puzzle together, though Terry corrected us. "Well, it's not like putting the whole plane back together. Generally, we're just looking at a portion of the plane, because normally we have a pretty good idea of what caused the accident. So we zero in on that."

And how could Terry tell. He went on. "Well, you know what that section is supposed to look like, and you know what damage would be caused in certain ways. So this is a kind of deductive science or art, and is basically the same kind of approach investigators use in investigating any wreck, whether it's an automobile or an aircraft. Fire or arson investigators use this type of approach too. You're trying to reconstruct what things were like before the accident or incident, so you can figure out what happened in what sequence and why."

In many cases, the local police or sheriff will turn up at the scene to see if a crime has been committed. Otherwise, it's up to the private or government investigators to continue any investigation. Terry offered an example.

"There was the case of a small plane that crashed around three in the morning in a small suburb east of San Francisco. But no one found the wreck until nine, and then, after the airport notified the insurance carrier, its adjuster asked me to check the scene and help out the sheriff's deputies in getting into the wreckage, so they might determine if there was a crime or not."

About an hour later, Terry arrived on the scene, and the deputies were waiting for him, not having started their investigation yet.

"They weren't sure where there would be fingerprints or not, since there were all these pieces of scattered wreckage and they wanted to be sure not to disturb anything when they went in to look for any bodies."

Then, after Terry helped the sheriff figure out what to do, the case took a bizarre turn.

"When we located the area where the cockpit fell we didn't find a body. But we found blood—evidence that the subject who flew the plane was injured. He even left behind his coat, his wallet and his glasses, so of course, we knew who it was. And then, once we knew that, it was easy to reconstruct what happened. Basically, the pilot was drunk and upset about something, so he broke into the airplane and stole it. And he had previously checked out on this kind of air-craft, which meant he could fly it. But the problem was he was so drunk, he never got the plane off the ground. Instead, he ran the plane off the end of the runway and tore through a fence and went down into a ditch, until someone who was flying in on final approach saw the wreckage and reported it."

What happened to the man? we wondered.

"Well, that was pretty bizarre, too," Terry commented. "It seemed like he might have walked away from all this, and simply disappeared. But then some fishermen discovered his body about two weeks later a quarter mile away from the accident scene. He had fallen into the creek as he was walking away and drowned."

But, while the police were involved in this case, since a crime had been committed—the theft of the plane, in most cases they weren't, and it is usually investigated by the NTSB, FAA, and insurance company investigators.

"For example, there was a tragedy at a shopping mall near where this other plane went down. A small plane crashed in the middle of this shopping center, and there were a number of deaths and numerous serious burn injuries. But it wasn't a criminal act. The law enforcement people were there for awhile, to determine if there was a crime. Their mission is to investigate a crime and bring criminal charges. But if there's no crime, as here, it's up to the private sector representing the individuals or companies involved to go in and find out what really happened. And then, if you represent the insurance carrier, the first step is to find out what happened and determine liability and mitigating damages. For instance, if it's a part that failed in addition to pilot error, the manufacturer of that part would become liable too. So you collect all this information, and then the lawyers and insurance companies sort it out."

Terry normally represented the defense in these cases, because that's the way he started—working for insurance companies. "And it's tough to go back and forth between the plaintiff and defense side. You're usually expected to take one side or the other. And besides, the defense side pays the bill, because it's the insurance company. With the plaintiff's side, sometimes the client takes months to pay or sometimes you may even get stiffed."

Several of Terry's cases involved helicopters that crashed in out-of-the-way places.

"In one case, this helicopter crashed in the middle of logging country, killing the pilot and seriously injuring the co-pilot. They were hauling logs, pulling them up on a cable hanging down from the aircraft, when the aircraft went down. And it was a big mess, because the eyewitnesses lived all over, and I ended up running all over Washington and Oregon tracking them down. I'd take a small plane myself, and then I'd fly to all these little places and I'd locate the people and ask them to meet me at the local airport. Then I'd take their statement and fly out again.

"Then, in another helicopter case in Oregon, the crash killed several people. We had to go through the bush, trying to find all bodies and plane parts that were scattered everywhere. It was like a big puzzle, just trying to find them, and then trying to put all these little technical pieces and eyewitness statements together to find out what happened.

"And then, in the event these cases developed into litigation, I had to be ready to testify in court. But then usually..." Terry looked a little relieved, "... most of these cases do settle before they come to trial. Based on the investigation reports, the lawyers and the insurance company have a pretty good idea of what happened and who's at fault, so they determine what the case is likely to be worth based on past ones of this sort, and then they settle. Here, for example, the lawyers and insurance companies would look at other losses and crashes to determine the likely amount."

In another case, a crash occurred because two young men got drunk. One, a licensed pilot, stole a plane at the local airport, and tried to show his friend all the tricks he could do. Unfortunately, in the course of showing how low he could fly, he crashed the plane into the side of a house at night and died. His passenger survived, only to file a lawsuit later naming several defendants, including the airport where the plane was parked.

"It was a crazy case from the beginning," Terry explained. "First of all, the rescuers involved ended up in a jurisdictional dispute over who would handle the case. This happened because the house the pilot crashed into was located right on a county line. So at first, these emergency response people arrived from both counties. But then, after they go there, instead of going to the aid of the pilot and the passenger in the aircraft, the rescuers spent about twenty minutes arguing as to whose jurisdiction it was. The reason was that they're all afraid that the plane was going to blow up any minute, since there's all this liquid flowing down the wreckage, and they think it's fuel. So of course they don't want to be placed at risk.

"Then, a California Highway Patrol officer came along, and immediately went to the wreckage, and found out that the liquid was water, because the plane hit a water pipe in the house and ruptured it. He started the rescue proceedings."

However, the next controversy was whether the aircraft operator or owner was liable.

"It was pretty amazing," Terry said. "The defendant tried to argue that the airport was at fault. In addition, the hangar contained a lock-box with the keys to the planes on it. The pilot who took the plane knew what the combination was to the lock because he had trained at this particular field before. Since this is how he got the keys to the plane which he crashed, the defendant tried to suggest the airport owner and operator were liable, which is questionable, because there was no expectation that someone who had trained there years before would use that knowledge to steal a plane which then crashed."

In any case, once the suit against the owner and operator was filed, it was Terry's job, representing the insurance company, to interview everybody connected with the case. When he did, he discovered that the official FAA investigators had obtained wrong information.

"As in all aircraft accidents, the FAA or NTSB does an official report," Terry explained. "Even relatively small ones, though if it's a really big accident, involving high liability, with lots of loss of life or lots of media attention, then the National Transportation Safety Board will investigate. In any case, when I looked at this report, I discovered that it claimed an unlicensed pilot stole the airplane, although I had discovered in my own investigation that he was definitely licensed and experienced. I even went to his family and photographed all his licenses. I passed this information to the FAA investigator, and he said he came to this conclusion because when he entered the name in the computer terminal, it came back negative—no record found. And he didn't think it necessary to check it again. Sometimes, though, this kind of error can actually affect liability, so it shows how really important it is to check these things out."

Here, the pilot's licensing had no effect on the case and it was eventually settled out of court. But as Terry pointed out, "You just never know."

And then, turning a little sad, he commented: "You know, even though we may talk about these cases from a liability viewpoint, it's also important to understand that each of these cases involves a tragedy. There's a death or there's a serious injury. Or people's lives have been turned around. So though I may be out there thinking about liability and monetary damages and spreading the risk, these kinds of cases are unfortunate, and you can't help but feel sad as you listen to people describe such cases. There are many people who can't handle this type of situation. But we deal with it every day. After a while, you learn how to separate yourself from all the emotional involvement, much like doctors and health professionals."

Terry concluded his discussion of airplane cases with one that was on the light side. It was a kind of welcome counterpoint after hearing him talk about all the destruction and death he had observed. In this case, someone had shoveled some snow off of a wing causing it damage.

"It was unbelievable," Terry exclaimed. "This guy rented an airplane, flew it to Tahoe, parked at the airport, and then it snowed overnight. While it was there, somebody used a metal shovel to clear the snow off the wings and the fuselage. The pilot then flew it home as if nothing had happened.

"After he returned it to the airport, the ground crew checked the plane the next day, and discovered these scrape marks all over it. They went to the pilot who rented it, and they asked him to explain, but he really couldn't.

"The insurance company is looking at several thousand dollars in repainting, and they want to find out what happened. That's where I came in. I went to the airport in Tahoe asking questions, and pretty soon I found a maintenance guy who said: 'Oh, yeah, I remember that. This guy came over and borrowed this metal snow shovel.' And then I found some eyewitnesses who saw him on the plane shoveling snow.

"And so then the insurance company was able to go over to this guy with the shovel and tell him to pay up, since we proved he was responsible."

Finally, we wondered what effect being an investigator had on Terry's personal life. And for Terry, as for many private eyes, the main effect was that the business made him more cautious and guarded—both about his physical security, and about others knowing personal things about him.

"I think, maybe I'm a little more security conscious than others, and this is especially true in the telecommunications area, because I know how easy it is for these things to be violated." In fact, as Terry pointed out, he had a very elaborate security system installed in his own building. Later when we left, he showed us how it took a series of phone calls and encoded button pushings to be successfully let out of the building and then to resecure it against any unwarranted visitors.

Then, in talking about his steps to take personal precautions to protect himself, Terry commented: "I think I'm probably a little more careful about my surroundings than the average person. I pay more attention to who's out there and who I am dealing with. But I think most investigators get that way after a while. I don't consider it paranoia. Rather, it's just being a little more careful, a little more aware of what's happening."

Going on to talk about the tendency of the investigator to be secretive, he observed: "Well, since as an investigator I know how easy it is to gather up information about someone, I'm probably a little more secretive and careful about whom I'm dealing with than the average person. Maybe a little more conservative than the average person too. Often the public thinks of the image of the flashy, flamboyant investigator, like the Tom Sellecks or earlier the Bogarts, but I don't think that's true. Generally, private investigators have a more low-profile, conservative way of relating to the world; more thoughtful, more cautious. I know I do."

Then, too, Terry pointed out, as part of this more conservative, secretive way of relating to others, many private investigators, himself included, tended to stick together and socialize with others in the field. "I think it's something that comes with the business, which is much like what I learned years ago in being a policeman. Generally, policemen, for the most part, tend to socialize with other policemen. Their work tends to keep them suspicious and cautious around others; it keeps them aloof; and I think it's somewhat similar in this business, too."

This concern with secrecy, combined with a desire not to be tarred with the incorrect popular persona of the private investigator, led Terry, like many other investigators, not to let others know what he did. Or as he put it: "Though a lot of my good friends are not in the business, such as one who runs a restaurant, another who is a general contractor, the majority of people who know me, including my neighbors, don't know what I do. I might tell them I investigate airplane accidents, but not say a licensed private investigator, because once you tell them that, they think you do what they've seen in the movies or on TV. They think you race around in fancy cars chasing women and shooting people and stuff like that, though the work's not really that way."

And finally, Terry seemed to think that private investigators, more than others, like to have a feeling of control over their environments.

"Generally, you could say that private investigators tend to be more protective of their personal life. It's part of that tendency to be more secretive, cautious and controlled."

The interview was almost over, and we wondered how this approach to life might affect his relationships with others he was close to. For instance, was he married? Single? Did he have kids? How did his work affect them?

Terry just looked at us mysteriously and wouldn't say. "Let's just say the answers are a few of my many secrets."

And then, the interview over, Terry carefully set his security system in motion by calling the appropriate numbers and punching in the correct codes, doused the lights, double and triple locked the door, and took us over to his car, where he had one last thing to show us—his radio control and communications system. It was amazing. The front of his car looked like a computer control room, with all sorts of radios, microphones, buttons and switches, plus a cellular telephone, two-way radio, and what looked like a screen with flashing radar.

"It's how I stay in touch and on top of things at every moment when I'm on the job, or even off the job," said Terry, and he hopped in the car. Then, just as he did, the phone rang, and he picked it up.

"Well, gotta go," he said. "About an important case." Then he rolled up the window quickly and was gone in his high-tech car on another high-tech case.

6

Pat Buckman: Surveillance and Undercover Work

We kept hearing about Pat Buckman, since several people we had already spoken to had worked for him on surveillance or undercover during their early days in the business or knew others who did. So we decided that he would be the ideal person to talk with about surveillance and undercover work.

Sam Brown and I arrived at his offices in the Potrero Hill section of San Francisco, a once industrial area of the city, now being refurbished with quaint-looking boutiques, delis, bookstores, and drop-in singles bars. The whole area seemed alive, vital, and even Pat's office had a kind of exhuberant, new corporate look as we walked up a flight of stairs into an office with an expanse of several desks, clacking typewriters, computer terminals, ringing phones, and abstract paintings on the walls.

It was quite a difference from the less officey offices of the other private investigators we had visited, who generally worked alone or with one or a few associates, and commonly had offices in their homes. But then Pat, over the years, had become more of a supervisor and business manager than an active investigator himself, handling about sixty to seventy new cases a month, and supervising a team of about a dozen operatives. At one time, Pat worked out in the field himself, doing a great deal of surveillance and undercover work, but now he mostly assigned his operatives to do this, while carefully preparing, supervising and debriefing them on each case.

Pat led us to a desk in the center of the bustling office, and we set up in the midst of the clacking machines. It felt a little like being in the middle of a stock brokerage, and Pat briefly commented: "Sorry about all the noise and confusion, but that's the way it is everyday. We're monitoring and coordinating so many cases."

And then with us juggling the tape recorders so that we could hopefully hear Pat above the uproar, the interview began.

Pat has a long history in this business—almost thirty years, having started doing investigations back in the early 1960s. Born in San Francisco, he got his B.A. in criminology from City College in San Francisco, and originally started out to become a fireman. He took the qualifying test shortly after serving in the Korean War. However, since this was the same test and qualifying list used for the police force and an opening for a cop came up, Pat decided to take the job. So he worked as a cop for four years. Then, after leaving the force, he managed a bar and a restaurant for about six months. While doing this, he was approached by a friend who ran a busy investigative services agency. He needed someone followed, and asked Pat to help out.

"I enjoyed the work and found I was good at it. It helped with my background of being a police officer, because that gave me a lot of contacts and I knew a lot of people. Also, cops learn how to get information, although there wasn't any formal training in those days. The appointments were just made on political considerations and you learned who to salute and how to follow the rules. But it provided a good source of contacts and information for being an investigator, and after I had a shot at following some people for my friend, I liked doing it, and decided to go into that business for myself."

Initially, Pat did the work in the field himself, and since those were the days of fault divorces, he did a great deal of surveillance work in domestic cases. "That was big business then, following errant spouses around, trying to get the goods on them for a divorce action. The idea was to show some kind of adultery or playing around, so there would be grounds for divorce. Now, you can't even bring evidence of infidelity. It has no bearing on the divorce, because there is no-fault divorce. But then it was the full-employment act for private detectives, because in those days, in so many divorces, the woman would cite mental cruelty. And if she could prove adultery, the man would have to give up about eighty percent of his income. She'd get the house, the car, the furniture. Our job was to help her get the evidence so she could get all this property. There was so much of this kind of work back then, you could really get rich and retire from it."

In fact, that's what Pat did for awhile—he retired to Hawaii and took it easy. But then, two years later, after his own divorce, in 1981, he returned to San Francisco to start up in business again. Most of the divorce work of the early years was gone, but now there was a new arena where surveillance and undercover work was especially important—in the corporate field and in child custody cases, so Pat shifted his focus to that, and gradually expanded into other areas, as well as building a team of people to work with him on different types of cases.

Though Pat's office is very high tech and systematized now, he still remembered the old days fondly.

"It was always exciting, never boring. Everyday you did something different, it kept you alert, and that's one of the things that attracted me to this business. Plus it was such quick easy money. For example, in those days, I could make enough money in two or three days to take the rest of the month off and go sailing, and I used to ocean race a lot. So I'd go sail in Tahiti or someplace exotic for awhile. Yes, it was pretty free and easy in those days."

Another fond memory of that time was the much greater informality.

"We weren't burdened with so much paper. Today, we have to do so much to keep formal records to protect ourselves. Back then, I used to call an attorney to tell him what I observed or overheard, tell him what the bill was, and that was that. But now we have to document everything. Things have become so much more formal, legalistic and sophisticated."

Then, too, the old divorce laws contributed to this free-wheeling way of life that exists in much of the romaniticized mystique of the investigator today.

"In those days, before the no-fault dissolution, there was a lot of divorce work. Because in those days a spouse, usually the man, would want to get something on his wife, so he wouldn't have to pay all that alimony or end up living in a hotel room while she kept the house. So we'd usually have a great time following around the wealthy spouses, usually the wives, trying to catch them in some kind of dalliance. I once followed the wife of a famous casino owner for eight weeks. We traveled to Hawaii, Mexico, Washington, D.C., Florida, to all these resorts, and it was great, like a vacation in high style."

Also, back then, Pat did a lot of locate-and-recover children cases himself. "And that was great too. There would be a lot of surveillance in a lot of foreign countries. It was a real globe-trotting life. I'd make enough money, say about $40,000 to snatch a kid, and then I wouldn't have to work for a couple of months, so I could sail off in my boat for awhile. It was just a terrific way to live, a kind of movie fantasy of what it's like to be a private eye. Today, it's really a business, with most private investigators working on their own, and the work is really hard, not glamorous at all."

Pat gave a few examples of the myth of the modern fantasy. "Well, for one thing, the glamour of tracking people through fancy hotels is only a small part of the business. Much of it is very dull, sitting around in cars on cold, lonely streets, waiting and watching for something to happen. And then, the films and TV show all this violence. But nobody can get hit over the head as many times in one lifetime as some of those private eyes on TV do and live. That old image has been so magnified that it's nearly satire. Today nobody works like that."

What is it like today in the areas of surveillance and undercover work where Pat specializes?

According to Pat, today, there is still some of the domestic checking up on spouses and lovers, but now much of the surveillance is done in corporate cases, following executives around. And there is an increasing number of child custody surveillances arising from court battles. We asked him to explain a little about each area in turn, starting with the corporate cases, which was currently his main type of surveillance work.

Why should investigators be needed to follow executives around?

"Because of competition. The company isn't so much concerned that the executive might be looking for another job, but more frequently that an executive might be involved in transferring proprietary information from his company to another for compensation. Perhaps he might be running a business on the side or engaged in some unfair business practice to gain an advantage for his company that might come back and hurt it later should public revelation follow."

What sort of unfair business practices? Pat went on.

"Sometimes a salesman might try to get some advance information in ways they shouldn't so they can do better in making a bid on a job, like when a company is working with some government agency, such as the Department of Defense. That kind of activity might initially help the company get the bid and look good for the salesman. But if this information comes out, taking this short-cut can get the company in trouble. A big company like GE or Boeing might just pay a moderate fine if one of their people is found to have done this. And then that person who did this could be fired, and that would be that. But if a little guy does this, say someone who does only about $20 million with the government, the fine would be a much larger percentage of his business, or he could be put on a blacklist for further projects, because it's a smaller company and the leadership would be held more responsible for what it's people do. That one act could destroy the company.

"Then, too, a company wants to make sure that some of their top people are not trading with competitors, information for money."

Pat gave an example.

"One time a company wondered why a competitor seemed to come up with some new products that had almost exactly the same new features it had just introduced within a few weeks or months earlier. Plus, the other company was able to get the jump by offering just about the same thing for a substantially lower price. This would have been possible if the other company did not have the high development costs they did in researching the new features, building the prototypes for experimental testing, and getting the product on the market. Thus, the first company suspected some internal espionage, and they hired us."

Pat described the case.

"We set up a surveillance targeting a few of the suspected executives who had access to the new research and development findings and marketing discussions of new products. We positioned some cars near the parking lot, and we followed the executives as they drove around or met with people. We also had some people on the street who were able to follow them into restaurants and other public places, and then could sit by these executives and overhear conversations.

"As we soon discovered, one of the executives was setting up meetings with a counterpart from the competition. We saw them together, photographed them, and in a few instances, heard a little of their conversation. And in one case, we snapped a picture of this executive showing the competition some drawings for a new product and then he gave the competition a report—the whole marketing strategy for the launch.

"It was incredible. Here this guy, number three in the company, making a six-figure salary, is selling out his own company for maybe $50,000. Well, after we got the evidence, the head of the company confronted him, and they worked out a settlement and he left. So that's where corporate surveillance can come in—to show if a person in the company is being honest or not, and then if he isn't, to confront him with the evidence, so he not only leaves but even can be made to reimburse the company for what he has done. And in some cases, there may even be criminal charges based on information turned over to the local D.A. if the person has broken any criminal laws."

Pat then explained a little about the ins and outs of child custody surveillances.

"Basically, what you usually have here are parents battling over issues of control, using the child as a pawn to their power games. What sometimes happens is one parent has custody, the other visiting rights, or maybe they can't agree over joint custody arrangements. So one parent goes off with the child, often over state lines, to keep the spouse with custody rights from seeing that child. And that's where we come in—to find the child, watch for an appropriate time, and then snatch the child back.

"It's presumably legal to do this, if the spouse who's your client has the custody papers from the court and the other parent has presumably violated the court orders by taking the child. However, it can be a really tricky area, because in the meantime the spouse with the child has gotten some papers granting custody for the child in another state; or maybe the parent and child have ended up in another country, with its own special laws. So it can be risky, and if you don't do everything right, it can be easy to end up in trouble with the law yourself."

Pat gave an example of a case where he had ended up briefly snatching the wrong kid.

"It was a case I was working on that took me back to the South. I had finally tracked down the client's son to a certain city and determined what school he was going to. We went there, and in the afternoon, while we were on surveillance by the school playground, there was a recess and all the kids came out to play. Well, the woman suddenly points: 'That's my kid,' and so I drove up close, jumped out with her, and we grabbed the kid, and we jumped back in the car. But then, when we got two blocks away, she suddenly announced: 'This is not my kid.'

"And that was a real heart stopper. So we drove back, dumped him off, just as all the other kids were going in from recess, and certainly he's going to be telling them this wild-eyed story about how a man and a woman picked him up and that's why he's late for class. After that, I headed out of town for awhile. After all, if the teacher believed his story, the school authorities are probably going to be calling the police. And then that's kidnapping—a heavy charge."

Pat looked disbelieving about the incident even now, more than fifteen years later. "I mean, can you believe that? The mother didn't even recognize her own kid. She says: 'That's my Johnnie,' very certainly. But then it wasn't her Johnnie at all."

So did he ever find the boy?

"Yeah, yeah, eventually," Pat said. "But we waited a few weeks. We wanted things to die down. And then, at another recess, we drove by, and this time we got the right kid. But this time, I had someone else do it. The whole situation was too nerve-wracking. I didn't want to be tied in with that previous attempt; so I just stayed out of town myself."

Then, turning to the domestic case area, Pat pointed out that there was much less domestic work now that there was no need for evidence in a divorce case to prove fault, though it was still a common area for surveillance. He discussed some of the main reasons.

"Sometimes the spouse just wants to know. He or she already suspects something, and really just seeks some confirmation. It can be hard to know the truth, but for many people, that's really better than being up in the air, guessing, suspecting, but never really knowing. They realize where they stand now and can deal with that."

Pat gave an example of one man whose wife he was investigating at the request of the man's attorney.

"The man was going through a divorce, and said he didn't care who the suspected lover was. He just wanted to know if his wife was screwing around when he was away on business trips. It was a no-fault divorce case, so whether she was or she wasn't wouldn't make any difference in the settlement; and the two of them were already having problems with communicating and fighting about things anyway. But he just wanted to know where he stood.

"And that's typical," Pat commented. "When anyone wants to know if their marital partner is screwing around, they usually know the score. They just want the confirmation by having somebody come back and tell them they know."

Why should they want this confirmation? Why was it better to know where they stood?

Pat went on. "Well, by knowing, the issue is out in the open. And then they can always confront the spouse and say: 'I know you're screwing Johnny, Mary, or whatever.' It's like a release or a confession that helps to clear the air."

Yet as Pat acknowledged, sometimes too much information about what their spouse was doing could create problems by triggering vengeful actions. That was one reason that he generally preferred to work directly with attorneys; they could choose what information to reveal to a client based on that individual's needs and temperament. There were times when Pat thought it best not to tell a client who the lover actually was.

"Sometimes it's not a good idea to tell the client something that will inflame him or her to the point they will harm their own case because of their jealousy or rage. For example, the guy who discovers his wife fooling around with his best friend might fly off the handle and kill him. So that's why the good domestic relations attorney knows he can't tell the client everything, and that's why I very seldom will take a case without an attorney. Because then the attorney can decide what to tell the client, since the information they give to their client is not everything we give to the attorney about what we have found out."

Pat gave a recent example. "In this one case I had on the Peninsula south of San Francisco, this client flew to Los Angeles several times a month, and he wondered about whether his wife was playing around on the side. He told his attorney: 'I don't care who it is. I just want to know if my wife is screwing around with someone while I'm gone.' After we watched her for a few days, we discovered the wife was having an affair with his brother, and I didn't want to tell him that, and his attorney agreed. 'Don't say that it's his brother,' the lawyer warned, 'because he'll kill him. He set his younger brother up in business, he loaned him money, he did everything he could to help him, and he won't be able to deal with this.' So I wrote up the report for the attorney without divulging that."

But what if the client wants to know, we wondered?

Pat hesitated a moment. "Well, that's why I prefer to work with attorneys. My report goes to the attorney, and he can decide what he wants to tell the client or what he doesn't want to tell. Also, when I work with an attorney, what I put in my report becomes work product, so it's confidential. But otherwise, if I work for a client directly, anybody could subpoena me and say: 'What did you talk about? What did your client ask you to do? What did you tell him or her? And I'd have to answer. But if I work for the client's attorney, other people can't ask me those things. So it's really safer for everyone. Plus the attorney can do that prescreening of information for the client.

"But still..." Pat spoke slowly, hesitantly, "...if a client who hired me directly did want that information, I would tell him if I had agreed to take that particular job. On the other hand, if I felt there might be some serious risk in telling a client information, which might set him off, such as finding out about a wife screwing a man's brother, I might not take the job in the first place. After all, you don't want to do something you know is going to contribute to one person seriously injuring or killing another. Certainly, the results of any investigation are a calculated risk—but if I sense the investigation might lead to a big blow-out, I certainly wouldn't do it. Which is why it's better to work with attorneys—they can help to screen out such problems and temper the results. They already understand the business, and they know the right moves."

Then, from the why's of surveillance, the conversation shifted to the how-to of surveillance. How, exactly, was a usual surveillance conducted?

And almost immediately Pat blew away the stereotype of the private eye lurking in doorways or standing nonchalantly on a street corner.

"Most of the time, you conduct a surveillance by car," he said. "You're more mobile that way. And generally you have a two-cars or two-man surveillance. Also, you typically use cars equipped with radios, so the two cars can be in radio contact with each other and send messages about the person under surveillance. Or, if possible, if the client has the budget for it, you may use three cars, because there's a better chance of maintaining contact with the person and not being seen, since the cars can readily trade off surveillance for awhile."

Pat gave a few examples of how a surveillance with two or more cars might work. "The problem with just one person on a surveillance, is that he or she can more easily lose the subject or be burned for following him. For instance, say there's just one person tailing the guy. He could go right; he could go left; he could just get across when the light changes and the guy behind him doesn't have enough time to react. Or say one person is following another on a long stretch of highway and is trying to at least keep the other in view. Well, if I saw a car following me for a very long time, I might wonder.

"By contrast, with a couple of cars or more, there are different ways of following. For example, there's the piggyback approach, in which two cars might travel on parallel streets. So then, one car might drop back, and then the other one might move ahead to follow for awhile. Or suppose the cars are following the guy on the freeway. They could take turns following, too. Say the guy takes a cloverleaf. The first guy may not take it, but the second guy will. Then, he may swing around and after they get through the cloverleaf, the third guy may pick him up. Meanwhile, the others will double back.

"On the other hand, if it's not possible to use more than one car, there are various tricks of the trade, and a good surveillance person will be able to keep a tail going most of the time."

For a moment, Pat hesitated, careful not to give away any inappropriate private eye secrets. But finally, he offered a few common ploys.

"One thing a good surveillance person will know is not to follow too closely. And it's important not to make eye contact. So the person won't normally stop right behind the driver and look in the mirror. More usually, the person will stop a car length or two away, with one or two cars between them. And then the person will also try to estimate in advance where the subject is likely to turn, so he or she can prepare and be in the lane to turn too. Or maybe the driver might take a calculated risk if he or she is pretty sure that the subject is going to a certain place and drive ahead of him for awhile. And then if the subject stops, normally the investigator will just keep going and stop ahead or perhaps park off on a side street, so that when the subject starts up again, he can pull out again and end up a few car lengths behind. It takes awhile, but after sometime you start to get a kind of sixth sense about these things. It's like you're flowing with the subject, almost like you are in his mind, so you can sense what he's going to do and better stay with him, but far enough out of sight, so he doesn't know you're there."

And then, if the subject holed up for awhile, there would be the stakeout. In turn, as Pat explained, there were some common tried and true techniques for handling this most effectively. One method is to park up the street to stay out of sight. Also, letting the police know in advance avoids the embarrassment of being checked out by them.

"We normally call the police as a matter of course and would be foolish not to, because if we don't, some neighbor will see this man or woman sitting in a car for a long time and will probably call the cops. And then they're going to show up, and the whole world is going to see us, which will blow the surveillance. Then, too, calling the police protects us if something happens in the area, such as an accident, shooting, or whatever, because we can explain in advance that we had a legitimate reason to be there, and don't end up getting caught up in the investigation of this other incident."

Pat also pointed out that simply giving the police an I.D. and explaining that the investigator was on a case was enough.

"We don't have to tell the police who we're following or why. All we have to tell them is who we are or that we're working on a civil matter. I'll just show my private investigator's card with my license, or my investigators working under my license will do the same, and then that's it. That's all the police need to know."

Also, Pat emphasized the importance of getting some background information on the subject before beginning the surveillance.

"Many people think you just go out and follow somebody. But before you do, you normally do a great deal of background work on them, which will increase the success rate tremendously."

How? Pat continued.

"Well, before you tail someone in a car, you find out what kind of vehicles they own, what kind they drive. You also get their description, maybe a photograph of them. Sometimes it also is important to know who the subject's best friends are and who they know, so you can tell if a person comes by or a car pulls up, is that a friend or what?"

Pat gave some examples of how this kind of information could help.

"Well, suppose it's fairly dark, and a person suddenly comes out of a nightclub and onto the street. Is this the subject you're waiting to follow? Maybe you can't make out the features distinctly, but if you know approximately how tall and how heavy this person is, that can help. Likewise, if it's a woman, it can be helpful to know in advance how she wears her hair, the color of it, whether she wears high heels, that sort of thing. Or if it's a man, you might find it helpful to know if he wears glasses or not, stoops or limps when he walks. Is he or she left-handed? Right-handed? Ambidextrous?

"Then, too, knowing in advance the kind of car driven can help you identify it when you suddenly see it on the street or coming out of a garage. The problem is that a lot of times you won't be able to see a person leave directly. They just go into a garage or big public place. And a lot of times you can't sit close enough to see who is coming or going. So you may just have to make an educated guess based on what you know about the type of car the person drives, the way he walks or moves, the kind of clothes he wears which you can only see in silhouette. And then you just hope you're right, because if not, it's easy to lose a subject this way."

On the other hand, being seen was always a concern, and Pat described some strategies for concealment, particularly after the subject had stopped moving around for awhile.

"If you can, you park in a position where you're not noticed. For example, say you're watching somebody's house. You can't just park in front of the guy's house. You'd be spotted right away. Instead, you might park down the block. However, the risk in that is when the guy leaves, you might lose him if he goes in the other direction, so it's usually best to bracket such a surveillance with two or more radio cars. Then, you can park the cars in different places, so that he has to pass one of them. And then the cars stay in radio communication with each other, so that if the subject does leave, the drivers can decide who is going to follow him first and where the other cars are going to go, so they can pick up the surveillance when the first car pulls off."

Yet, even with all this planning, there could still be problems.

"One of the main problems," Pat commented, "is the neighbors start wondering about you sitting there after awhile. And then maybe some neighbor or some of their kids may come up to you and ask you what you are doing. Well, you hope this doesn't happen, but if it does, and you become too noticeable, even a block or two away, then you have to move."

And the other big problem for most investigators was not being able to move.

"You just can't leave your car or your post when you're on a surveillance, because that could be the very moment when the subject suddenly decides to leave himself. And then you've missed him, and you may not even know it. So you absolutely have to stay there and you have to stay awake, which sometimes can be hard to do.... And then there's the boredom of the loneliness. It's not like on the movies or in TV. Instead, the time can just drag, and meanwhile, you're sitting or standing there, just trying to stay awake and pay attention. Plus another problem can be just going to the bathroom or eating, because you can't get out, and you can't leave anything on the street. You have to bring any food into the car with you before the surveillance, and if you have to go to the bathroom, well, you just have to improvise, say by urinating into a milk carton. And meanwhile, you're hoping against hope that this isn't the moment the subject chooses to leave, while you've got your fly open and you're peeing into a milk carton. That's actually happened to a couple of my investigators. But when the subject suddenly appears or leaves, the investigator has to be ready to take off too, call of nature or not.

Usually, the way Pat described it, an investigator would be on his own on the street or in a car on a surveillance, so it could be a lonely business, especially when the subject stopped someplace for awhile or went to sleep for the night, while the investigator had to stay nearby watching and waiting. "And sometimes it had to be hard to stay awake for those long hours," Pat observed.

However, there were also some special surveillances where the investigator watching had to blend into a crowd or the surrounding activities, such as bowling in a nearby lane if the person under surveillance was a bowler. And then, often two investigators might work together to both better follow or watch the subject and fit in.

Pat explained. "Well, if you are following people who are going to plays or to places where social activities are going on, it can look more normal to have two people there, particularly a man and a woman. If the subject is going to a society ball, I wouldn't go there by myself or send an operative alone. After all, anyone alone would stick out. So I would go with another operative, a woman, and she'd be wearing a mink coat, whether she rents it or owns it, while I'd be in my tuxedo like everyone else."

But would he have to take another operative to a social gathering? What about just taking a date?

Pat shook his head. "Not a good idea. If you took a date, you'd have to be very careful it was the right kind of person, one who could carry off the acting as well as you can. You just can't take anyone. For instance, some of my female operatives can't take their boyfriends as much as they might like to because they're not cool enough to carry off the scene."

And what about taking a date along without telling him what was happening, so he could just act his natural self?

Again Pat shook his head, and even more vigorously. "Impossible. First of all, you wouldn't have your date very long, because all of a sudden you might have to be taking off in the middle of the evening, when the subject suddenly ups and leaves, and your date may not be very understanding when you say you have to leave immediately and say something like: 'I have to get my car because he's going to his limo, and I have to get behind his limo.' Because then your date may protest saying something like 'Well, I want to see the end of the opera,' so the idea of taking non-professionals along on a job doesn't work very well.

"And besides," Pat went on, "there's the problem of confidentiality. You bring someone, say an acquaintance, and even if the surveillance goes well, the next day at the office, they're out there talking about it. So you're asking for trouble if you let outside people know your business, and that includes your girlfriend or boyfriend, wife or husband, father or mother, children—anybody. You're just asking for trouble. Because even if people don't mean any harm by it, everybody talks, everybody converses. And what's more fun than talking about what a private investigator does? Everyone's fascinated by the business—so they talk, and your confidential cases can end up all over town."

The conversation turned to the kinds of equipment and vehicles used to make it easier to watch or follow people. One device was a transponder, which Pat told of putting on a car when he was following a trucker believed by his boss to be stealing things from a warehouse.

"It's a small electronic device, like ones designed for airplanes. The airplane has this device that emits electronic beeps or signals, so the ground controller can tell how far away it is and in what direction. It's about the size of a silver dollar, and it has a magnetized antenna which sends outside the signals, and so if you slap it on or underneath some object or vehicle that is moving, you can use it to locate the person with that object or in that vehicle."

Typically, Pat used these devices on inside jobs where the owner of the vehicle had the suspicion that someone in his organization was involved in some sort of theft or illegal activity and wanted him followed. "They're particularly good in commercial work," he observed. "Say someone is hijacking trucks, or maybe it's a liquor truck that's always losing ten cases of this or that, so the owner suspects the driver is unloading this somewhere. It might be harder following these guys, because you can't get too close to them, since they have a kind of sixth sense when they're being followed. So it's easier using a transponder. Then you can let the driver out of your sight, but you still know where he is, and after he stops you can close in."

Pat also pointed out that using these devices was perfectly legal the way he used them, since he had the permission of the owner to place them there. It might not always be legal to just slap a transponder on anyone's property, because of invasion of privacy issues, though Pat didn't know the full ins and outs of the law. "I just know you can't buy them legally, at least here in California, unless you are working on something along with the police or have a client say you are working on an internal theft or other internal matter. But normally we're using transponders for an internal theft and usually have some cooperation with the local police, and so we just tell them we have a transponder, and that's all we need to do.

"Besides, that's the only way we would want to use them. I wouldn't want to go into someone's home and put one on the guy's car when it's in the garage. That might be considered trespassing. And besides, the devices are fairly sophisticated, expensive pieces of equipment, and you would normally never get them back if you used them without someone's permission. I certainly would never go back for them."

And what about using vans with all their sophisticated listening or observing equipment? Pat didn't think it a good idea, although there were certain advantages. "You can film from inside so much easier, and no one can see you because the windows are one way glass, or because you can see through a telescope on top which is angled like a periscope camera. And of course you can have all sorts of receiving and recording devices inside. But the problem with a van is it's so limited, very expensive, and you can't use it that much. It isn't good for any type of moving surveillance, because if you follow someone in a van, you can get burned very easily or you can have trouble keeping up. A van is very noticeable, and it's hard to keep up with someone darting in and out of traffic. Also, parking's tougher just to find a spot, and when you do park on the street, it's kind of obvious.

"About the only time a van is of use is for a one location surveillance, and when it's in a location where it can fit in. For example, you might use the van if you're watching a dock, or if you are keeping surveillance and you want to watch from a couple of blocks away."

We talked a little about cameras. If Pat used anything, he normally would take stills with a small Minox. But most times he didn't use a video or film camera. Why not?

"Well, normally, you don't need to video or film anyone to show what they are doing. Generally, it's enough to just take a 35mm picture showing who the person is or who he or she is with, though sometimes a client may think a video is necessary. But it really isn't. For example, one time, a client said he wanted a video of his wife kissing her boyfriend, but the attorney told him it wasn't necessary. Just a picture was all he needed."

When might a film or video be needed?

"Well, usually, filming in surveillance is just used to show buys or when people are selling something. For example, the film might be used to show them in the act of stealing goods out of a truck or buying drugs or some other item they shouldn't, because here a photo alone might not be enough to show what is going on. But then, this type of surveillance is usually stationary. We have time to set up cameras in a special location, such as an apartment house across the street. But otherwise, if you are dealing with moving subjects, a film of the activity usually isn't practical. It's hard to take and usually you don't need it."

And what about concealed cameras or cameras that didn't look like cameras, I asked. Did he ever use those? I described how I had once cut a little hole in a purse and set up a place in it for a little camera, when I was experimenting with private investigation work in my college days.

Pat was quite skeptical. "Oh, sure you can do that. But what are you really going to get? Such hidden cameras are just not practical for the everyday surveillance. For one thing, they're hard to aim. You don't know what you'll actually get. Also, you might be more noticeable trying to get the camera in the right position in the bag or other hidden location. To get such a picture when I'm not sure about what I'm aiming at, I'd have to get real close, and it might be hard for me to take a picture without the subject seeing me. But in most surveillances, you never see me. I'm just off in the background someplace or blending in with the crowd, and I wouldn't want to do anything to suddenly draw attention to myself."

Thus, Pat usually favored a small camera like a fast film Minox. "You can just hold it up, move, click real fast, and then you've got your picture. In fact, some of the new fast films go up to ASA 3200, so you can take a picture in almost any available light."

Such pictures were often used as a negotiation tool in reaching a settlement.

"They offer your client a kind of a wedge. For example, the lawyer pulls a picture out in the negotiations, and the other side wonders: 'Oh, God, what else do they know?' A picture is a good, graphic way of saying that you know what's going on. Without the picture, the other side might think you just have suspicions, or they might think they can argue that your client is wrong or mistaken, that things aren't what the client may suspect. But with the picture, they know you know, and that can help people get to the bargaining table and cut a better deal for your client."

Pat gave an example. "I was working on a case back East in a state that still has a fault divorce law, and I followed this woman around for several weeks. It took a long time to get any evidence on her, because she wasn't doing anything, just traveling around and staying in nice resorts. But then, finally, after eight weeks, she met someone, and I got some pretty good pictures at the pool."

According to Pat, the husband hadn't really suspected his wife of anything and wasn't concerned about whether or not she was involved with someone else. He just wanted some relief in their pending divorce action. "The man had long since stopped loving her, and a divorce was planned. He just wanted to know if she was playing around for leverage in a financial settlement. Usually, when somebody's getting divorced, there's a good chance there's some infidelity going on, and he hoped this might be the case. He wanted help in obtaining proof."

How much help? "We saved him more than a million dollars," Pat smiled. "And there wasn't even a trial, so I didn't have to testify. They settled, because since he had the pictures, she suddenly dropped her high demands. It was a fault state where adultery is still a grounds for a divorce action, and now he had the evidence, so she quickly gave in."

Pat also described his experiences in following people, some of them all over the globe. And the clients were willing to fund these long expeditions because of the high amount of money or strong emotions involved. Many of these cases involved chasing down people who had stolen valuable properties; others involved looking for parents who had run off with their kids in child snatchings, when they didn't have custody.

"In one case, I followed a man all the way through Europe over to Yugoslavia and then to Trieste in Italy, before I found out where he had his kid hidden. In another case, I traveled all over Central and South America looking for some stolen materials before I located them. As for the woman I followed for eight weeks in a divorce case, I tracked her to Hawaii and Mexico, then to Portland, Oregon, and Las Vegas. I was on her trail the whole time."

As Pat pointed out, it helped to do advance work to find out a little about where the subject was going, such as the flight he or she was taking. Then he could arrange to be on that flight too, or at least be there to meet it. Also, Pat usually tried to be in a nearby hotel room, sometimes next door, so he could readily watch the subject's room. Sometimes, he found a place across the corridor or across the street. And then he took along a variety of clothes so he could readily fit into whatever locale that person might be going to. "You just want to be able to blend in so the person doesn't see you. Even though you may be near them for weeks, they still don't realize you're there. And it helps that most people don't imagine that someone is following them, so they're not always looking around or alert. Most just don't pay attention, and that makes it easier to stay with them without them suspecting a tail."

Still, there were times when Pat did lose people, usually because of unanticipated circumstances.

"You lose people for some of the damnedest reasons. For example, a guy gets on the airplane and you get on the plane with him. Now normally, you would just expect to follow him out, while staying a respectful distance behind. But then, suppose there's a mechanical problem, and now all passengers have to leave the plane unexpectedly. This once happened to me, where the plane had to return for repairs, and the stewardesses opened both doors. I saw the subject start going out through the front, and I tried to follow him. But suddenly, the stewardess was in front of me announcing the remaining passengers had to go out the back exit. After he got off, my man got on a bus which went one way, and I was loaded on a bus that went another. After that, I lost him. He didn't take the next flight, so maybe he changed his plans. And here I was in Rome, after trailing him for two weeks. When that happens, it's hard to explain to the client, though, of course, you're without blame. This sort of thing does happen."

Did Pat still get paid if there was such a misadventure?

"Of course," Pat said. "I always get paid in advance. I don't work without the money. And the clients have to understand there are no guarantees. The investigator can only do the best he can; and there are always contingencies that can screw up a search. You can't always be prepared for any eventuality."

Then, turning to another topic, we talked about the undercover work that Pat or his operative did. In the early years, Pat did this himself, but now he mainly had associates go in and assume other identifies or roles so they could observe and get evidence on someone suspected of wrong doing.

"Mostly we do corporate undercover work—for companies that have suspicions, usually about a theft or drugs, and usually the problem involves someone in the warehouse who's taking merchandise or buying or selling drugs. Only a small percentage of the work involves white collar or office workers."

How would Pat set up an undercover arrangement?

"Basically, you begin by getting the undercover operative in and getting him accepted by the people who work there. And even before he (at least it's usually a he) goes in, you develop a background history for him, which includes his name, number, current and past addresses, past work, a whole resume. He has to memorize it. He literally has to become that new person, so it seems natural.

"And then you arrange to get that operative hired, and the way it is normally done, maybe only one or two people in the whole company will know, and in some companies only the head of security or maybe the head of personnel will be advised, and they are sworn to secrecy. Then, no one else will talk to that person about the case, except me, and I'll debrief him or her about what appears to be going on."

Another question was how did Pat find these people. Were these people who already knew the business or would be likely to get hired if they applied for the job? Did he just advertise to find them?

Pat shook his head vigorously. "No, I don't place ads, though some people do. But it's risky to advertise, and I know investigators who have gotten burned frequently for advertising. They put someone in and that person joins forces with the culprits. So I strictly go on personnel recommendations or use somebody who has worked for me before on something else.

"And as for past training, in most of the jobs it's pretty easy to learn the business, such as working in a warehouse. It's more difficult in the corporate setting, because usually you can only get in executive secretaries and bookkeeping types, and then you need someone with some experience in this area. But if it's a general kind of job, a well-rounded person with a worldly way about him makes a good undercover operative—for example, someone who's been a truck driver, a car salesman, a real estate salesman, someone who has bounced around and done a little of this or that."

When the person was hired, Pat would give him or her a careful rundown on what to look for and how to act, so the new employee would be at ease, get the necessary information, and not be revealed. "Sure, it helps if the person already has some experience with the kind of world he is supposed to step into, such as a drug culture. They have to understand some of the terminology, or we'll give them a crash course in what this world is like. And also, he or she needs to be prepared for someone asking them if they're an undercover operative. It happens all the time. Someone approaches them to test them, and they have to know how to say no convincingly, seem amazed with conviction, or properly play dumb. Otherwise, if they hesitate for a minute and seem embarrassed, they're dead—maybe even literally. It can be a rough world out there."

Once in the company, the operative is instructed initially to just hang out, though he would have a general idea of what he was looking for, too.

"The idea is just to get to know everyone else at first. He or she should just act naturally; do the job as best as possible without outperforming their fellow workers. And they should pretty much go along with whatever the other employees do. For example, when there's something everyone is disgruntled about, they should be disgruntled. When they all say some guy is an asshole, they should say something like: 'I hate that son of a bitch, too.' Or if people are talking about drugs openly, a guy might say something like: 'I got loaded last night, and this girl had some grass, and it just about killed me.'

But Pat warned about asking questions. "It's not a good idea to do that. When you're undercover, it's best not to ask any questions. Just observe, and let them tell you—that's our instructions to our operatives."

In fact, he indicated he didn't expect an undercover person to start bringing in any information for several weeks. "When people are involved in some kind of wrongdoing in a company, they suspect others may be checking up on them all the time, and they're very suspicious of everybody and very careful. And they have a kind of sixth sense about when someone might be undercover. That's why it's not a good idea to try to do undercover work too fast. Usually, you can't find out anything in a couple of weeks. And I don't want the operatives I put in to even try. It's too risky. Rather, they should just learn their job, be a regular guy, go out and have a beer when the others do, that kind of thing."

And what if the others were taking drugs in a drug case? Should the operative do that too?

Pat shook his head. "No, they don't take drugs. It's illegal, so I can't have the operatives doing that. Another reason is that the drugs can hurt the person's powers of observation and reason, so they can become careless. They can say things they shouldn't, reveal too much. Or they can get screwed up mentally and become part of the group, instead of observing, so drugs are a no-no. And I just tell them to offer excuses, whatever seems most reasonable. They might say, for instance, something like 'I'm on rehab; I'm on probation, I've got to pee in the bottle every week; I go to AA meetings.' And then, if they mention some excuse, they should be able to back it up. If they claim they're in AA—they should know when the AA meetings are and should go there a few times."

But then, if they couldn't do drugs themselves in a drug case, how would they elicit the information the employer wanted, such as who was using or selling drugs.

"Easy. If an undercover agent just hangs out for awhile, people will start to feel comfortable around him. They won't think he's a threat. And once people think someone isn't a threat, they do drugs pretty openly. Also, if you have any expertise in drugs"—Pat pointed to one of his people who worked undercover many times, a man in his thirties who looked like an accountant—"you can see someone who is under the influence of drugs. Like Mike there, who spent seven years undercover buying and selling drugs for a D.A. before he came to work with me. You just notice the slower than usual speech, the slightly glazed eyes, the spaciness or the hyper-kinetic feeling about the person, that sort of thing."

Then, Pat spoke a little about working with the operative once he was in the company.

"Usually, we'll talk each day—on the phone, or we'll meet, or the person will write up a brief report. It's important to stay in touch, though of course we take precautions. I don't want anyone seeing the operative meeting with me. So we use drops, special meeting places, communication signals, that sort of thing. Or I'll send a different person at times to get the report. The important thing is that the operative should report everything about his observations, not edit them or make any decisions about the worth of his observations. This way, I can decide what's valuable or not, and I can use this in dealing with the corporate security chief or other contact in the organization to decide how everything fits in and what we want to know."

Pat also noted that sometimes he might have more than one operative in a particular place. "If the place is pretty big, you might need this. Or maybe the company isn't sure exactly what division is involved in a particular problem. So two or more operatives might be useful, say in one warehouse in different sections, or maybe in different offices of the company. But then normally, they won't even know each other. No one will know but the company contact. And sometimes there might be different contacts who know about each one."

And what about pay? Did the operative get paid a salary for his work on the job?

"Of course," said Pat. "Besides getting paid for being an operative, the operative gets a W2 form. He's paid just like everybody else. Everything is normal. In fact, usually the payroll people don't know. They think he's just another normal employee."

We had been talking mostly about men working in the warehouse to do undercover work. What about women? To what extent were women involved in the field?

"It's a minority," Pat commented, "because most undercover work is done in a job that is dominated by males, such as in warehouses, truck driving, or on the docks. Women are used in just a small number of the cases, such as the office work, when we'll use a secretary or receptionist. And sometimes, in a hospital or clinic case, we might use a female nurse; for example, one of my investigators is also an RN, available whenever I need her. But mostly no—this is one of the areas of investigation that is largely dominated by men."

Pat gave a few examples of undercover cases he had worked on. One typical one was an office cocaine case.

"This manufacturing company knew it had a big office problem with people buying and selling drugs, but it didn't know who. The bosses suspected something, because there had been some problems with declining productivity and an increase in accident rates, and then in the course of an internal theft investigation, while I was interviewing one of the secretaries, she confessed to having a cocaine problem and getting drugs in the office, though she wouldn't say from whom.

"Soon after she was fired because of a particular theft investigation, we put a woman in the company who started off as a file clerk. And we just told her to wait and watch. It took us six months for her to start seeing anything, but it was worth the wait, because after that, some of the other employees asked her if she wanted to buy some coke from others in the company. Eventually, we found about a dozen people involved, and ultimately nine or ten people were arrested."

Were the police involved in this or other cases involving criminal activity?

Pat shook his head again. "No, not in the initial investigation; just after the fact. We don't get the police involved in the beginning. You become a liaison or agent for the police or district attorney, and I don't want to have an agency relationship, because then, I'm encumbered with the Miranda rights requirement in interviewing people and all the other restrictions on search or seizure or privacy that relate to the police. For example, if I'm working with the police, I would have to tell suspects their rights during an interview, but I don't have to do that as a private investigator. And if an undercover operator is looking through private files and gets some evidence there, there could be some restrictions that any such evidence or information from that evidence might be excluded, because of restrictions on searching without a warrant or seeing something that isn't in plain view. So there are cases where the suspects could get off because the evidence or information can't be used if I'm working with the cops. So I don't. But then, after the fact, if there is a crime involved, I call the police. If we've found cocaine, I would tell the cops our discovery and ask them to make an arrest."

In another even more dramatic undercover case, Pat spent some time behind bars—though not for anything he did, but because he was investigating possible corruption in the jails.

"The authorities thought there was something funny going on in the local lockup, where the prisoners would be sent for short sentences or if they were waiting for a prelim or trial. And I did three months there, which was definitely not fun. It was like being there for three years, and I hated every minute."

What did Pat do?

"I was treated like a regular prisoner. I was locked up, had to eat the same junk, I went out to exercise with the regular prisoners. And I sat around being bored much of the time, just like the other prisoners. About the only contact I had with anyone else was when I had a visitor or I met with my supposed lawyer, actually contacts from the outside who wanted a report on my observations in the case."

And what was Pat looking for?

"Drugs. The authorities believed the guards were supplying the prisoners with drugs and getting some money for it. And then, if the prisoners wanted an extra favor or wanted to make an extra phone call, the guards would let them do it for some extra money. So I just waited, became part of the prison population, and eventually, they approached me to ask if I wanted to buy drugs or wanted anything else, such as moving to another cell. In fact, I found that if the prisoners didn't play along and come up with money, the guards would do things to harass them, like put them in a cell with a bunch of guys they didn't like. And some of the non-players who didn't come up with money actually got roughed up this way."

But how did the prisoners get money if they were in jail?

"Oh, prisoner's can get money when they're in jail. They might make a little doing prison work. But mainly, they can get it from their visitors. If a prisoner said he didn't have any money, the guards would just tell him to get his visitors to bring him some money. And then, when the visitors arrived, the guards would just let them pass the prisoners the money. So it was a real scam the guards were pulling off. But after a few months, I observed them taking money from prisoners. We cracked that case. Several guards became prisoners themselves, and I was glad to get out of jail when the job was over. It's an experience I certainly wouldn't care to repeat."

What sort of risks were there for an undercover operative, besides getting burned? And had any of Pat's operatives ever been injured as a result of their work?

"Well, it definitely is a risky business," he agreed. "After all you're depending on people's trust to carry the role off; and people can feel very betrayed and hurt, even vengeful, if they discover someone is not who he seems; if he has been reporting on them. The operative always has to be very careful. He always has to remember his role. Probably the biggest risk for the operative is to be careless and do something that exposes himself, perhaps because he starts to feel so confident and sure of himself or natural in his role he can let himself go, or he just forgets. For example, he makes a phone call he shouldn't make from work, one which connects him to his real role in life, or he gets drunk when he's with the group out drinking and he starts talking.

"The problem with letting go, with getting drunk, is the operative is likely to make a mistake. This whole undercover business involves walking a line that is so thin between who you are, and who you are supposed to be, that the longer you walk it, the easier it is to fall off. So the operative has to pretend like a good actor. And he has to develop that actor's personality, that old method approach, where he really gets into and lives that role. It's a tough business, and when the person goes to work or does anything with others from this new undercover life, he has to be really into it. He has to truly feel and be that part. And it can be much more difficult, even impossible to maintain, in an altered state."

And yet not to join with the others when they did indulge? It seemed hard to think the others would believe when he held back.

"Well, then, we'll use supporting evidence to back up his story. For example, suppose an operative calls me to say 'I don't think the guy believed me when I told him the probation story about why I can't do drugs.' Then, I'll contact probation, maybe have his 'probation officer' call him at work. Or I'll have the probation department do up some papers, so his fellow employees can see them. The key is to help him support his role, so others believe and he doesn't get burned."

But then, with all these precautions, what if the person was exposed. Might he get hurt?

Pat claimed this hadn't happened to any of his people in years.

"But it happens. It has happened. I know some other investigators who had operatives involved in a major theft involving silicon chips. In another case, the operative was in on a drug ring. Well, when that happens, people have been seriously hurt. Some people haven't been found. They don't come back to work or report anywhere else. So we're talking serious business here. There are real dangers, and the person going in needs to know about them, so he won't get careless and get caught."

What about the opposite problem—the undercover person who became so involved with the people he was observing or liked them so much that he didn't want to report on them anymore? Had Pat experienced this?

"No, it hasn't happened to me, though it has to a few other people I know, and it's something you have to guard against in this business. For instance, someone starts saying or thinking: 'This guy I'm supposed to get to know. Well, he's really a nice guy.' Well, that's when I'd tell him, 'Hey, wait a minute, you took this job, and if he's such a nice guy, why is he stealing from our client, who's paying me and paying you.' The point is when this issue comes up, you have to stop the operative from getting sympathetic, and remind him of the logic of what he's doing. Sure, the problem happens; but if you see the operative is starting to get soft on the people he's working with, it's important to remind him of the job he's supposed to do, and make him understand that even if the person seems to be Mr. Nice Guy, he's doing something wrong that has to be stopped."

We had one final question about operatives. How did Pat go about getting the person out at the end of the job and protect his cover?

"Easy. Usually, the employee gets terminated for cause. He may steal something and get caught. He may come to work drunk. Usually, these cases don't come to trial, since the employees who get caught as a result of these operations just get dismissed, have to repay what they've taken. If there's an arrest, everyone usually just pleas out. So you never have to reveal that there was an operative in there or who he was, as you might if his testimony was needed in court. Rather, the operative is just normally pulled out a little while before any bust or exposure happens, so it doesn't seem like his leaving has anything to do with the bust. And then, with him out safely, the employer can then act on the reports, without anyone suspecting that the undercover plant was the cause the employer finding out whatever he did."

Finally, we wanted to know how this work had affected Pat's personal life.

He laughed. "A whole lot. It effects everyone. I know I won't have a typical personal life. Nobody in this business does. It just can't happen. Because I can't say what I'm going to do tomorrow or even where I'm going to be tomorrow. Say some guy comes in with the right amount of money for a new case. Well, in a matter of hours, I could be gone on another assignment. And that's the way it is for most people in this business. You just don't know from one day to the next."

Also, like some of the other investigators we spoke to, Pat was very private about his personal life.

"I don't like to talk about my personal life, because I won't have a personal life that's personal if I start talking about it. I'm a very private person."

He also furthered this privacy by living alone in the country. "I used to be married, though not anymore. The work was kind of a strain on the marriage. It was just too unpredictable and crazy for my former wife. But then that's how it is for many people in the business—hard on relationships, because it's difficult for others to understand. In any case, now I live in the country a long ways from anyone, and I don't want anyone to know where I live. Not even people in the industry. I like living alone very quietly, and I don't even have a phone in my name, so I'm not in the phone book. No one can reach me unless they're one of the very few people who knows.

"And I don't tell most people what I do either," Pat added. "I don't have any friends in my neighborhood. I don't know any of my neighbors. In fact, that's why I went to the country. The closest people live a quarter of a mile away. And when I run into people anywhere who ask about me, I just tell them I'm retired. I relax or play golf all day. So no one needs to know, and I like to keep it that way. Very private. After all, this is a very private business, and I like to keep things private. I think most people in the business do, you know."

And with that, the interview ended. Pat had things to do, some very private things, so of course, we had to go.

7

Jordan Douglas: Doing Insurance and Personal Injury Investigations

It was time for our last interview, with Jordan Douglas, an investigator who specializes in insurance and personal injury cases. We arrived at the address Jordan had given us, an Irish bar with the feel of an old-world tavern located near the hustle and bustle of Fisherman's Wharf. The place was dark, with only a few dim lights, so that the bartender seemed almost silhouetted against the long mirror that ran the length of the bar. There were only a few patrons, none of them Jordan, hunched over their glasses and settled in for some serious drinking.

Were we in the right place? "Oh, yes," said the bartender knowingly. "Jordan sometimes works here behind the bar." We squeezed in through what seemed like an open pantry, with boxes of bottles, olives, and cans of juice, then made our way along the uneven stairs, grabbing on the walls from time to time for support. And then, finally, behind a patched wooden door we found Jordan's office, which had the feel of an artist's attic garret. It was small, with wood planks along the sides, and a few scattered desks and file cabinets, plus a computer.

As Jordan, about forty, with a James Bond/Rockford look, led us in, we noticed a black trenchcoat hanging on a standing rack and a large map of Las Vegas on one wall, and an equally large pinup poster of a girl in a bikini across from it. "Oh, I like going to Las Vegas and seeing showgirls," Jordan said, as if to explain. "And you're the first noninvestigator that's been to my office in three years. I don't spend a lot of time here, since if I'm sitting in my office, I'm generally not making any money. The money is out in the streets someplace doing investigations. So I just need a place to store a few things, get out of the rain, have a phone, and take care of administrative details. And I meet my clients at their offices anyway, since they don't want to take the time to come here. So I don't really need a glamorous office, and I rather like this one."

"Well, it has a certain charm," I agreed, thinking that if anyone fit the media image of the daredevil, romantic, woman-collecting, globe-trotting, danger-dealing, trench-coated private eye, Jordan certainly did—and his attic office hideaway with its combination artist and locker room look certainly fit the image.

But then, as Jordan described what he actually did, the glitzy image began slipping away, to be replaced by the hard everyday reality of investigating mostly insurance and personal injury cases.

When we interviewed him, Jordan had just turned forty and had been a private eye for twelve years, six of them with his own company. Jordan worked as an international financial analyst in Iran, after getting a degree in economics from a California university. But then, after the Shah got kicked out of Iran in 1979, Jordan and the rest of the people in the company were too. That's when he returned to the States and first got into the private investigator business.

So how did he end up working in Iran in the first place?

"I just started working for the company's overseas division," Jordan told us. "And they had operations in twenty or thirty countries, and they just happened to send me there. They could have sent me anywhere, but chose Iran. I worked there for five years, and I

commutted back and forth to San Francisco doing business fore-
casts, analyzing business plans, and other types of business projects.
When the Shah was ousted, Khomeni's people nationalized the company, so there was literally no more work to do. And within the
next two years, its interests in other countries—Vietnam, Guatemala,
El Salvador, Lebanon and Argentina—were either sold or nationalized, or the U.S. companies there were ousted for some political
reason or another. Eventually, the remaining companies of the international division were sold to a Swiss outfit, so I found myself looking for other work in the business field or doing something else.

"At that point, a lawyer friend offered me the opportunity to do
some investigations for him, and since he was using another agency
for his investigative work, I ended up going over there. I really
didn't know anything about investigations at the time, though I had
this strong analytical background because of my degree in economics, so I started as this club investigator. And that meant basically
doing research, checking records, serving subpoenas, doing interviews here and there, working mostly part-time at some of the less
glamorous parts of the investigation, not making very much, and
working meanwhile at other things to help pay the bills. I drove a
cab, I tended bar, and I built up enough hours to get my own
license. And then, six years ago, I decided to strike out on my
own."

As Jordan described it, that was even harder than working for
someone else for the first few years. "It was really tough, really
tough, I had to continue to work moonlighting jobs, while I was getting the agency started. In fact, I work downstairs in the bar two
shifts a month in exchange for this office. I started out with just one
client. It takes time to build up your business. So it was really a
struggle, though gradually I found myself specializing in insurance
defense work, and mostly personal injury cases. Then I contacted
attorneys and law firms that represent insurance companies, or got
my clients by referral, so it just ended up happening that way.
About ninety percent of my business is defense work, working for
the insurance companies and more specifically for the law firms that
represent them. Only about ten percent of my work is for plaintiffs."

According to Jordan, he was finally getting through this initial
cash crunch, and starting to catch up to his friends he had graduated

with who were now making around six-figure incomes in the business field. "So it's a real hard business, and you can go through a great deal of financial stress in the beginning. Just about everybody in this business does. Why? Because this is a very difficult business to market. You're selling credibility, you're selling reliability, you're selling yourself, and it takes time to get known and develop a reputation in this business. Besides, you're trying to work for either people that are in trouble or represent people in trouble, so you're not dealing with happy people or people who are on top of the world. And that can really mess up your social life and be very stressful. I mean, it's like 'no money, no honey.' In the beginning, it ruins your whole social life. It ruins your bank book. I wouldn't want any kids I might have to do this. But I love it, and now I can't imagine myself doing anything else."

Now that his business was starting to flourish, he even had several people working for him part-time on various cases. So now he spent about half his time involved as a business administrator and marketing to get new clients, in addition to doing some of the investigation work—mainly interviews and locating people and assets himself.

So what did Jordan like about the business, despite all the hardships he had gone through during his first decade in the field?

"This is a weird business, because you are dealing with people who are either desperate or they represent somebody who is desperate, or they otherwise have some sort of problem. And yet for me the rewards of the business come from the challenges. For example, locating people—I get a real kick of that. It's like playing a game of cat and mouse, where I'm the cat and the person I'm seeking is the mouse, and I enjoy the search. Also, I think one of the rewards is trying to pull together all of the information about a case into a logical, objective and factual picture, like putting a jigsaw puzzle together.

"And then the other thing that has led me to stay in this business is that I've never gotten bored with it. Each case has some underlying similarities, but each is different. There are different locales, different types of people, different types of situations. I'd gotten bored when I'd been doing other jobs where I was doing something repetitious, such as driving a taxi or tending a bar or working in an ordinary office environment. But these cases have just enough differences to keep my interest. And then, I like getting out; doing things outdoors; not being in the office.

Jordan then began to tell us a little about what he did as an insurance investigator, working mainly on personal injury cases.

"Well, mostly in this field you're trying to figure out what happened in the accident, how the person was hurt, who was responsible for what happened, and what kind of damages occurred. So a lot of this is pretty routine, everyday stuff. It's not the great train robbery type of cases. You're basically trying to piece together the facts through trading down and interviewing people who were eyewitnesses or who otherwise have knowledge about the incident, and then putting this information together as a logical, sequential report of what occurred so a lawyer can say: 'Oh, this is what they said happened,' and have it hold up in court if the case comes to that."

Unfortunately, as Jordan pointed out, one of the things that made these cases so difficult at times was that as an insurance investigator he was usually dealing with cases that were three to five years old.

"The reason it takes so long, is because when an insurance company gets a claim against some business or a homeowner or an automobile driver or other party for an accident, it goes to a claims adjuster or claims representative. Then, every effort is made to settle it without litigation. The company doesn't want it, because litigation is quite expensive. For instance, if the case is just a little fender-bender or a little slip and fall accident, there can be $10,000 to $20,000 in legal bills. Or if it's a construction case where there's a large housing development involved, or if it's one involving product defects, warranty defects, design defects, or other sorts of defects, you can end up with $500,000 worth of legal bills real fast. While the plaintiff's attorneys may be working on a contingency basis, so they get a percentage of only what they win, the defense attorneys are working on an hourly basis, which can range anywhere from $75 for an associate or paralegal to $100 for a junior partner to $200 or $300 an hour for the people whose names are on the letterhead. So with all the back and forth at court and the paperwork, costs can really mount up.

"So that's why the insurance companies usually will spend a couple of years or more trying to settle the matter. Say it's a relatively modest minor thing—somebody slips on a sidewalk or trips over your dogs or something on the steps. The insurance people might offer perhaps $15,000; a bigger case, they'll offer a little more. But then, suppose the plaintiff's attorney comes back, saying no, 'I want a million.' Well, things can break down.

"And so, when I get the case, that's the point after which a lawsuit has been filed and they haven't been able to work out an agreement and are going through the procedure to fight the claim at court. Eventually, there might still be a settlement, but now they have to get ready for trial. And the investigation is important, because there are big dollars at stake on both sides, and they hinge on exactly what happened and who's at fault."

"So if the insurance company wanted to settle so much, why did these cases end up in litigation? Did it seem like the plaintiff was usually being unreasonable? Or was it the insurance company that wasn't being fair enough in coming up with enough money?"

"I don't really know," Jordan conceded. "These cases can often go either way, and each side may have a different interpretation of the worth of the case. Besides juries are so uncertain. You just never know exactly what they are going to do. In any case, the point is that these things can drag on for years and when it seems like they can't be settled, that's when I'm asked to do a thorough investigation to help the insurance company prepare for trial."

But three to five years? We were amazed by the age of the cases Jordan handled. So why didn't the insurance companies just do this investigation in the beginning when their claims people first got the case?

"Well, usually there is some preliminary work done by an in-house investigator for the insurance company. And usually the plaintiff's attorney will do a preliminary investigation too. But then, since there is hope of a quick settlement, the insurance company doesn't want to commit to an expensive, thorough investigation at the beginning, because they're trying to settle the case and don't want to go to trial. And usually, they're figuring on a settlement of about three times the cost of the medical expenses for an injury. So say someone trips and breaks something and has $5,000 worth of medical bills, a reasonable settlement for that type of injury would be about $15,000. So the insurance company is not going to spend $4,000 for a typical investigation in such a case. They're going to try to settle it, and most of the time, they do.

"So that's why in the beginning a full-scale investigation isn't done. The company has done some overview work, but there's a reluctance to do an in-depth investigation, since they're anticipating that the case will be settled and go away. But now, with the suits filed, and several years of litigation with legal paperwork thrown back and forth, with a trial date looming, they need this real nuts and bolts investigation to see what's really going on."

It sounded, from Jordan's description, like it might be to any plaintiff's advantage just to prolong the case, since all the potential expenses mounting up might encourage the insurance company to give even more just to make the case go away. So how could Jordan's investigation help, beyond just adding still more expenses?

"Well, you just never know what's going to happen at a trial. And certainly the economic factor is one consideration, because a trial will go on for two or three weeks, and it costs several thousand dollars a day, with all the legal experts and perhaps $700 an hour worth of legal talent—three or four attorneys—sitting in a courtroom for eight hours. It really adds up—say ten days in a courtroom; $5,000 a day, that's $50,000. And then you throw it to the jury. If they agree with the jury, that's $50,000 on top of what the jury says. So you just don't know."

Jordan pulled out several of his files and flipped through them. "So you see, that's why a good percentage of these civil cases don't actually make it to trial or don't make it completely through the trial. Frequently, a trial starts and then a settlement is reached. While most of my cases are scheduled or headed for trial, and all attempts to settle them prior to picking a jury have failed, neither side really wants a trial, because trials are not only expensive but also such a gamble. After all, you've got twelve people, and you can lay everything out in front of them, and then you still never know which way it's going to go. In reality, truth and justice does not prevail. And not only could the jurors go either way, the amount of money they decide in damages, if any, could be all over the place. Say the plaintiff is suing for a million; they could give him $10,000;

or even several million more. So you just don't know; and the issues aren't black and white. Just about anything could be the result.

"So that's why the investigation at this stage is so important, because maybe the trial can be avoided. This might be possible because an in-depth investigation provides a much clearer idea of what the outcome of the trial might be—so maybe if the plaintiff sees his case is weak now, he might withdraw it. Or maybe it will give everyone a better idea of the likely outcome or damages value of the case, so maybe a settlement might still be worked out, even at this late date."

What did such an investigation cost in a typical case?

Jordan looked thoughtful, finding it hard to decide what was typical. "Well, it can run around $500 to $10,000 roughly, depending on what is required. Say if surveillance is required to determine whether people are really injured or how severely and how that injury has affected their lives, this could be an expensive ordeal. Or if it's necessary to take a lot of statements, and witnesses are hard to find after all this time, because people move around, that could add up expenses too. But generally, a typical case might average around $1,000 to $5,000, if there are no major problems—and then, of course, if a case goes to trial, the company's lawyer will have expenses for expert testimony, say from an expert to look at the construction of a building or road where an accident occurred or a doctor to review a particular claimant's medical bills. And then, if a trial date is imminent, there are also expenses for firms to create posters and maps and buildboards and other graphic exhibits to be shown to the jury. So the investigation may be just a small part of the litigation costs—today litigation costs so much; and the hope is that a good investigation can stop the litigation process and bring everyone to the settlement table. Compared to everything else, it sure costs a lot less."

So what sort of work did Jordan do in a typical case? This time the question was a lot easier than trying to estimate costs.

"Well, most cases involve locating people," he said. "It's a very common thing to have to find them. The reason is not that they're hiding or on the run, but because we live in a mobile society, and these cases are usually old news. These events happened mostly three to five years ago, and so the witnesses who saw something or had a conversation or some dealings with the subject matter of this litigation are often not around. They don't live in the same place; they don't have the same employer. So it's hard to get in touch with them again. They've moved somewhere else.

"Now it may sound like a big manhunt looking for these people, but it's just a question of tracking them down, because their lives have gone on. They've moved across the street, to another neighborhood, to another town, to another state. So I have to find out where."

But how? Jordan went on.

"Well, there are several steps you go through. One is to use various information sources, like voter registration records. Also, you can find out where they were last known to live and start from there. The idea is to trace their steps, and you can combine a few public information sources that you access with a little field work, such as knocking on doors, talking to their former neighbors, or talking to their former employers, who may know where they went next. Then, those leads may point you in the right direction so you can either find them or have more information to continue the search. And eventually, you hope to find them."

And did Jordan? "I never miss." Then, he pointed out that he preferred to do it himself, rather than use a skip tracer working for him, as some private investigators do. "I just want to make sure it's done right," he said.

Then, he described the second major type of work he did on a typical case—interviewing people.

"That's the other major part of the job—talking to people to find out what they know about the incident or the people or equipment involved in it. And then, usually, if I can I get statements, written and signed summaries of what they just told me about the case. The process is pretty much the same whether the situation is an auto accident, business dispute, or employment conflict. Whatever the problem is, after I've located the witnesses, I frequently have to contact them and hear what they have to say."

So what types of cases did Jordan usually work on? He quickly reviewed the major types of accidents or insurance claims.

"Well, I do virtually everything there is from auto accidents to slip and falls in grocery stores to slip and falls on the streets. Also, I get involved in a lot of business disputes. Often these are contract disputes or disagreements between people about something that has gone awry, such as merchandise not delivered or damaged, and litigation has resulted. Then, too, I do a lot of construction work, where people are not happy with whatever they had built. In fact, that's a common problem—anytime anything's built, there's a lot of litigation associated with that. And then, I do a lot of medical malpractice, where a doctor or health professional has allegedly done something wrong. Also, a lot of wrongful death litigation, where someone dies as a result of an accident, malpractice or some other reason, and the spouse, parent, estate or other appropriate party is trying to get compensated for that wrong."

Now we wondered about some of the cases Jordan had handled. Was there anything that stood out as particularly interesting or exciting?

For a moment, he pondered. "Well, I don't think any of these kind of cases are particularly thrilling. It's not like I'm dealing with Scotland Yard type murders or mysteries. So I don't really get thrilled on cases. I don't know how anyone could."

Instead, Jordan just described some typical cases. Yet, while they may not have been packed with chills and excitement, there was a certain fascination in these cases, as we listened to Jordan describe how he pieced together the bits of evidence to suggest what really happened, and in one case, suggested that some people involved in claiming an accident had really committed a crime.

He began by describing a typical auto accident, or "fender-bender" as he called it. However, in this case, there were also several deaths, and he had to determine which party to the initial collision which triggered a pile up and several explosions was at fault or bore most of the blame.

"It was a really gruesome accident that happened on Highway 101. A big freight truck hit a car, and then a bunch of cars behind them piled up and several of them exploded, so there were a lot of deaths involved and a big freeway mess that tied up traffic for miles. So there were millions and millions of dollars at stake, since people got killed. Besides just damage to vehicles and personal injuries, there were wrongful death actions. And if the truck driver was guilty of gross negligence, say if he was speeding, there could be triple damages as well. So it was a big, big case, and the lawyer or the insurance company representing the trucker wanted me to check things out."

So Jordan had to locate the five witnesses who were listed in the original police report as being at the accident. "But what was strange about this case, was that only three of these people actually had a very good view of what they saw, and some of the stories were conflicting."

Jordan also commented on the willingness of people to help—the kind of "good samaritan" pull to be helpful, though logically it might not make any sense.

"Very frequently you find that people really do want to be helpful, which makes it possible to find out what happened. In reality, though being helpful is the opposite of what anybody would rationally do, because once someone gets involved in a case, it's almost not worth it. The person is just going to get harangued by lawyers to give depositions and may have to appear in court, and all he'll get is a $35 witness fee. Yet, people do get involved, and I suppose that's mainly because what goes around comes around, so that sometime, they may be involved in an accident and someone will help them out."

Anyway, in this case, this desire to be helpful had ended up with five witnesses who were willing to be involved, although in two cases, Jordan felt some doubt about the witnesses motives, and one of them had the potential to distort the whole case.

"Three of these witnesses clearly were in a physical position to see what they said they saw. But one of them I don't think was even really there—just trying to help. And curiously, another one saw something that was virtually the opposite of what the other three who could see agreed they saw.

"So it really created a kind of jigsaw puzzle with a piece that didn't fit. I mean, that's what these cases are very much like, where each witness has a little piece of the puzzle. These accident cases are like that, because they usually happen in a situation where the witness's attention is initially somewhere else. But then, all of a sudden, there's a sight or sound that draws the witness's attention. And by the time he or she turns or gets over there and looks, within a couple of seconds, maybe three or four, it's all over. So the witness might not have seen the start. Or he might only have seen the end of it. Or he might just have seen the middle. So he often has just seen a piece of it, and it's important as an investigator to sort out what each person really did see. After all, it's great when people are helpful and they really did witness something, but it just messes things up when they just speculate or say something that's wrong."

Unfortunately, in this case, Jordan had two witnesses who he thought were doing just that—one speculating, the other giving wrong information that was messing up the case.

"I don't think the one guy was there and able to see anything because he was too far behind. He just described himself as being in the wrong location to have seen what he said he saw. And then the other guy who could have seen things gave a version of the accident scenario and sequence was completely opposite of the other three."

Thus, Jordan had to sort things out to try to come up with a consistent portrait of what really occurred. But how?

"Well, I had to sit down with this guy who had the opposite opinion to see why he might have that and be so sure of it. And it turned out that this was a very strong, opinionated guy who was very certain of himself and his observational powers. So I had to spend some time with him. Actually I met with him three times, and at one of our meetings, I drew a map of that particular section of the freeway to scale. Then, using this diagram, I spent some time pointing out to him very diplomatically that if he was so many feet behind this freight truck in the particular lane where he claimed to be and if the car the truck hit was over there and another car just behind it, that he physically could not have seen what he claimed. I had to be very diplomatic in doing this, because he was so very outspoken and sure of himself, and his ego was really getting in the way. So I had to smooth things over so he could lower his ego enough to realize that 'Yes, this is where I was, and so on, I couldn't have seen that.'"

So what was it he was claiming to see that was different from what the others agreed happened?

"Well, that this freight truck was only going fifty miles and hour, and lots of room ahead of it, and this car cut in front of it, while the other witnesses seemed to think the truck was going too fast, was driving too close to the car ahead, and didn't put on the brakes soon enough. That kind of disparity can really change things, because it raises questions about who is really at fault, and that changes the picture in dollars and cents. And my clients call me to save them money if I can. Anyway, it took awhile, but this guy finally realized he couldn't have actually seen what he said, because he would have had to look through a sixty-foot-long semi-trailer that had closed in and had been right there between him and the accident at the time of the crash."

So why should this driver say all these things if they weren't true?

Jordan looked puzzled. "It's always been a mystery to me. I did look into his background, because I suspected that he or someone in his family either worked for a trucking company or maybe even that trucking company which owned the truck involved in the accident, because it was very clear-cut that the large truck was in the wrong. But then I never did find out if there was such a connection. However, I did have to discount his version because it didn't make sense in light of the other accounts. And once I got him to realize that his version couldn't have been correct, he finally backed down. I don't think he came up with that version maliciously; I think he really thought he saw what he did; but then sometimes our perceptions can play tricks on us when we would rather see something else, and perhaps that is what occurred here. In any case, the role of the investigator is to sort such things out."

And what of the helpful good samaritan who Jordan didn't think could see at all? Why should he give such a story? What was motivating him?

Again, Jordan could only speculate. "I think he just wanted to help. I think he was about a quarter mile or more behind the vehicle, and then when he came to the accident, he saw it was a real dramatic one involving this large truck and all these cars that exploded. So he maybe just felt like giving a statement to help the victims by blaming the driver of the truck. Who knows? My job is just to find the truth, whatever it is, whether it's favorable or not to my client."

As we were about to ask another question, the phone rang. It was a client, giving Jordan some new instructions in a pending wrongful death case involving a baby which allegedly fell out of a baby buggy, hit his head and died.

"But did it really happen that way?" Jordan commented, after he got off the phone and wrote down a few notes on the case. "That's what I'm trying to find out.

"The case is now in trial, because all attempts to settle have failed. Basically it involves the death of a child about a year and a half. The parents who are the plaintiffs are saying that it's the fault of the manufacturer of the baby buggy, and I'm representing the manufacturer—or more precisely working for the manufacturer's lawyer. In any case, the parents are saying that the child was in this little buggy, and the mother was wheeling it across the floor when it hit a little bump between the rooms and tipped over. The child fell out, hit his forehead, experienced some hemorrhaging inside his head, and was rushed to the hospital, where he died within a day. So the parents are claiming wrongful death; that the baby buggy was defective so it tipped over when it shouldn't, and therefore they have been deprived of the joy and companionship of this child for however long they would have lived. They're saying that the design of the stroller was faulty, because it should not have been able to tip over. So they're asking for major money."

But was it? Jordan didn't seem to think so. In fact, he thought maybe the parents were at fault and his investigation was trying to prove this.

"Look at it this way. This baby buggy company isn't some kind of shlock outfit that just threw together a faulty product. It's a very large, prestigious worldwide company, and if it did that sort of thing, made shlock, it wouldn't still be in business.

"And then it has turned out with further examination that this little child had other bruises that couldn't have been sustained if this stroller dumped over just once. So the whole issue of child abuse is being considered, and I'm trying to investigate several areas hoping to recreate what happened in the five or six days preceding this child's death. Specifically, I'm trying to find out where the child went, who was with it, was it physically abused, and if so by whom."

What Jordan was saying was startling, suggesting a potential bombshell in the case. Could the parents have actually claimed the buggy was at fault, when the buggy had nothing to do with the child's death? when the parents themselves, or one of them, might have been the ones responsible?

"Very, very possible, but very difficult to prove. In this particular case, there were only two witnesses to what actually happened—the child and the mother, and one of them is dead, and the other one definitely isn't going to admit responsibility. She is going to stick with the story that she and her husband told, that this is what happened—the buggy tipped over. Because obviously, if she or he said anything otherwise, such as admitting something like: 'Yeah, maybe the baby was screaming and I swatted it a couple of times,' or 'The baby fell of a bed when I did this or that to it,' that person is going to be in jail for a long, long time.

"So this makes it a very tricky case. But given my clients' and my suspicions, what I'm doing now is a background search in trying to piece together the events of that child's last few days to see if there was any abuse going on. But the investigation is quite tricky, because it involves identifying, locating and talking to friends and associates, babysitters, anyone who knew this couple, and then getting them to answer some very sensitive questions, such as 'Did the parents ever swat their kid around when the kid was crying?' 'How did they shut it up?'—things like that. And it's a very sensitive issue, because it's hard to ask somebody something like: 'Does your neighbor, friend, or associate bash their kid around?' People may not know, or want to admit it if they do, or they may not want to get involved because they have had a good relationship with the parents. It's a very, very tough thing to talk about, whether they know anything or not."

So how did Jordan approach the people to talk to them about this? And did he say who he was?

At once he bristled a little. "Of course, I always tell people exactly who I am. It's a requirement that private investigators must do this in getting a statement; you cannot misrepresent yourself, so I'm always very straightforward about this, particularly in dealing with such a sensitive topic. I think that part of the mystique of private eyes is that they misrepresent themselves or that they pose as somebody else, and certainly that does happen in certain situations, such as when an investigator is working undercover or conducting a surveillance. But in field investigations like this where you actually interview witnesses, and their statements may be used in court proceedings, you've got to be up front. For one thing, if you aren't and this comes out, which it probably will, the statements aren't admissible. Also, if you're trying to bullshit somebody, they're going to spot that too, and they're probably going to end the interview and throw you out."

So did Jordan have to tell the person which side he was representing in doing the investigation?

"Yes, that's a requirement, too. Sometimes an investigator might just say he or she is investigating a case, and not clarify exactly for which side. But if the person asks you, you have to tell him or her which side you are with. One of the quickest ways to lose your license would be not to do that. And besides, I think it's ethically very important to be up front. So I tell the witness from the start."

What about the mother? Had he talked to her yet?

Jordan shook his head. "No, because she's off limits, since she's represented by the attorney for the other side."

And her husband?

"That's the same story. The husband and wife are like one entity in this case. So they're off limits because I can only speak to their attorney since they're represented. And there's no point in talking to him, because he's not going to tell me anything harmful to his client. And even if they weren't represented by an attorney, it's not in their interest to talk to me or say anything other than their original story. So, no I haven't talked to either of them and won't."

We suddenly thought about another spin on the case. What about the possibility that there could be a combination of causes—that the parents both abused the child and he fell out of the buggy.

Jordan nodded. "Yeah, that's a possibility too, and we've been checking out whether the buggy could tip over as well." Although he wasn't doing this checking himself, he had arranged to get an expert on baby buggy construction run the test.

"And what we're looking at, is what it would take to knock the buggy over. The guy we're using is a physicist who understands these technical things about force and weight. And then we're doing a simulation. For example, he's found out how much the baby weighed when it died—nineteen pounds, and now he's going to be putting nineteen pounds in the buggy and determine the center of gravity. And then, the accident will be re-created, and he'll look at the exact number of foot pounds of force or pressure needed to tip the buggy over with that center of gravity. Well, his theory is that in this particular case, the baby would not have been strong enough to tip the buggy over for another five or ten years. But then it's necessary to prove this theory, so that's what this accident reconstruction is designed to show—that the baby couldn't have tipped the buggy over alone, and in that case, the accident must have been caused by some other means, such as the mother or father tipping over the buggy or child abuse or a combination of the two."

It sounded like an amazing turn of events if Jordan and the expert could prove this. But then, what if they did? What if they established that the mother or father did in fact abuse the child, to cause the death? Would there be criminal charges? And would Jordan or the lawyer in the case contact the D.A.?

"Definitely," he replied. "And I would probably be the one to contact them, since I've been doing the investigation that helped to show the mother or father's guilt. Also, it's important to do this, because if there are criminal charges or a conviction, it helps our case, and we would probably win. But at the same time, getting the D.A. involved helps to bring someone to justice for something. So these cases are not only about money, though they may sometimes seem that way. They're about truth and justice too, or at least trying to get as close to that as possible."

Moreover, as Jordan pointed out, if there were criminal charges and a conviction, the insurance company might even have some recourse to get back all the money it had put up to defend the baby buggy company, as well as some additional money in penalties.

"The couple might be pursued under the insurance fraud statutes, because they might be potentially guilty not only of child abuse, but of insurance fraud, too, which has its own set of penalties. Besides any criminal charges, the insurance company that had to defend this fraudulent lawsuit for the accused company would be entitled to sue these people as well, and would be entitled to triple damages if it won. So if it put out $200,000 to defend this suit, and the suit turns out to be bogus to begin with, the company would be potentially entitled to $600,000. But then, winning that could be tough, and collecting any money might be even tougher, since the couple might have no money, particularly if they end up fighting criminal charges or spending some time in jail. And besides, insurance companies don't like to get involved in such suits, because of all the bad press. So probably that would be the end of the case if we can show the abuse, and the insurance company would just take its losses."

We had one last question on the case. Did Jordan have any predictions about where the case was going or what might be a likely outcome at this point?

He shook his head. "Well, it's still up in the air, and no one knows. There's only one witness, and I think we have been able to successfully challenge her story. But then, there are twelve people sitting on the jury, and it doesn't matter what I think. It only matters what they think, and in these jury cases, the verdict can go any way. Maybe they'll be swayed by the evidence of abuse and the testimony that the buggy couldn't tip over. Or maybe they'll believe the mother, take pity on her for losing her baby, and decide the company should be held responsible, particularly because it has so much money."

But Jordan and the clients he represented weren't only up against fickle, uncertain juries. As he described, the whole personal injury/insurance world he worked in was really a hardball, dog-eat-dog type of world, where the lawyers maneuvered around each other like sharks, to mix a few metaphors, since there was so much money at stake. In a sense, Jordan's investigation provided a way to help ground the battle of the lawyers in a kind of fact-based reality. Even so, he encountered a world where wildly high demands and claims were routinely made and fought against, and where sometimes even requests to lie were urged upon him to help some law firm win a case, although he turned these down.

"It's really an amazing battle out there," he said. "There are millions riding on the outcome in some cases. It's like two armies confronting each other with all the resources they can muster, trying to win. And one reason this happens is that the civil justice system is adversarial, as is the criminal justice system. But then sometimes it can seem crazy what the plaintiff's ask for. They're trying to create a better bargaining position to improve what they ultimately gain, of course. But the figures can often bear no resemblence to any sort of reason.

"For instance, a person can trip and fall, say he slips on a grape in a grocery store, and all of a sudden, he's asking for $200,000 or $300,000 for a little sprain. Or a dog nips somebody in the leg, and the person's claiming $190,000 in damages."

So where did the plaintiff's get these figures from? And were they at all realistic, in that the cases settled around those figures?

"No, they're not at all realistic. The plaintiff's lawyers just start out high, say at $200,000, and they would be happy to get a tenth of that, say $20,000. I suppose from a certain point of view it's ridiculous, but then, because the system is adversarial and both sides are playing hardball, that's the way it works, with each side trying to outfight the other, and flinging around offers and counteroffers like so much ammunition and shields to block a blow. In turn, I and other investigators have found that the plaintiff's side tends to be a little bit more imaginative than the defense in coming up with figures, since they're under an obligation to their clients to maximize the value of the particular case. In fact, they could be sued for malpractice if they didn't do this. So you end up with this very high, seemingly outrageous demand, so they can get the maximum possible for their client."

I recalled one of my own cases years before when a toy manufacturer didn't return some models of puzzles and games, despite my repeated requests for them for several months, and a lawyer sued him. "The manufacturer just didn't get around for returning them, but the lawyer sued him for $10 million claiming fraud, conversion, misrepresentation, copyright infringement, all sorts of things. And then we finally settled for $2,000."

"Yeah, that's typical," Jordan said. "The lawyer thinks big, but then settles small when reality sets in. Still, in these kinds of personal injury cases, the plaintiff's lawyer frequently has some extra cards on his side which can substantially up the verdict or the settlement, because there's an injured person, and frequently sympathy goes out to him, regardless of whose at fault. And then another advantage he has is that this little guy is up against the big insurance company that's got millions or billions of dollars. Plus there's this person who may never be the same again. And maybe he can't work, or is in a wheelchair, or has to depend on a nurse, or something like that.

"Anyway, in battling out what this guy or his family will get, both sides play their little hardball games in this adversarial system. But then, I try to avoid taking sides in the battle, even though one side hires me. Instead, as the investigator, I see my role as trying to be as objective as possible. So I go out, find out what happened like a journalist doing a story, and then I come back saying: 'Here's the news. And if you don't like it, that's unfortunate, but this is what it is. If the news is good, I'm really happy. But if it's bad, well, that's the way it is. My job is just to get the news, good or bad.'"

However, as Jordan reported, not all law firms that contacted him were happy with this neutral, just-the-facts approach, and instead wanted him to bend, massage, manipulate or otherwise alter the facts that turned up in his reports, and in his experience, it was only some plaintiff's firms that asked him to do this.

"They asked me to lie and/or alter the results of my investigation that would not have been favorable to the plaintiff's side of the case," Jordan explained. "And none of the defense firms I have worked for ever asked me to do that."

He seemed to think this kind of approach was fairly frequent in the business. "At least it's more common than we'd like to think. After all, it's a war out there, and I know other investigators who have had this experience too."

So what kinds of things was he sometimes asked to alter or lie about? Though again he emphasized, "I wouldn't do that.

"Suppose I find a witness that is totally unfavorable to the law firm's side of the case. They might ask me to forget I even talk to that person and not report any conversation to them. And that interferes with the investigation and the evidence in the case. It eliminates that piece of evidence, unless the other side should find it independently. For example, say the firm gave me a list of six witnesses to interview about an auto accident. Then what I'm asked to do is summarize only the results of interviewing five of them to eliminate that one piece of bad news from the case. And then, as long as the information is not in my report, the firm doesn't have to report on the results of my contact with that witness to the opposite.

Otherwise, if something's in my report, there's the obligation to turn over the results of my investigation in court or in discovery. But if it's not in my report, then in essence the firm don't know about it."

But Jordan turned the client down. "I just don't feel that's how you should deal with people," he said. "Maybe because of my old-fashioned work ethnic or because I come from pioneer stock. But I just wouldn't do it."

Another client he turned down was one who wanted him to manipulate the results of a store survey to show that it wasn't carrying a particular product.

"Basically, the client wanted me to do a stocking survey, in which I canvas a group of stores selling a particular product to see if it is in stock. I told him the way I would normally do it, which would be to pick twenty stores at random, go in. If the product was there, I would tell him, and then he could do whatever he wanted with this information. But he wanted me to go to more stores, about forty, and then say I went to the twenty stores which didn't happen to have this product. But I told him that I would only do the project if I gave him a real factual summary of what I did. I wasn't about to say I just went to twenty stores when I went to forty, and so I guess he found someone else to do this. After all, it is possible to find investigators to do these things, though the professional, ethical ones in the business wouldn't do it."

And then, shortly after this experience, Jordan had an even more incredible one—a law firm he had never worked for before blatantly asked him to lie.

"I was going around with my brochures soliciting new business about six months ago, and I dropped a brochure off for an office manager for this large plaintiff's law firm. Then, a couple of days later, she phoned back and explained that the company had a hard time keeping investigators, since they were in the business of suing people and sometimes they needed their investigators to say things for them to help their case. 'But many of these investigators we have used in the past have had a hard time lying for us,' she told me, and we want somebody to lie. Do you have a problem with that?' I could hardly believe it. I had never even met this person and this was over the phone, and here she was asking me that.

"Well, I told her if she was just talking about a little incidental point or a kind of unimportant adjunct to the case the firm wanted left out of a report that might be one thing. But if she was talking about leaving out or altering major details provided by important witnesses that was something else, and I wouldn't do it. As I told her, 'It's just not worth it to me. I have my reputation and ethics to think about, and I don't need the job that much.'

"So that was that. But I was really flabbergasted that this well-known law firm would even consider doing what she suggested. For example, she actually wanted me to come up with another witness they could use, someone who could support their side of the story. So I would be actually creating witnesses with invented testimonies, and she also wanted me to misrepresent the testimony of another witness. I suppose the law firm felt they would never need to use any of this information in court, that they could just use it to provide a wedge for getting a better settlement in negotiations. But for whatever reason they wanted this, I didn't want to be involved. Sure it's a war out there, but at a certain point, I think one side can go too far. After all, there are rules of what's accepted in warfare, and I think this goes way beyond. It's like using chemical warfare or suddenly dishing out some napalm to destroy villages with women and children, when you know such weapons aren't allowed in the fight."

We had been talking about the battles of the lawyers that basically took place in the board rooms with reams of paper, documents, offers and counteroffers, and sometimes lies. But what about on the street? What were the dangers out there? And had Jordan encountered any danger himself?

"No, usually these kinds of investigations are pretty routine and safe. Because you're usually talking to fairly respectable working people or companies with money; you're not tracking down criminals or violent people on the streets."

But then, there was the time that one man Jordan was trying to subpoena for a case pulled a gun on him.

"It was about eight years ago, and I was trying to serve a subpoena to come to a deposition on a biker type who lived in way out in the boonies in the East Bay about forty miles east of San Francisco. This was a construction case, where some kind of equipment that was installed and welded into place had sprung a leak, and there was a claim that the part wasn't strong enough to stand up under pressure, and this man had been working on the job site as one of the iron workers or welders who installed the part. He wasn't a real crucial witness, but at least he had a little information about what happened.

"Well, I had spoken to this man a couple of times before, and I had even gotten a signed statement from him. But now the case was going to trial and we needed a deposition. However, this witness suddenly decided he did not want to get involved. Anyway, when I got to the door, I knocked, explained why I was there, and then he opens the door up to this chain, and this shotgun barrel comes out. And I could hear several other guys in the place just behind him.

"So I was scared, damn scared as I found myself standing at the doorway looking at that thing. I felt my heart pounding away. And then, I remembered an old story that says if somebody points a gun at you and has not pulled the trigger within five seconds, he's not going to. And all of a sudden, I realized that the five seconds had passed, and I was still alive. So suddenly, I felt my self-confidence return, and I told him, 'No, come on, put the goddamn thing away,' and I found myself acting very brave. And then finally he did. He even accepted the subpoena. Then, after that, I was sure glad to get in my car and get away. After all, I didn't want him to suddenly change his mind and maybe shoot."

So why was the man so resistant, we wondered. Could he have been liable for his own role in the accident?

"No, no, nothing like that," Jordan said quickly. "He wasn't even being sued and wouldn't be. It's just that he had been contacted over the course of the case so many times by so many different people— after all, there were investigators for about half a dozen plaintiff's lawyers, and then there was me representing the defense. And we had each contacted him several times. So all of a sudden, he just had enough. That's one of the unfortunate things about these complex cases—they just drag on so long and there are so many people involved, each with his own lawyer. And this was just his way of saying enough. But then, I was able to convince him, so at least he was willing to cooperate one more time."

However, while this incident soon calmed down into just another routine subpoena service, in another case Jordan was actually arrested. It happened about eight years ago when he first met Sam Brown, and they were both serving papers during a labor dispute, at Fisherman's Wharf in San Francisco.

"It was really wild," Jordan reported. "I had to serve a temporary restraining order on someone who was picketing in front of a particular restaurant during a strike. Well, it was already a very tense situation, because the paperwork had been flying back and forth between the lawyers for the restaurant and the lawyers for the union, as commonly happens in these adversarial situations. So anyway, with all these orders and cancelling orders, the workers and the owners were really angry at each other, and the scene was like a real tinderbox. Just about anything could set it off, and that's one reason the restaurant was seeking a restraining order against these guys. The picketer was one of these big tough troublemaker types who had been egging the other guys on.

"So anyway, that's what the setting was like when I went down to serve my papers, at around eleven in the evening. "About fifty people who used to work for this restaurant—waiters, bartenders, cooks, kitchen help, you name it—were marching around in a circle, accompanied by about another fifty union supporters. Well, I was dressed like a tourist, wearing a fancy leather jacket, and I had this big packet of information with the subpoena under my jacket. At first, I wandered along casually, like I was going to go to the edge of the wharf to look at the seals, and then I tried to edge my way casually over to this group to get as close to this guy as possible. However, he seemed to be real hard to get, because he was in the middle of this picket line, surrounded by a group of other workers, and then, when he noticed me and realized what was going on, that I was there trying to serve him with some papers, he and the other people in the line started rushing around inn a circle. So I just darted into the group and I wove my way in to serve him, and I tapped him on the shoulder and when he turned around, I handed him the papers. Everything was perfectly legal, but then suddenly, as I was turning to go, this guy bellowed out, 'He hit me,' and the next thing I knew, this police officer who had just arrived at the scene came over and arrested me. And now this guy is claiming I hit him on the arm, and he even opened his jacket and pulled up his sleeve to show the officer that he had scratches on his left arm where I supposedly hit him.

"Well, it was all a lie. I barely tapped him on his shoulder, and he was wearing a heavy jacket. At most, I might have brushed by one of the picketers as I tried to get through to serve him. But then, the officer asked me for identification, and I didn't have any ID on me, so the cop arrested me for assault and battery and took me in."

So what happened? And did this count as a service?

"Yeah, it counted," said Jordan. "It was perfectly good. But then I had to cool my heels for a while in the local pen, while they wrote up the charges and I arranged to make bail. But then, nothing ever came of it. The D.A. just dismissed the charges before the case ever came to court; I didn't even have to go to a preliminary hearing, which is when the D.A. tries to show the judge he has a case. I think the D.A. could see that I was just doing my job, and the case wouldn't hold up if he tried to pursue it. But the whole thing was still a real hassle, and it still counts as an arrest. So I have an arrest record for just doing my job."

Jordan frowned slightly at the irony of injustice of it all, and then we turned to another topic.

He spoke a little about the medical malpractice cases he worked on, generally defending doctors, since he mainly did insurance defense work.

"It's a very, very technical field, since the case revolves around whether the doctor should or shouldn't have done this or that, and proving this depends on bringing in medical experts who can talk about the current standard of reasonable care in the field, to show if the doctor did or didn't do the right thing. So there are doctors and other health care practitioners used to show that.

"But where I come in is in showing whether the person really does have the particular injury he claims. Say a person claims to have had this particular operation or surgery done, and now can no longer play the piano, or even walk out to the mailbox. Well, my job would be to show if his statement is really true. For example, I might be hired to get a picture of that guy out at the mailbox or playing the piano, to punch holes in the so-called victim's story. It's essentially what's called "life-style verification," to show what the person's life-style is really like, and to show whether his claims about a restricted life-style are really true.

"I was asked to go out on this insurance case where the woman claimed that her recent operation had left her nearly paralyzed, so she had to spend most of her time in a wheelchair, and for the rest, she had to get about using a case. Well, the doctors who examined her for the insurance company were suspicious, because they didn't find anything organically wrong, and they said the results of her surgery, which was for a tumor that had been growing near her spine, had been good. So presumably, she should be able to walk with ease, though she claimed she couldn't.

"Well, that's why they asked me to get involved, to check her story out. And so I did. I stationed myself near her house and I watched with binoculars for awhile. Then, after I got a sense of who was in the house, I found a time when everyone was out, and I made a delivery and made an excuse, so she would have to go get some identification to sign for it. Well, I noticed that she seemed to get around okay. She wasn't using a wheelchair, walker or cane, and then after a few more days, I managed to snap some pictures of her working in her garden in the backyard of her house, which showed her easily walking around. So between those observations and the pictures, that was the end of the case. The lawyers who hired me just showed the results to her lawyer, and they knew they didn't have a prayer."

Could the doctor or his lawyers have gone after her criminally? Or could they have sued her for a false claim themselves?

"Maybe, maybe not," Jordan said. "These kind of things can be hard to prove. Say she had thought she was paralyzed, but suddenly she found herself cured. Maybe she could have argued that. Anyway, the family didn't have very much money—that's why they tried to push the case. But at least the insurance company didn't have to pay her anything. So they were happy about that."

Jordan also had some experiences going undercover, despite his insurance/personal injury specialty, and we talked briefly about this. In a few cases, he did bar checks to see if the bartender was honest. "What you're trying to do is see if whatever has been sold gets rung up, and then later what you paid and any bar tapes can be compared." Also, in some of his most memorable cases, he played the role of an accountant, a drug dealer, an investor at a stock brokerage house and a plumber. He briefly described what happened.

"I took the role of an accountant and auditor in a large, well-know manufacturing company, because a key employee was suspected of pilfering large amounts of money out of her boss' desk, and he wanted her—actually his secretary—caught so he could have the grounds to dismiss her.

"Well, I knew the bills were in there, and we set up the office so the drawer was wired with an alarm. A little silent flasher was connected to my own desk which was located near the office. That way, after the alarm went off I could see the office clearly, and nobody else could come and go without me noticing. And then, I just came to the office, pretending to do my job and waiting when the boss left his for something to happen. When he was gone, there would be no reason for anyone to open his desk drawer, so if the secretary did, that would be our way of trapping her. After a couple of days of this, I was just sitting there, looking through some records, when the little flasher thing went off, and I knew that someone had actually gone in there, opened the drawer, and taken some money. When I got to the door, I saw the secretary standing in the office looking through the files, which would be perfectly natural. But I knew from the alarm that she had also touched the money in some way. Then, after I saw the secretary leave, I went in there, checked the drawer myself, and found the money was gone—there was $3,000 missing. My job then was just to keep my eyes on her and follow her without arousing her suspicions until she left the property, because she hasn't really stolen anything until she does.

"And then, once she walked out at the end of the day, two of the other people involved in the sting were waiting outside to confront her. They found these hundred-dollar bills on her. So we had the proof, because we had recorded the serial numbers and xeroxed them. There was no way she could innocently claim that this was her own money. We had her dead to rights, which is important in these kind of cases, because if you don't have it all down pat, the person can claim false arrest, unlawful termination, or things like that, and the whole thing can backfire. That's because in these employment cases, where you accuse someone of dishonesty, you're dealing with his or her livelihood. So unless you have all your facts straight, all benefit of doubt generally goes to the employee. And you also can have twelve people on a jury who are either employees now or have been at one time. So you've got to be able to trace the theft from step A to B to show it occurred and very clearly that the employee did it."

Because the evidence was so clear in this case, there was no trial, so Jordan didn't have to testify, though normally, in such a case, he would to describe his observations.

"In this case, she just gave back the money and quietly left. And the boss dropped pressing any criminal charges. He just wanted her out and the money back. He didn't want the bad press of getting involved in a criminal case and maybe a trial."

In the drug case, Jordan assumed the role as a dealer because a lawyer for a bigwig drug dealer who was nabbed in a hotel suspected a setup—that the cops had enlisted the aid of the maids there to rifle through the luggage and drawers of guests who fit the drug dealer's profile. The maids were to provide the police department information on that guest which would help in making a subsequent arrest.

"But that's actually illegal and an invasion of the privacy of the guests if the police were doing that," Jordan said. "And the drug dealer was trying to show this. Then he could say he was wrongfully arrested, because the police shouldn't have had the evidence against him they did, so then that would be thrown out. Without the evidence, the police wouldn't have probable cause to arrest him. So the case would be dismissed, and he would be free. On the other hand, the reason the police might be doing this is that they didn't have sufficient reason or probably cause to arrest the dealer, though because of a tip, they suspected he was doing something. So it was their way of getting around the usual legal restrictions to make the arrest when they were pretty sure the man was doing something wrong. But then that's wrong too; the police aren't supposed to do this, and that's why any evidence they get in this way would be thrown out—to protect the individual from oppressive police actions, whether guilty or not."

So what actually happened, we wondered after our civics lesson. Jordan went on.

"Well, in this case, I came in with a couple of bags of flour that looked much like powered cocaine. And then I left a scale and some snow seals and other stuff laying around in the room. I also flashed a lot of money at the bar, and I was always on the pay phone. I essentially did the old 'Miami Vice' number, to make it apparent that I was hot and heavy in the drug trade. And then, I also left a briefcase around where I had some flour packed in plastic bags, as well as some bags in the drawers. Then, finally, I had a tape recorder secreted in the lid of the case, and it was triggered with sound, so that when the maids came into the room, it would record everything they did. If they went through the desk drawers or opened the case, it would pick that up."

The scheme sounded ingenious. But did it work?

"Unfortunately, the maids never tried doing it to me or to another investigator they sent in. So we never found out if they were doing it or not. And eventually the guy just pled to a deal. After all, he was really running a coke business—he just couldn't beat the rap."

As for the plumber and investor roles, Jordan just hung around in a plumbing supply house and in a stock brokerage house respectively until he observed some signs of embezzlement. And after seeing the suspected parties helping themselves to the cash drawer when they thought no one was looking, he just reported his observations, and the employers took it from there.

Now we asked Jordan the question we had asked all of the other private eyes we had spoken to—what did being in this business do to his personal life? And like most of the others, he found it had a dramatic effect because of the unpredictability, the financial insecurities in the beginning, and the battle against the mistaken mystique of the glamorous and gallivanting private eye.

"First of all, the field has a big effect on your social and personal life, because it's an unpredictable business. You go out there to work on a case, and there's no set procedure on how to do something. There are some general ideas but you are dealing in unknown territory. And then, once you get out there, you don't know what is going to happen, where you are going to be, how much time it is going to take.

"For example, you knock on someone's door to do an interview. Well, you don't know what's going on there; you don't know what they have to say; you don't know anything about the situation you're getting into. Or if you're sitting out there drinking coffee on a surveillance, you don't know when they're going to leave.

"So in reality, you just know the nuts and bolts of the job, but beyond that, you really don't know what you're doing. You know in a general way what could happen and in a general way how to deal with whatever happens. It's a tough job, and that can't help but carry over into your personal life. You talk to most people who go to work. They know what they're doing now; they know what they're going to be doing tomorrow and the next day.

"I have a girlfriend I live with now, and she asks me: 'What time will you be home?' And I say, 'Well, I think I'll be knocking the surveillance off at 5:15, so I should be home by 6:00.' But then, when the time comes, I could be on the freeway heading from Sacramento at 5:15 behind this guy. Or then maybe he might jump on an airplane and I'm heading out of state or out of the country. So ultimately, I just don't know, and the people in my life have to learn to live with this, though there are many people who can't."

What about at least letting people know when plans got changed, when appointments would be missed. Couldn't that at least calm down some of the unpredictability?

"Unfortunately, that's not always possible. You just suddenly have to take off. You can't get to a phone." And then Jordan didn't have a cellular phone in his car, because he so often used different cars or rental cars when out on the road in different places. "It's just a gypsy sort of life sometimes in many areas of the business, and it's not a comfortable world for many people, so it can be very hard on relationships."

Then, too, the financial problems of starting out in the field could create difficulties in relationships too. Earlier Jordan had described the basic problem as "no money, no honey," and now he elaborated on how the financial hurdles he faced had affected him.

"Just about the only thing that's predictable in this business is knowing that financially you're going to be broke for six more years of doing this line of work when you start out without a license and have to work for somebody else, because they pay peanuts. Maybe $15 or $20 and hour, $25 tops, and you're busting your ass doing all this crazy, unpredictable work. And then it takes several years to get your business established too, so until then, you can live like an artist in a garret." Jordan pointed around his own garretlike office to underscore the idea.

"Well, when you're living like that, it can be very hard to have a serious relationship with anyone. It's not like the experience of most of my contemporaries, the guys I went to college with. Now they're lawyers, vice presidents in companies, big shot sales types, managers of businesses or department stores, and they're pulling in close to six figures. And meanwhile, for the last few years, I've ended up a couple of months behind on the rent."

On the other hand, on the plus side, Jordan did find that because of the mystique of the private eye, some women might be initially attracted to him, just because of the work he did, so they were willing to put up with the unpredictable hours and the occasionally cancelled dates, as well as with the fact that Jordan had little money to take them out.

Then, too, in the beginning, another problem interfering with relationships was the many hours spent in moonlighting to help pay the rent. For instance, in Jordan's case, he had been doing this since he started in the business twelve years ago, until about the last eighteen months before we interviewed him. "And when you're doing that," he commented, "you can get real stressed out. You get stressed on your day job doing all sorts of oddball things in investigations, and then, on top of that, you may be spending a few nights a week slinging gin, driving a hack, or something like that. So it can be a real struggle, not only to make it financially but to keep a relationship going too."

In fact, as Jordan explained, this way of life was one reason he had never been married, though he was engaged now and planned to wed soon.

"I've finally come through the hard times. Before this, because of my work, I don't see how I could have gotten married. And I think this situation is true for a lot of private investigators in a similar situation, because you're dealing with really adverse financial conditions for a long time and oddball hours and oddball schedules, which is not really conducive to a family life."

We had one last question. So now, having gone through this long struggle, knowing what he knows about the business now, would

Jordan do it again? He looked at us long and thoughtfully, then finally answered:

"Well, it's a tough, tough business, and I would never allow a child of mine to do it and I would never encourage anyone else to do it. And I know I've paid a lot of dues to get where I am. I feel the hard part is behind me now, though I've underestimated how much dues were required to get here. For besides being an investigator, you've got to be a salesman, a marketing man, a businessman and more in order to make it. But now, having done it, I feel like I'm stuck with this career."

Jordan paused for a few moments, thinking, reflecting.

"Why am I stuck with this? Because I've passed the big four-O, and I don't think the crazy combination of skills it takes to be good in this business transfers to any other profession very well. But then I love it too because of all the variety and challenge. It's never boring. And now that those periods of anguish are behind me, I think the financial future looks bright. I've built up my client base; I've got people working for me; I'm good at what I do; and I'm truly optimistic about eventually getting caught up with the people I went to college with who are making those hundred grand incomes. Maybe if I had to do it over knowing what I do now, I wouldn't have done it. But I have, and now that the struggle is over, I know there's no going back. And besides, I really love what I do."

And on that note the interview ended—with a kind of mixture of realism and optimism about what the life and work of a private eye was all about. It seemed like a fitting conclusion.

Then, carefully, very carefully, Jordan led us down the rickety wooden stairs back to the bar, as we clung to the walls so as not to fall. Then, as we waved goodbye, he headed off on another case.

"Though at least my girlfriend said she would wait for me for a late dinner," Jordan said. "I just hope it won't be too late again," he added with the hint of an ironic grin.

8

Anne Davis: Defending the Criminal and Helping the Plaintiff in Civil Cases

This interview with Anne Davis, who specializes in criminal defense work, took us to a large well-furnished flat high on a hill overlooking the ocean in San Francisco. It had a trendy, modern look, with bright yellow curtains by the wide windows with a sweeping view of the water, and abstract and minimalist paintings on the walls. A long white couch with black throw pillows and a circular glass coffee table in the middle of the room contributed to this arty effect.

Anne welcomed us with a cheery hello, and as we set up our taperecorders on the glass coffee table, she returned with some wine and cheese to create a comfortable, mellow mood.

Before launching on her experiences in the business, Anne described her own varied background. After college, she spent some years as a hip bohemian artist. "I felt like I wanted to try everything and really experience life to its fullest," Anne told us, "so I tried all sorts of jobs, and even tried to make it in the art world in New York for awhile. I worked as a temp in several big companies for a few years, spent some time working as a waitress, and worked in a department store selling toys. I even tried singing in some small New York clubs, and I tried going into partnership with some friends to run a small restaurant. So even before I got into this business, I was always a very independent, adventurous type of person, and I think it takes someone like that to do well in this field.

By the mid-1970s, Anne was frustrated with her career as an artist and looking to make a switch. She decided to become an investigator.

"Well, after trying to break into the art and music scene in New York, which was very hard to do, I decided I wanted to do something different, which was interesting, too, but where I was also sure I could get paid. I found I liked excitement, things that were constantly changing, and I didn't want a typical 9 to 5 job stuck in an office. Also, I wanted a job that would bring all of my skills together. After much soul-searching, it occurred to me that being a private investigator would enable me to do this, I could work independently, work out in the field; there would be projects of variety and excitement. And so, after deciding this is what I wanted to do in the early 1970s, when I was about thirty, I focused on making this happen. I just kept imagining myself doing this, and then, within a couple of days, I met a private investigator at the restaurant where I worked. I told him I was interested in doing the work and I felt I could do it. He gave me a go at a job.

"I did well at the work, and then he gave me another job interviewing witnesses for a case, and then another job, and then I met another detective who I apprenticed with for about four years, working with him part-time, doing this sort of work."

"Then, after about eight years of working for other investigators, I had built up enough time and experience in the field—about 6,000 hours minimum is required. So I got my own license, and that's what I've been doing ever since, working mostly for attorneys and sometimes with other private investigators. I've been doing both civil cases and criminal defense work, though eventually I began to specialize in the criminal defense area. And mostly, I have been able to do well, because if you do a good job, you get referrals. Because that's the way it works in this business, since it's based so much on referral and word of mouth. The attorneys hear you're efficient and they come after you. So my business just kept growing."

Anne remained excited and motivated by investigative work because not only did she like the continual variety and challenge, but she liked the independence the business offered. "I really do like working alone, and I usually do, because I like my independence. Still, it can be fun working with someone, because you can laugh and you can joke and you can get the energy up. But even though I usually work alone, I still work closely with the attorneys.

"Also, I like the idea of being able to call the shots, decide what's the best approach to use in investigating a case. I can make the decisions and take the responsibility. And I like the idea of being able to help my clients: I get a great satisfaction helping people and seeing the gain from my work on a case."

Since most investigators have traditionally been men and the field has traditionally had a macho, tough-guy image (though increasingly, there are more and more women investigators), we asked Anne about what's it like to be a woman in the field. Were there any special differences she noticed, any extra dangers in being a woman in the field?

"Well, I think sometimes a woman has an advantage in interviewing witnesses and others, because a lot of times she can get the information better than a man, and a lot of attorneys know this and will prefer to hire a woman investigator on such cases. The reason is that a woman can seem more empathetic and understanding, so people are more willing to talk. The usual and most effective approach to getting information is not through the stereotypical tough private eye threatening 'You better tell me what you know,' and then perhaps pushing the witness or the suspect up against a wall or using other macho techniques to squeeze out information. Rather, it's usually better to use a sympathetic approach, showing that you want to understand, and then perhaps use an appeal to fairness, which is what I do.

"Also, I think a witness may be more willing to speak to a woman private investigator because she's less threatening to a lot of witnesses. Say an investigator is out pounding on someone's door at eight at night and the person looks out and sees a big guy. The door is less likely to be open to him as to someone like me. I don't look so scary."

But what about the opposite side of her being less threatening? Was there any additional danger to her? Anne shook her head. "I don't think so," she said. "The very dangerous places, such as the projects, where there are drugs and frequent shootings, I won't go, although I did for many years. And in the kinds of cases I do, any danger is already in the past, because I'm investigating an accident, shooting, assault, or other incident *after* it has already occurred."

Also, Anne thought the presence of a woman investigator was particularly helpful in certain types of sensitive cases, such as a rape. "I think a lot of attorneys realize that a woman can handle these things in a more delicate manner," Anne commented. "And we appear less threatening to the witness or victim than a big male. So a lot of times I'll get cases that are very, very delicate. The attorneys feel I'll be able to handle the witnesses better."

On the other side, however, there were some disadvantages, mainly because Anne, like other women investigators, sometimes encountered the old boy network of investigators with traditional women-don't-do-as-well attitudes, which limited her in getting certain cases.

"This is less of a problem than in the past, but there's an old boy network in this business, as well as every other business. It's a kind of male club, and many men who are part of this don't want to let woman in, especially when a woman is in business for herself as a competitor. Yet when a woman is good, they will respect her and know of her work. I feel that myself."

Anne described an experience of another woman investigator. "She was working with three investigators who were partners, and they wanted a woman in their firm. But they didn't want to take a woman in as a partner, which goes back to these traditional attitudes. The woman did feel held back a little at the time, because she would have preferred to go into business with a partner. But eventually, as attitudes have been changing and women are finding more acceptance, she did find someone to work with closely while setting up her own practice. This close working arrangement helped, because in this business it's important to get feedback from your associates and others in the field."

Over time, Anne noted similar changes in the field. In the early days, when she first started, it was harder to break in and get referrals, though now she felt it was a good and growing field for female investigators.

"But they have to have certain kinds of qualities." Anne explained "Independent, adventurous—like me, I guess. A person has to be willing to be a risk-taker. You can't be a timid or reticent person. And you need insatiable curiosity too."

In fact, according to Anne, there were certain fields that women did particularly well at. "Undercover work—that's a good field for women, because they can blend in very easily in different situations. And they are very good in criminal work, because the main thing here is to be able to talk to people, interview them, and get a statement. The idea is to get the facts for testimony!"

Yet, even while women might be especially good in certain fields, there was still the disadvantage of getting paid a little less for their work. "But isn't that the way just about everywhere," Anne commented, citing her own experience in the field, where she generally charged $60 an hour, whereas most of the men doing the same work charged $75 to $85.

Anne also pointed out that the women in the field didn't tend to stick together or help each other. She found she had few women attorneys as clients, although defense work is one of the areas to which women attorneys have gravitated. "It has surprised me," she acknowledged, "but I have found that the women attorneys I have known tend to prefer to hire men as their investigators. I think it may have something to do with prefering a balance of the male and female mental energy; maybe they think that works together best."

I mentioned a book I had worked on with another author (*Women to Women: From Sabotage to Support* by Judith Briles) about women sabotaging each other in the workplace or feeling resistant to working together because there was a kind of jealousy and resentment between women. And Anne acknowledged that this kind of dynamic might be a factor though she wasn't sure. "But perhaps as more and more women enter the field, more and more women will be working together in the future," she suggested hopefully.

And finally we wondered if being a woman might affect the way the attorneys she worked with treated her, perhaps feeling they could direct or control her more because she is a woman.

"Not at all," said Anne. "I don't see myself deferring to any of the attorneys I work with, because I don't let anybody push me around or intimidate me, and I don't let any one tell me how to do something. I'll have a discussion about the ways to go about investigating an incident with my clients, and I want to understand my client's theory of the case, so I can look for the type of information that will be relevant to supporting that particular theory.

"In fact," Anne added, "I wonder if we should be talking about people and personalities in this field rather than about the differences between men and women. I think it's possible to make too much of the differences, because the qualities of a good investigator are the qualities of a good investigator male or female. But yes, very definitely, it's a field with more and more opportunities for women, and in the years ahead, there should be more and more women in the field."

The the conversation turned to the type of work Anne does. What types of cases did she work on? What did she do?

Anne began outlining the types of cases. "The most common criminal ones I've been involved with are rapes, robberies, murders, and assaults and batteries—the usual sorts of major crimes which require a defense. And I've defended all types of people from all walks of life, including lawyers, psychologists, police officers, and doctors. It's been just about anybody, because everybody has problems. I've also represented various companies involved in litigation, including some insurance companies and manufacturing corporations.

And in some types of situations, I've worked both sides—which many people in this business do—though not the same case, of course. For example, in some cases I've tried to help in defending a police officer who has gotten into trouble and been accused of something. And in others I've had clients who say that the police officers beat them up. Then, in either event, I have to check out the story. Was it true? Was the officer provoked? Was the person resisting arrest? Or was the officer or person just a bad apple? The cases can go either way, and it's my job to find out what really occurred."

Anne also pointed out that, like other defense investigators, she worked mainly for private defense attorneys, although she, like many other investigators, would take several court appointed cases each year. These were the cases assigned to a private attorney if the public defender couldn't handle it, generally because the latter was already handling a co-defendant in the case, so there would be a conflict of interest.

"Most of us in defense work try to take a few of these," Anne explained, "because it's a way of helping the indigent. And it's really a public service, because you lose money on those cases. That happens because you're not working for your regular fee, and you're fronting all the costs in addition to your time. Then you have to wait for the city, the county, the state, or the feds to pay you, and that's typically three to six or eight months down the road. So if you took a full load of these cases, there's no way you could stay in business. But as an occasional job, it's a nice thing to do—and I feel it helps to fulfill one's duty as a citizen."

What happens when Anne gets a case? She explained.

"The first thing that happens is somebody is generally charged by the police and district attorney, and then the defense attorney gets the case and calls me in on it. The attorney fills me in on the case and tells me what witnesses he thinks I should contact who might have knowledge about whatever incident occurred and what they might say. Then, usually, I will talk to the defendant in the case too. I want to meet with him or her and learn that person's story and understanding of the case. Oftentimes I will find that the defendant doesn't even tell his or her attorney things I'm told. I don't know why, but sometimes the defendant forgets, the attorney doesn't have the time to go into the details in depth, or maybe I just inspire trust. But in any case, like most investigators, whatever information I get, I will pass it onto the defense attorney. And that's true whether the information is favorable to the case or not. It's important that the attorney knows everything—the weaknesses as well as the strengths, so he or she can be prepared to deal with whatever comes up."

Normally, according to Anne, this first meeting with the attorney focuses on reviewing the police report and talking to the client. After these preliminaries, a course of action can be determined.

"Usually, you proceed on this because this reflects the police version of what happened and what led to the arrest by the local police,

FBI, DEA, or whatever other government agency is involved. Also, the city district attorney, federal prosecutor, or other prosecuting agency charging the defendant bases their charges on this report. Thus it's good to have this background information, so we know what we're dealing with, what the charges and accusations are. Additionally, the police reports will list any witnesses the authorities have talked to, and if the defendant made a statement, the report will include that, too.

"In some cases, an attorney will ask me to get going on a case before he has the report, generally because there has been some delay in getting it from the prosecutor, perhaps because the prosecutor isn't sure what the charges should be. But normally, the attorneys don't like to go ahead before they see the report."

So just how accurate was this report?

"Well, it varies. Sometimes they're not accurate at all, and often there are even mistakes in spelling. But they help you see what type of officers are involved in the incident, and what they claim they have against the defendant. The reports also are usually pretty good as far as providing leads, since they list all the witnesses and victims that the police spoke to, and include their addresses, and a phone number if the person has one. So they're good for follow-up contact.

"However, the authorities initially on the scene don't do the same type of interviewing that later police investigators might do or that I might do, so the report's not as in-depth. The police usually don't have the time for this kind of in-depth interviewing, and leave that for the prosecutor's investigators to do when they go back and follow up. But if the police do get any statements from anyone, they will write those up, and include them in the report, too."

What kind of mistakes might they make? What kinds of things were usually left out in these initial reports? Anne gave some examples.

"Well, I've seen a lot of these mistakes especially in traffic accident reports. Usually it's a highway patrol report. But a lot of times an officer from another unit may cover this, and he may not be knowledgeable about accidents, so that when he draws up the accident scene, it's not accurate at all. There may be mistakes on where the roads are relative to each other or errors in the distances of the vehicles and things like that.

"Or sometimes an officer may get mixed up where there are a number of events and witnesses connected with the same case. For example, I have one police report now involving three auto burglaries. After the police officer interviewed the witnesses, he got mixed up on what witness went with what location and with what burglary.

"When you follow up, you want to look for these errors and try to correct them. Then, too, the police may refer to things in the report which they don't have time to check out, and these leads can be helpful too. One time I had a police report that referred to a man named Jerry who lived down the street near the corner where a fight started, and he was listed in the report as being on the porch watching. But the police never bothered to interview him, and when I located him, he turned out to be the one witness we needed to support the story of the man we were defending. It was a grudge assault case, where one man was accusing the other of waiting on the street to attack him. Jerry had been on the porch while the man was waiting for our client, and when I spoke to him, he revealed this."

Anne also explained the importance of having an understanding of the lawyer's theory or approach to the defense at the start of an investigation.

"Each case is so different, and the way you investigate it depends so much on how the lawyer thinks he wants to defend it. I'm now working on a robbery case with a confession, for example, and when you have a confession, your defense is going to be different than it would be if there was some question as to whether or not your client committed the act, whatever it is. If the person has admitted something, or if it's very clear that the prosecutor has an open and shut case to prove the defendant did it, you will generally focus the investigation on finding character references who can help to make your client seem like a better person, or others who might be able to help explain why he did it, to present him in a more sympathetic light. For instance, they can help to show he was under a tremendous amount of stress, that he was provoked, that he was ill and delusional, or that there might be mitigating circumstances.

"On the other hand, if it's not clear that the person did it, I might investigate to prove an alibi. Or I might try to show he had a different life pattern than this type of crime shows. For example, in a really involved murder case, investigators will do a complete and thorough check on the defendant from his earliest years. They'll go to his hometown, talk to his schoolteachers, to the people who knew him at church, to old employers, to friends. The idea is to get a full profile on the defendant's life, so you can show the kind of person he is. You want to find any information you can to help show that he couldn't have committed this crime, because he's just not that kind of person."

Or if the person did do it, another tack, apart from getting character witnesses, might be to show that the offense wasn't as bad as it might seem at first. So the investigation might try to find evidence that the offense was really less serious or done in self-defense. As Anne commended:

"Say there's an assault. The investigation might show it isn't quite what it seems. Suppose somebody is charged with assault with a deadly weapon, such as a knife. He might have a defense in that he was only holding the knife, not using it as a deadly weapon. Or perhaps he had the weapon and used it; but maybe this was because somebody was moving in on him with a deadly weapon; so he acted only to protect himself."

Anne also stressed the importance of using a fairly straightforward approach in contacting witnesses to get information and statements.

"You can sometimes be creative in your approach to get someone to talk to you, describing yourself as a friend of someone whom person knows. But this kind of approach, if you use it at all, is really just appropriate in civil cases, because you have a little more leeway in what you can say or do. You may be able to get away with something like going to a neighbor with a phony story to find out about somebody in the neighborhood. But in a criminal case, you generally have to be straightforward, because if you misrepresent yourself to get an interview it can rebound against you and the attorney, in that any evidence you come up with from that interview may be excluded because of the deception. Then the attorney may end up not being able to make a crucial point to support his client. So you can't misrepresent yourself in such cases or it could ruin the case for everybody.

"Thus, in criminal work, you normally just tell everyone you talk to upfront what defendant and attorney you are representing, and then you question them about what you want to know."

Anne also noted that the defendant was usually a good source of witnesses, apart from those listed in the police report.

"The defendant may know a number of witnesses not in the report, who may have either seen the incident or know something about it, know someone who does, or at least could be good character witnesses for him, such as an employer or former employer, relative or long-term friend with a good job. So I'll usually talk to the defendant first, who sometimes is in jail."

Anne described how she went about interviewing witnesses, emphasizing the importance of getting a signed statement.

"It helps if you can get a signed statement from witnesses, because then, it's clear what they are saying about what they know. They've had a chance to review what they've said and agree with it, although the statement itself isn't evidence. They still would have to be called on to testify or give a formal deposition to use anything they say if there is a trial. But at least this clarifies their testimony and suggests they will be cooperative. However, even if I can't get a statement, the witnesses' comments will be useful in helping the lawyer know what they know or would say, so I'll report that, too."

As Anne explained, many people might talk to her, yet be reluctant to sign anything. "Usually, if you can't get a signed statement from someone within an hour of talking to them, you're not going to get one. And the reason is that people are more and more reluctant to sign anything. They're afraid of the formality, they are concerned that it could be used against them in some way, or maybe they're concerned about committing themselves to something. I think it's because people are getting more sophisticated about legal matters. And some may be aware that later these statements might be used if they testify to contradict what they are saying on the stand, so they may be afraid of getting tripped up by signing something now. However, I'm not out there to manufacture facts. I just want people to tell the truth."

So if someone was willing to actually sign a statement, how did Anne go about getting this?

"Well, a statement is really like a summary of the facts as reported by the witness, a tightening up of what they have said.

Basically, what I want to include is the witness' position, how he or she knows the client, for how long, what the relationship to the client is, and what he or she can say about the incident, whatever it may be. When I'm doing the interview, I just take notes on what is said, and usually people ramble all over the place when they talk. I reorganize some of their thoughts to make everything more coherent. I have them read the statement over and make any corrections, and I tell them not to sign if it's not what they told me. But if it is, I ask them to sign it, and at this point, almost everyone does." Anne also observed that sometimes she had to play the role of a social worker or psychologist. "Especially with some defendants, you have to do this," she said. "A lot of times, these defendants are very, very scared, and they need a lot of support. So you have to hold their hand all the way through the case, because they feel their whole life or future depends on the outcome, and often it does. Usually, the lawyers don't do this hand-holding, because they don't have the time or just don't feel comfortable in this kind of role. They leave the hand-holding to me because I do that real well, and it takes the pressure off them."

We wondered about the question of danger as Anne was going around trying to find and talk to these witnesses.

Anne shook her head, "Not really. Everybody thinks there is a lot of danger, but there really isn't. For one thing, when you're working for the defense, you are trying to find witnesses to help the defendant, and they're often friends or other people who want to do what they can to be of assistance. And if they are living in really dangerous neighborhoods, I won't travel there but will arrange to meet the witness somewhere else, or I will have someone who looks real tough accompany me.

Anne gave an example of how she once used a police escort to help her go into public housing project areas.

"Usually, if I'm going into the projects, I will arrange to go during the day, when it is safest, even when I'm with someone. Once, I found myself there alone unexpectedly, and when a patrol car came around the block, which frequently happens there, I flagged the officer down. Then I introduced myself as an investigator and explained my mission. The cops were really helpful, and didn't ask a lot of questions. Instead, they just accompanied me, and when we got to the right floor, they waited down the hall out of view, while I went to the place and pounded on the door."

Was it common for the police to do this? "I don't think so. At least not for the average investigator. But I think they did this for me, as they might for another woman investigator, because they can see I'm a woman. And they know it would be dangerous for me to go in alone.

"But now, with all the crack, I'm hesitant to go into these projects at all anymore. That's because it's like a war zone down there with all the dealers, crackheads, and prostitutes, who'll do anything for crack. So someone might put a knife in someone else over practically nothing, even twenty-five cents."

Thus, in recent years, Anne has rejected a number of cases. "For example, I turned down one where a family was wiped out, killed by people involved in the crack cocaine business. It would have taken me into the worst areas of a large city. Up until a few years ago I still might have gone there. But not now. I just don't feel safe, because of the violent drug scene there."

Unfortunately, as Anne explained, one of the private eye myths was that the investigator was right there on the scene of the crime along with the police. But it wasn't quite that way. Normally, she had to wait until much later to gain access, if at all. As Anne put it:

"Take the Angela Lansbury crime thrillers on TV. She's always right on the scene. But in reality, the cops wouldn't let her in there. She wouldn't be allowed. The only way you can possibly go there is after the fact, and that's if someone will let you in. I've had cases, for example, where I've been hired by the family because they feel the police officers didn't do a good enough job in investigating the crime, and then when I went back, I was able to get all the evidence they had, see the place, and then try to uncover more.

"But in other cases, no, it hasn't been easy. For instance, on one big kidnapping case, there were three jurisdictions of police officers involved, because the man came from one town, he was staying with the victim in another, and he had taken the victim into the third. Well, I believed from talking to people who knew him that the so-called victim had actually gone with the man willingly and engaged in some crimes with him and then tried to change her story to make it seem like she was his victim when they got caught. But I was not able to get access to the house where they had been staying to check out my theory, because some other people were living there, and they didn't want to let me in.

"But then, of course," Anne added, "if the crime scene was a public place, you can always go back there once the police investigation is over."

Additionally, Anne stressed the importance of starting an investigation early.

"You want to get to the witnesses as soon as possible, while the memory of the incident is fresh in their minds or while they're still in the area. Today, people often move around a lot, and it can be hard to find some witnesses if you wait too long. And then, too, it's better to get to the witnesses first, before the other side does.

"If the prosecution gets there first, they may tell the witnesses that they don't have to speak to me, or even make it sound like they shouldn't, which they aren't supposed to do. Or possibly, the prosecution's interviewer may suggest some things about the defendant that aren't true, which could affect what the witness says to me. On the other hand, if I get there first, I can help the person understand that he is free to speak to the prosecution investigators or not, that he can choose, because sometimes, when the prosecution investigators get there with their badges and all, people feel compelled to talk, when they don't have to."

Anne also had her ways of getting reluctant witnesses to talk when she felt they really did know something about the case that could help her client.

"Sometimes people may be willing to tell the truth if they get subpoenaed and go to court, because once they're in a courtroom with a judge and a jury, it's hard to back out or lie. Yet, when you first approach them, a lot of people will do everything they can to avoid being subpoenaed to testify. They'll often lie to you and tell you they don't know anything about the crime, because they don't want to be involved. But if I'm pretty sure they really do know, I will suggest the lawyer subpoena them, because once on the stand, they will tell the truth. A good example of this happened when I was investigating a murder at a bar. The bartender had supposedly been murdered by another worker at the bar, and I was asked to verify some statements in the police report. One man I interviewed who worked there too, said he wouldn't give me a written statement, though he told me he had received threats from the man who was involved in the murder. But when I asked him if he was subpoenaed to testify, would he tell the truth about what he knew, and he said yes."

However, Anne had a caution about subpoenaing reluctant witnesses. "As long as you're pretty sure of what a reluctant witness will say, it's usually fine to subpoena him to get him into court. But you really want to avoid calling in or subpoenaing anybody unless you know what he or she is going to say. So that's what I'm there to find out for the attorney, and if I'm really not sure what to expect, I'll usually recommend skipping the witness.

"Usually I try to appeal to people's sense of fairness if I feel they're trying not to talk because they don't want to get involved. And almost always, we either get someone to talk, so we know what to expect, or we just don't call them."

Finally, before going on to describe some of her most interesting cases, Ann spoke a little about interviewing someone in jail.

"Actually, it's sometimes easier, because the defendant is usually really glad to see you. After all, the prisoners don't get too many visitors, so they're delighted to see someone to break up the routine."

But then, the interview itself was much like any other. "When you go into the jail," Anne explained, "you ask for an attorney-client room, which is a small enclosed room with a couple of chairs. And it's completely private, though the guards can peer in through the window in the door if they want. If I'm taking a statement from a witness, however, it's pretty much the same as taking a statement anywhere, except the setting's different. If I'm talking to the defendant, though, I wouldn't get a statement." Anne explained the intricacies of the law. "And the reason for that is if the defendant gives a signed statement, then that may become something that's discoverable to the other side, because a party to the case has made a formal statement. But if I just take my own notes, these are considered confidential. It's considered part of what's called the attorney's 'work product,' since I'm acting as the agent of the attorney. So I can show my notes to the attorney, and that's completely confidential."

By contrast, signed statements from witnesses in the jail or any-where were usually fully protected, since the defense didn't have to reveal its own witnesses. "But sometimes," Anne cautioned, "the other side might be entitled to an investigator's reports and state-ments under certain circumstances, so the investigator has to be aware of the little twists and turns in the law in knowing what to do."

Then the conversation turned to Anne's more memorable cases. She brought out some bulging case files to help her remember and rifled through them as memories flooded back. And as she related them, each one seemed not only a little drama or tragedy about someone's life but also a snapshot portrait or clue about what worked or didn't in dealing with the criminal justice system, juries and the courts.

In one case, Anne tried to help a man who had murdered a teenager. A girl from a small country town in Wyoming came to San Francisco and was befriended by an older man in his thirties. He had helped her out by lending her money, helped her find an apart-ment, and then had suddenly killed her in a fit of anger when she dumped him for a younger man. And he had confessed to the kil-ling, so the lawyer felt the only hope was in showing he was really a normally good, respectable man who had just gone crazy when he was a little drunk, and this woman to whom he had given so much betrayed and abandoned him.

"It was a particularly gruesome case," Anne said. "So many stab wounds, so much blood. It seemed like the work of a monster. Our client was this normally kind, gentle man—a successful accountant who had recently lost his own wife. He was in a very lonely, vulnerable period in his life.

"Well, when he met this woman, he felt very paternal and protec-tive. He really loved her. All of a sudden, she turned on him, and she did so in such a cruel, unexpected way. He had taken her out to celebrate her birthday, and it seemed like they had a wonderful time. When he took her home, she announced that while she appre-ciated his attentions, now they were through, and she needed to move on to other things. Well, I guess the man couldn't deal with that, so he just went crazy. He became hysterical, got a knife, and nearly decapitated the girl. He admitted that.

"It was a very hard, really delicate case to deal with, because here's this basically quiet, respectable, generous man, and now his life is totally ruined by this one incident. But on the other hand he killed someone.

"Anyway, the lawyer's strategy in this case was to play up the good qualities of this man and show how basically good he was to demonstrate how he could be distraught enough to commit murder. And at the same time the defense wanted to show that this girl was not such a sweet innocent. My job was to go out and find people who knew him and worked with him, and also contact people from the man's family who would come to the trial and testify as to how good a person he was."

What happened? Anne went on, slowly leading up to the climax of the case. "Well, after I found out that the girl had been seeing several men on the side and had worked briefly as a hooker when she first came to San Francisco, I tried to find more information to show that she really wasn't this sweet innocent but had been using our client. I found people who had seen her in bars and were willing to testify about her past as a hooker.

"And then, after I spoke to some of the man's relatives and business associates, I arranged for them to come and testify. They were real pillars of the community, fine, clean-living honest, respectable, successful folks, and we hoped they'd make a good impression, and help make the jury more sympathetic to the man."

What was the verdict?

Anne turned very serious. "Well, unfortunately, it was just a theory to make the man seem good and the girl a manipulative villain but the jury didn't buy it. They convicted the defendant of first-degree murder anyway. Now they definitely would have convicted him of something, since he had confessed to a murder. But maybe the jury might have come in on manslaughter or second-degree murder or something else with a lighter sentence. But no. First degree."

Yet in Anne's view, the investigation and the lawyer's theory wasn't to blame for this. "I think maybe it would have helped if the attorney had put the defendant on the stand to tell his story. But the attorney didn't want to do that, though there is always that choice— to have the defendant testify or not. It's not a good idea if the defendant doesn't present himself very well, or has a long record that can come up if the defendant speaks for himself. But here was this good man with nothing bad in his background, and the jury probably wanted to hear from him, because his intentions, his state of mind, was so important to the outcome of this case.

"In any case, it's hard to know whether that would have helped and why the jurors decided as they did. But then, you never know with jurors. So here apparently, they didn't buy the lawyer's good guy/bad girl theory and voted to convict. And it's really sad. This man in his late thirties with a successful career and his whole life in front of him, and then in a few seconds he messes up.

"So very sad." She snapped shut the file. "But you do what you can. And even the best of strategies or investigations may not work. With judges and juries you can never tell. The best you can do, as in gambling, is to improve odds."

Anne then related a case about date-rape and it had a happy outcome—an acquittal—because the jury ended up feeling uncertain of what really happened due to the conflicting stories. Yet Anne was quite sure her client was telling the truth, that he was not guilty, and the the girl was making up the story because she felt guilty after having had sex and was afraid of angering her very conservative parents.

"The only two people who knew exactly what happened in this case would be the girl and the guy, but I believed my client, because he gave me a detailed story of what happened that night, and I check out every detail. I didn't catch him in any lies, which is the worst thing that can happen in an attorney-client relationship.

"When I spoke to him, he didn't deny the intercourse. But he said the girl didn't object, and the way he described it, it sounded like she either consented or acted in a way that could be reasonably understood as consent, in which case there was no rape. Basically, they went out for dinner and a movie, and afterward he invited her to drive out to the beach, and she said yes. As they were walking along the beach in an isolated area, he propositioned her, and she didn't say no. Is that rape? I'm not sure. And the jury wasn't sure either. So we got an acquittal, but if they convicted him, this twenty-five-year-old kid was looking at about twenty-five years."

How did Anne's investigation help him? And how did the young man's own story make the difference?

"I think the single most important piece of evidence I found in the case was the name of a woman listed in the police report as one of the people who had been at the restaurant that night while the couple was there. Now there wasn't anything in the report about this woman's relationships to the man or the supposed victim.

"The police never checked it, but what my client told me was true, and this woman turned out to be our most important witness. When I found her, it turned out she knew the woman from the neighborhood; they occasionally met each other at some local singles' events, and she described the woman as something of a flirt, which really helped my client's case, because this woman was trying to come across as a nice, conservative, even naive girl who got taken advantage of or was raped. I think this woman's testimony put some doubt in the jury's mind about her complaint.

"It also helped that my client was forthright about other things that happened that evening. For example, he said that while they were walking on the beach, before he had sex with the woman, he asked her if she wanted to smoke some grass, and she did. Well, when the woman was on the stand and we asked her about going to the beach, she just described taking a walk but said nothing about the joint. So I think my client's version sounded more believable. After all, why would he admit to something that was incriminating, which he didn't have to. But he did, I believe, because he was telling the whole truth, while the girl was not."

But why should she lie? Why should she try to get this guy punished for raping her if he did not?

"Probably because when she came home, it was very late, and she ran into her roommate, who is also her cousin, and she was looking very disheveled. So she was probably afraid her cousin might say something and this might get back to her parents, who she knew would be very disapproving, since they were a fairly close, religious family.

"And that's probably when it happened. She felt she had to come up with an explanation, and she said she was assaulted. She didn't even tell her cousin rape, just assault. So then her cousin told her to call the police, and she felt she was trapped by her story, and so she did. When the police came, they asked her if she was raped, and she said yes. Probably, if her cousin had been asleep in the other room, she would have just gone to bed, and that would have been the end of the matter. But now she was on the spot, and I think she was just very embarrassed by the whole situation, and she was trying to save face in front of the police and the other girl."

Since we had just been talking about the importance of telling the truth and how it could make the difference between a successful defense and a conviction, we wondered whether Anne found people generally truthful, how did she know? How did she persuade people to be truthful?

"Of course, it's always a concern if the defendant or a witness is telling you the truth and if they're telling you everything, because you have to know everything. It can be a disaster to get into court and have a surprise witness or have something come out that you didn't know about, because you aren't prepared. And you have to explain to the defendants that they are really hurting themselves by not telling you these things. They may not tell you because they are embarrassed about what they have done or hope these things won't come out if they say nothing. But they do."

In general did Anne find the defendants she worked with truthful or not?

She shook her head and looked confused. "I used to think I knew, but I don't know anymore. I like to think they are telling the truth. And if their story checks out when I go out or there are other people who verify what they said, that helps to reassure me. Of course, there are always those defendants who will get people to lie for them. I hate it when it happens, but it does occur, and sometimes you just can't tell."

This was one reason that Anne always checked out a defendant's or witness's story—not only to back it up with other evidence, but in part to satisfy herself that she had been told the truth.

Anne offered an example. "Suppose a defendant tells me that he saw something and that a friend was there with him at the time. I certainly will want to talk with his friend and find out what he saw, as well as making sure the friend backs his claim.

"Of course, I let the defendant know I'm planning to check out his story and that I'm not taking everything totally on faith. And the attorney tells him that too. In addition, I explain to them, emphatically, that it's very important that I'm told the truth, because otherwise what the defendant says will only come back to haunt him.

"Even so, some may lie, although on many cases, I usually meet with the same defendant again and again, as the investigation continues, to check out new information I have found or let him know if I haven't been able to find any support for what he was telling me, and then sometimes the real truth will come out. As you do your investigation, you may come up with more questions and want to go over things with them to get things clearer or in more detail.

"I certainly let people know when I know or think they're lying to me. I don't let them think that they're fooling me, because then they'll just think they can continue to do this."

So how could Anne be so sure that someone was lying? Anne gave an example from a recent killing she was investigating.

"It's a case where a man in his early thirties was killed for revenge after a barroom argument, and I know who did it."

How could she think she knew?

Anne explained. "I think a certain man did it and that he lied, because this person was the last to see the victim alive, and he also lost some money to the victim in a gambling wager, which he couldn't really afford. Then he lied to the cops, and when I interviewed him, he lied to me. I know he lied, because he had a lot of different stories. The things he told me didn't check out with the things he told to the cops. He lied to his girlfriend, he lied about his background, he lied about everything. For example, in talking about the incident, he lied about where he was, what time he was there, even that he was there at all. He said he wasn't in the victim's house when it happened; he said he was at home. But I have a witness who saw him in the victim's house, and others who saw him leave the bar later that night, but earlier than he said he did. So it's very clear to me he lied and lied, and he did so because he was guilty. It's very clear."

So how did the defendants or witnesses usually react to a confrontation about their lies.

Anne paused thoughtfully. "Well, it depends on what type of liar each one is. After all, there are defendants and witnesses who will deny anything to the end, no matter what I say I know, such as this guy in the revenge killing case who lied about everything. But then, many others will admit they were trying to mislead you."

In any event, whether she was able to extract the truth or not, Anne reported the findings of her investigation to the attorney she was working for.

"I give them the truth. I tell them whatever I find. I tell them everything. The good, the bad; whatever people tell me, including the lies. Some investigators don't; they leave some things out, perhaps because they aren't sure some piece of information or a lie may be helpful. I pass on everything, including whether a person will make a good witness, even though he's telling the truth. And there can be a difference, because even though what the person is saying is helpful and true, he may not be a good witness because he's shy, backward, or doesn't look good. So the judge or jurors may not like him or believe him. Thus, since the investigator is normally the first person to see the witness, it's important to describe him or her to the attorney and let him know what kind of a witness that person will make, so the attorney can make a decision about whether to use the witness.

"Also, by telling the attorney everything, that helps him know how strong or weak his case is. That's why, if I find the defendant wasn't telling the whole truth, I'll let the attorney know that too. I never hold anything back."

After this brief diversion into the ins and outs of dealing with lying, Anne turned back to her case files. Now she pointed out how some of her cases involved a kind of journey of discovery into human nature.

"Sometimes you really see the worst of a person, as well as the best, in doing these investigations. You see not only the lies and the deceit but the depths of human greed and inhumanity."

Anne described a case of a trustee of an old man's property who couldn't be trusted. The trustee was appointed the conservator for this old man, because he was a cousin who lived nearby. The trustee proceeded to take just about everything he could from the man's property—both while the old man was alive and then after he died—as administrator of the estate. But then some of the relatives who were beneficiaries began to suspect something was wrong and triggered an investigation.

"To some extent, many trustees who administer estates, including the probate attorneys, will take what they can get from these estates. But this man really went much further than even everyday venal trustees normally go."

Anne explained what happened.

"The relatives first suspected him when there was an accounting, which is a normal procedure when there is an estate. After many months, the executor or conservator of the estate was to account for all the moneys and what has been spent. And in this case, the accounting just didn't make sense; the numbers and the reasons for many of the expenses just didn't jibe.

"For example, the trustee bought a lot of things for himself out of the money in the fund he was in charge of. And there was no way to justify these purchases, though he tried to. He bought himself things like an expensive stereo and a new car and charged them to the old man, who was incompetent and under this man's conservatorship at the time. Some other suspicious expenses were $10,000 worth of plane trips, theater tickets, and dinners in expensive restaurants. How could you justify such expenses for a ninety-year-old man in a wheelchair?"

So how did this trustee think he could get away with such expenses in an accounting? How could he think someone might not suspect something was wrong?

Anne looked equally mystified. "That's what we don't really understand. But sometimes people seem to think their web of lies will protect them. In this case the trustee perjured in declarations and lied continuously in interviews. He just made things up. When I checked them out, I found they were not true.

"There were a lot of expensive abstract paintings in the house, for example. The trustee said he sold them to a gallery. But when I talked to the gallery owners, they never heard of him and they never had a showing of the items. And the trustee used this supposed sale, which never happened, to justify some travel expenses. I found that he lied about just about everything."

How did this apparently evil, deceitful man end up being entrusted with this estate? Anne related the sad story.

"He was a cousin who lived in the same community, though they had never been especially close. He was even listed in the will, though in a nominal way. And then when this old man has a close call in the hospital, this cousin showed up with his own lawyer, he talked him out of his long-time attorney, and had him sign another will giving him the right to be the executor as well as to care for the old man. And the attorney had the papers drawn up right there in the hospital, and then the cousin just took over, and ravaged this estate for the next two years."

In fact, as Anne explained, the trustee involved some of his friends and associates in the ravaging and concealment process, which sometimes made the investigation very difficult.

Somehow, despite the hurdles, Anne had managed to piece what happened in the case together, though now it was still up to the beneficiaries' attorney, who hired her to investigate, to prove all of these allegations in court. And then, if he proved them, there would only be monetary damages or penalties, since this was still just a civil case.

But what about criminal charges, we wondered, since the cousin's conduct seemed so outrageous.

"Well, the criminal charges are a possibility. But when you have a civil case, you cannot threaten the other side with criminal charges, though they may be all there, as here. However, at some point, the attorney may let the D.A. know, and then the D.A. can decide whether or not to step in."

Would Anne still be involved if that happened?

"Well, I've already done the work to lay the groundwork for what's been going on, and the D.A.'s office will certainly want to know about that. But if the D.A. decides to prosecute and file criminal charges, then his people would do their own investigations too. However, they still would probably use my investigations and I'd probably become a witness."

This involvement of a private investigator as a witness for the D.A. in a criminal case wasn't typical. But then, this wasn't a typical case.

"It just amazes me how this trustee could be so convincing and venal," Anne commented. "And then to think he could get away with all this, too. But then, you sometimes see real evil in this business . . .and real stupidity, too."

Another interesting case started out as a simple eviction by a landlord who owned a few properties. The incident began when an earthquake cracked some pipes in a building. It took several weeks to repair the damage, although otherwise the building had been deemed safe by the city authorities. One of the men in the building not only didn't pay his rent during this time, as did the other tenants, but it turned out he was also making a great deal of noise when he came home late at night and bothering the tenants in other ways. So the landlord lost two other tenants.

"That's when the landlord brought me in," Anne explained," to help them in getting information they could use in pressing the eviction against this man."

But first, Anne gave a general background on eviction cases. "I work a lot of them, and frequently they become very heated, because they involve something so very basic—people's homes. A lot of retaliatory measures can occur both leading up to and after the eviction notice filing."

Anne described a common scenario. "Sometimes a building may lose its gas for awhile, so it becomes very inconvenient for the tenants, such as happened in this case. They can't cook, perhaps they have no hot water, and maybe the situation continues for quite a long time, because the manager of the building can't get a plumber out there. There have even been cases where it may take up to three months to get the problem repaired. And this case happened after the earthquake, which was a time when resources for repairs were already strained anyway.

"Well, what often happens in the meantime is the tenants stop paying their rent. And normally the landlords will let that rent money go when there is a serious problem. They don't go after the tenants for the rent while the problem is going on. But once the gas is turned back on, or the serious problem ends, it's time to start paying the rent again. However, what sometimes happens, as here, is some people find a reason that they shouldn't have to pay the rent, and that's when the landlords bring me in. They want to know a little about the people who aren't paying rent or are otherwise causing trouble. One particular concern is whether these people have a history of filing lawsuits. There are some people who just file lawsuits all the time, usually nuisance suits, and then much of the time the other side pays them off just to get them out of their hair.

"In this case, the landlord had a tenant who had not only stopped paying his rent even after the gas leak was fixed, but also was responsible for the landlord losing two other tenants. He was just a very inconsiderate, aggressive type of person, who didn't care about other people. The landlord sent him an eviction notice, and then the man countersued, saying there was something wrong with his apartment.

"The landlord wanted me to check him out and his complaint as well. In a case like this, the first step is to talk to the city and county departments which set the standards for housing to see if anything is seriously wrong. I spoke to the building inspector normally in charge of these things to find out just how bad the leak was and whether it was a serious health hazard. The inspector said it was only a cosmetic problem, not dangerous, and not causing the man any inconvenience at all. Even though the leak had been triggered by the earthquake, it wasn't a serious problem. The man was just taking advantage of the situation to get out of his rent. It quickly appeared that he had no reason to withhold the rent, though these people who file the lawsuits will get their own attorneys on the slightest excuse and they'll fight because they want the money.

"Anyway, the other key aspect of this type of case is interviewing the other tenants who feel disturbed by this person. I located the ones who left because of him, and then I heard their stories. And they told me some real incredible ones of how this man really went all out in making noise sometimes to get back at people if they complained. For example, one time at two in the morning, when he was moving furniture around and the neighbor asked him to stop, he turned on his stereo full blast for thirty minutes.

Anne pulled out a sheaf of letters from her case file. "Just listen to a couple of letters," she said. "This will show you what this man was really like." She changed the names of the parties involved as she read some brief excerpts: " 'My name is Don Allen, a former tenant who lived there with my wife, Judy. We found the landlord, Nancy Williams, very helpful, and if we had any problems in our unit, which were very few, they were always taken care of very promptly.

" 'We didn't have much contact with the man who lived upstairs, but when we did, he made us feel very uncomfortable. He glared at us when we happened to pass in the hall, and one day later we had an argument about the noise he made. He was coming back from a softball game holding a bat, and for a moment, I thought he was going to hit me with this. So I was very scared. Then, another time I heard him stomping around upstairs, like he was kicking something, and I heard some crashing sound, like dishes being thrown around.

" 'So eventually, we started to feel so uncomfortable with him living upstairs that we decided to move.' "

Letters from the other vacating tenants sounded much the same. "The man on the top floor made us feel very nervous. . . ." "We think the man has some emotional problems."

"So all this helped the landlord in building his case for eviction of the man and in fighting his countersuit," Anne said.

If that wasn't already enough, Anne dug up some background information that revealed the man was a very violent person with a history of fighting.

Background checks can be really important in these cases," Anne commented, "because they show what the person is like: what he's done in the past. For example, maybe the person is a convicted felon, someone with a past record as a troublemaker. Who knows? So you start with the public record, then talk to the family, business contacts, or friends. You see where it goes, and in this case the man turned out to be potentially very dangerous."

Anne flipped through the file for a few moments, thoughtfully pulling together a few documents and reports.

"To start with, he was a man who ran out on his former wife and had assumed another identity ten years earlier. He had used several names. As I discovered from papers I found in the public records, he had never bothered to divorce his wife, and I learned he had taken her for a lot of money before he left.

"And then he fled to another state to get away from it all, and he managed to fade into this other life for many years. He even moved in with another woman for awhile, and he married a third before getting a divorce, while still married to his first wife. So he was really quite strange.

"And the amazing thing about all this is that you start out with what you think is a simple eviction case, but then you discover it can lead you into discovering some very strange things about people and human nature. This business, what you find—it never ceases to amaze."

What happened in this case? What happened to the man?

"The landlord got him out of the building. They won the eviction, the countersuit was dismissed, and that's all they cared about. They never expected to get any back rent from him. They just wanted him out." As Anne observed, "In these kinds of cases, it's always possible to go back and sue in small claims court. But a lot of these tenants like her don't have the money. So after they leave, it's difficult or impossible to find them again. Normally, the landlord is glad they're gone. Which is what occurred in this case."

Then, Anne pulled out another old file that showed still another example of the dark side of human nature. This one was a combination of deception, envy, jealousy, and greed.

"It's one of the worst wrongful termination cases I've ever seen," said Anne. "The heads of the company just decided they didn't like this woman, wanted to get rid of her, and tried to set her up."

Anne described what happened. "I must have spoken to about thirty people in the case, and I found they all supported my client. Basically, what happened was that the company charged her with improper activities with a client. They claimed she had an affair with him, which compromised their dealings with his firm, and so they fired her. But that wasn't the real reason at all. In fact, the man had been trying to date this girl and had a history of going out with women in that company. He kept trying to call my client. He left messages with her secretary trying to get her to join him for dinner. But apart from a few strictly business lunches, there was nothing improper at all.

"But there were a lot of things the company tried to do to my client to insult and humiliate her—I'll call her Nanci. For example, Nanci, who's in her thirties, happens to be a fairly heavy-set woman. One day, one of the managers of the company stopped by Nanci's desk, which was near several other people, and in a very loud voice, began making disparaging remarks about Nanci's weight, suggesting that she might look much better if she lost weight, and recommending she join a diet program the manager was involved in. Well, at the time, Nanci didn't say anything about this.

She just sat quietly and took it. But it's an example of how mean-spirited these people could be. The company wanted her out, and they were trying to get her out in any way they could. And when they couldn't provoke her to leave or do something to get herself fired, they simply set her up with these phony improper-behavior-with-a-client charges."

But why should they want to do all that, we wondered.

"Because," said Anne, "this woman didn't agree with many of the company's policies. For example, the company did things to discriminate against minority groups, such as telling her not to hire a Hispanic or promote a very capable Samoan who worked for her. In addition, she knew that the company did some questionable things with their accounting and production activities to get around state and federal laws, and she spoke to her supervisor about this. The company was afraid of her. Maybe she might say something to others outside the company. At first they suggested she leave; then they tried to make it tough for her so she would do so; and finally, after she had been with the company for more than five years, they fired her based on this alleged affair with a client. She sued them for a few million dollars, and she ended up getting about $250,000. But while the suit was going—on for about three years—the company made it difficult for her. Or at least she thinks it was the company. One night someone broke into her apartment and stole some things; another night, while she and a friend were at the theater, someone knifed her tires. And when she started her own business, it was broken into and trashed a couple of times. So after she left the company, it was very hard for her to go with her life."

Anne closed the file. "So you see," she commented, "some of these civil cases can really end up being dirtier than the criminal ones, because the people are always arguing about money. Often they'll engage in criminal or almost criminal actions to get what they can."

And in this case? Had there been criminal charges or could there be?

"That's up to the D.A.," said Lucy. "They know about the burglary, the slashed tires, and the trashing. But as to who did it—all of that is so hard to prove."

In flipping through her files, Anne quickly skimmed by some

cases on corruption and cases where justice somehow didn't seem to work.

"You really see another side of life in this business," she commented. "And these problems can affect people in all walks of life—from the man on the street to the beat cop, and sometimes, even lawyers and judges."

Anne pointed up an example from a collection case she had handled.

"Collection agencies can be very lucrative. And there are a number of illegal things that an agency can do to increase its profits. But some do it, such as this one, and in this case, we found them out."

What sort of things?

"An agency can play games with the way the payments come in and are posted. They actually collect a whole lot more than they post, and then they don't pay the client the full amount they collected. They pay a much smaller percentage of what they collect by cheating their clients. And we found out, because we were working with a woman who was suing her company, and she gave us facts."

Then, onto another case. This time one that involved complaints against the police in a city in Southern California.

"It was a seemingly routine robbery case, and it took several years to get to a preliminary hearing, which is very unusual. Most take only a few months. But in this case there were dozens of motions about police misconduct, and each one had to be investigated. For example, my client told me he had been beaten up by the police when they caught him on the street, claiming he had run away from the scene of the crime, though he maintained he was just walking on the street and happened to be dressed like the suspect. That allegation had to be checked out. And then the lawyer I was working with filed what is called a Pitchess motion, named after a defendant called Pitchess who complained about the police. Basically this motion allows you to get all the complaints that have been made against the officer in question. Anyway, with all the legal wrangling back and forth, because, of course, the other side did not want to produce all these complaints, it took us about five years to finally get them.

"Meanwhile, the case was dragged out by a blizzard of briefs, legal arguments, and no-shows. Because our client was complaining about police beatings and being set up, and there were quite a few cops involved in the bust, we had to subpoena them many times to come to hearings. Then they wouldn't show up. And then there would be some excuse, like they were on vacation, sick-leave, called out on an emergency, or some other such thing. So much of the time the hearings were just put over. Anyway, we finally won. The motion was granted, the judge had his doubts about the case against my client, the charges were dismissed. But it took a very long long time. It's one of the basic problems of the current criminal justice systems. Things take so long to resolve."

Unfortunately, in working these cases, Anne, like other private investigators, didn't always get much cooperation or interest from the police at times when they could have used it. And sometimes this could create problems in finding someone, even in preventing a shooting, such as in the case of a Persian family that hired her to find their runaway son.

Anne began with some general comments about problems of private eyes and the police. "Though I have a few good friends on the force, in general, private eyes don't get any cooperation from the police. Why? One reason is they don't like it if you're checking out the fact that they didn't do their own job right in some of these cases. Or they think the private eye shouldn't be involved—that the police should be working the case. Or they are just overworked and overwhelmed, and they don't have the time to get involved. So it can be difficult to get them interested."

Anne gave an example of a case where she found evidence proving who killed a young boy for $2,000, after the police had given up and his parents asked her to investigate. "We did everything we could to try to get police attention in going after this guy when we found the evidence, but we couldn't get them interested. They said they didn't feel there was enough of a case. But more probably it was a question of priorities. This was just a small-time killing, probably the result of an unpaid debt in a drug buy or a feud over a girl, and the police have fifty or more homicides to investigate at any one time. And it's hard to get them to resurrect a case that they have previously dropped. They give it a shot in the beginning, but afterward, if they run into dead ends, they can lose interest, and it's hard to bring that back after the fact. They just have too many other things going on."

Anne faced these sort of problems in the runaway kids case. "It was one of these interethnic, interfamily conflicts," she began. "This Persian family hired me to get back their seventeen-year-old son, who had run off with an eighteen-year-old Jewish girl. The kids were very much in love, but the family didn't like it, because the girl was very independent and they didn't like the idea of their son being with a girl of a different faith. The father was really frantic, because this boy was turning eighteen within six months, which meant he would be his own boss. So the family was really desperate to get him back. The boy had run away to stay with the girl once before, though he came back because the kids needed some money. Now he had been gone for about two weeks, and his family was afraid this time it was for good."

The family contacted the police, Anne explained. But after feeling frustrated by police inaction, they came to her.

"Basically, what happened," Anne went on, "was they filed a missing persons report on their son, let's call him Abdul, and on his girlfriend, whom we'll call Linda. When the police didn't have any luck after a few weeks, the father went to another city where he knew the girl had some contacts. The father paid off some people and found a cousin of Linda's who was a kind of new-age healer. She told him where the kids were hiding, living in this kind of hippie community, where a lot of students lived. So he went to the local police and told them about the missing persons report filed in San Francisco and how he had traced his son to this house. The police drove by the house, but they wouldn't go in. They said this was really a private matter, and this looked like a perfectly ordinary house, and they had no real reason to go there. So that's how things were when the family, call them the Saids, came to me.

"At first, I wasn't sure exactly what I could do about this. I wasn't sure what I could say to talk my way in to see if the kids were there. Or even if I did find this boy, how could I get him to come home. But after talking to the missing person's police officer in San Francisco, I discovered there was a warrant for the girl's arrest on some other charge, although I couldn't find out exactly what this was for, because of the confidentiality of juvenile records.

It could be something minor, even a traffic violation, but I thought this might help to get the local police interested in going out to the house again—now with not just a missing person's report, but a warrant, too, and I knew where the girl was supposed to be. But they still weren't interested. There's such a shortage of officers that the police don't go out and pick people up on warrants very often unless there's a real bad crime.

"So I felt like I had hit a dead end with the cops, though I did have a college-age friend who worked part-time as an investigator, and I thought maybe he might have a better chance of getting into the house to make contact with the boy and find out what was really going on."

But first, Anne wanted to go over her plan with the parents, to see if they agreed with this approach, and get a retainer.

"I wanted to explain that we would probably be using surveillance and follow them out of the house, so it might take several days. But we couldn't just go busting in there because there were many people living there, and that might provoke a confrontation. We'd do our best though to get him back.

"And then, the most amazing thing happened. As I was sitting there with the parents, and the father was ready to sign the retainer check, there was a knock at the door. It was Abdul and Linda. They were back to try to get some more money before taking off again. So finally, here's this chance to arrest the girl on the warrant and get back the girl. But can I get the San Francisco police to do it? And can I get out of here without the boy or girl seeing me? If so, if the police can make the arrest now, that could take care of the whole thing, and I wouldn't have to go to the other town and follow the kids around.

"It was like a scene from a movie. While the mother was downstairs talking to the kids in the living room, the father rushed me into the back bedroom, and I hid in the bathroom for a few minutes. Meanwhile, the kids were still in the living room talking. Finally, the mother got them to go into the kitchen, and the father rushed me downstairs out the front door to the garage, and I ran to the police station which is about eight blocks away from the home."

But why did Anne have to go through all this, we wondered. After all, the boy was back at the home. Couldn't the parents have just gotten him back voluntarily now?

Anne shook her head. "No, because Abdul was a very defiant young man, and as long as he was with Linda the parents couldn't hold him there. He was determined not to live there. They just wanted some money, because as I discovered later from the father, Linda was pregnant. Anyway, who knows why he wanted to leave. Maybe conflicts in the home, or he felt his parents' rules were too restrictive. Though the parents couldn't understand it, he liked hanging out with this girl better than staying at home, though he still wanted his parents to help."

What happened? Did Anne get the boy back?

"I went to the police station. And it was really difficult getting them concerned. It was a Saturday afternoon; there were only a few cops in the station; and it was hard to get them very interested, though I explained I was a private investigator, showed them my card, and told them what I was doing. Meanwhile, I was feeling more and more frustrated, as I tried to point out the urgency of acting quickly. There wasn't much time, since the kids wouldn't be at this house very long. But the officer on duty just looking at me like he wasn't sure whether or not to buy my story or whether acting now was really so urgent. Then, finally, he asked me about the warrant. Fortunately, I had the warrant number, and when he punched it into the computer, and he saw this was true, he agreed the police should do something, and said he would arrange to have a patrol car meet me at the corner near the house in ten minutes. 'And please hurry,' I said as I left, 'because the kids are going to leave the house.'"

"So I went to the corner to wait. And ten minutes passes, eleven, twelve. Meanwhile, I'm watching the house which is down the street in the middle of the block, hoping against hope that these kids won't leave."

"Finally, after about fifteen minutes, a patrol car finally pulled up, and the police officer asked me to get in. And again, he wanted to know about the warrant. "How sure are you about it,' he asked me. And I explained about how the police sergeant had punched it into the computer. 'So I'm very very sure about it,' I said. And then I kept telling him, 'Please, please, we've got to go up the block. At least to the middle of the block, so we can see the house. Because they might leave at any time, and we don't know the direction they'll be traveling.

"Just as he was about to start the car, a message came over the radio. There'd been a stabbing in the neighborhood. So he hit the gas and drove up the street. And suddenly, there we were at the house, and I saw the father outside on the ground screaming: 'He stabbed me, my son stabbed me.' And he was pointing north, saying: 'They went that way. They went that way.'"

"Now, finally, the policeman really was excited, and he tore off at eighty miles an hour. As he roared along, the people at the side of the road were pointing too. And then, finally, with another cop car that had joined us, we raced out to the beach. We spotted Abdul's car parked on the side of the road, and he was out there running into the bushes. I jumped out of the car with the police at that point, because I wanted to see what's happening. I felt somewhat responsible because if I could have gotten the cops out there sooner, we could have saved the kid from getting into this fight with his father and using a weapon.

"And then the cops cornered and cuffed him. When the cops asked me if this was the boy I was looking for, I said very sadly, yes, he's the one. The situation was very sad, because Abdul not only had his relationship with the girl broken up, but he's up on charges for the assault, stabbing, car chase, and resisting arrest, and he created a deep rift with his parents. And none of this need have happened if it had been possible to interest the police in the first place."

So in the fifteen minutes or so after Anne left, what had happened at the house to cause this tragedy? Later, from what the police told her, Anne was able to put together the last pieces.

"Apparently, they started arguing about him taking off with this girl again, and when the kids left, his father tried to chase them. He caught him and started punching. That's when the kid stabbed his father, though just in the arm. So in the end, this situation created a real break in this family, and the man didn't get his son back anyway, though he did get him away from his girlfriend."

It was a case that left Anne feeling unnerved. "I just feel it didn't have a very good outcome for anybody. It was one of those things that probably should have been settled by better communication in the family, not getting the police, private investigators, and all these social service agencies involved. And then the man didn't pay me all he had agreed to either. Though I had done all the work he wanted, he said he didn't get back his son, though if anything, it was his fault for hitting the boy that things turned out as they did."

After hearing Anne describe all of these extensive investigations involved in mounting a defense, we wondered about the costs, and was it difficult for the average defendant to afford this.

Anne shook her head sadly. "That's the big problem for the average defendant. The costs of a defense are just astronomical. The really poor ones get taken care of by the Public Defender's Office or a private attorney assigned to the case if the Defender's Office can't handle it because of a conflict. But the average middle class defendant or his family can really go broke. Typically, the good attorney wants about $25,000 or $30,000 to take it to trial, with about $5,000 to $6,000 earmarked for the average investigation. Well, someone from the middle or working class just doesn't have that kind of money."

So what do they do?

"Mortgage their house. Borrow from friends or relatives. A single case, a single slip in life, can be a real disaster. For example, one of my cases now is an assault with a deadly weapon. A guy who got in a fight with another at a beach party, and one thing led to another. And he and his family have no money, and they don't know what they're going to do. It's really sad."

But what about the person who was wrongly accused of something by someone else? After the trial was over and the case dismissed or acquitted, did he have any recourse? Could he get back the money he spent or other damages after the truth came out, such as in the date-rape case described earlier, where the girl had lied and set the man up? Couldn't the person who was put through the agony and expense of a criminal trial have some grounds for suing and collecting from the person who did this?

"Well, maybe in theory they could. But in truth, most people who are involved in something like this are so glad that it's over, they just want to put it behind them. They've spent so much money; the whole thing has been so emotionally exhausting. They just don't want to spend any more time, money, or emotional energy.

"And one of the reasons things are so expensive and so draining," Anne added, "is that the courts are in such a mess. Some things drag on and on, and costs mount up. So it's hard for the middle class to afford a good defense anymore. And then, when it's over, should they win, they just want out."

Since Anne had mentioned the problems with the courts, we wondered if she had to go in there often to testify as a witness about what she had found.

Anne shook her head. "I'm called to testify fairly often, but I don't testify very much. And that's the way it usually is for investigators. It's odd, but what typically happens is the lawyer changes his mind at the last minute or the case is settled or there is a continuance or something else.

"Usually, what occurs is I get a subpoena to show up at a certain time. Many times I've shown up and waited for hours. But then at other times, after I get the subpoena, the lawyer will tell me that I can just wait at home or do something else, as long as I'm available for a call when he needs me. And that's the more usual way, because these cases are so uncertain in the courts. There are delays, continuances. The lawyer never knows how long things are going to take or when exactly he'll need a witness. And if I'm just waiting around idly in court, he has to pay me. So it's better if I can be on call."

We had just a few last questions. Were there any special dangers in probing around for information on criminal matters? (Apart from potentially dangerous areas, such as the projects, which she avoided.)

"Not really," Anne said. "After all, I'm mainly seeking information to help the defendant, so many of the people I speak to are going to want to help. And the people on the other side are the D.A. and his or her investigators, so it's not like I'm walking into a den of thieves with hitmen who are going to try to off me because of the information I'm getting. Any battle against this information will be at court."

However, this didn't mean that the witnesses she spoke to were always necessarily positive and supportive, because sometimes she was trying to interview the victim or friends of the victim.

"And then," Anne commented, "it may be that the D.A. or the

D.A.'s investigators have gotten to the witnesses first, and often tell these people something like: 'This person is going to be around asking questions about the case and you don't have to talk to them.' Well, they're not supposed to say that. They can actually get in trouble for interfering with a witness or victim in a case, if that comes out. But it happens, and if it does, I try to appeal to the witness's fairness and say I just want to know the truth. And then usually he will talk, though the police or their investigators won't. But as for any danger from this process—no, not really. I just make sure that the place where I'm going to meet the person to talk is safe."

Then, very briefly, Anne spoke a little about her experience in serving subpoenas, which sometimes had the potential for being more dangerous than just talking to people in an investigation.

"After all," said Anne, "sometimes you're giving someone who may be very reluctant a notice to appear, though I didn't have any serious problems myself when I did this in my early years in this business. However, an even greater problem than the danger is just being able to find someone sometimes, since some people can be very elusive. They suspect a subpoena is coming, so they hide or try to pretend they are someone else. But early on I got a reputation for being able to serve subpoenas that no one else could serve."

So how did she do this?

"Persistence, creativity," Anne continued. "For example, I would pretend I was doing a flower delivery. I would put on a little apron and have some flowers. And then I would have a little board for people to sign for the flowers. People want to open the door for flowers. And then I'd serve the subpoena too. Or sometimes I'd get their signature to compare it with their signature on other documents. And it wasn't too expensive either. I wouldn't use expensive flowers. Just a bunch of daisies, or maybe I'd pick some flowers from the garden."

Anne paused for a moment thoughtfully. "However, that's one approach I'm not sure I'd use again, because about a year ago, there was a flower bomb in San Francisco."

So what were some of her other strategies?

Anne went on. "Well, once in a while, you have to follow someone to a place where you can serve them. For example, suppose a guy lives behind an iron gate and a long driveway in an expensive community. You can't just go up to the front door and ring the bell. So there have been times I have followed people to gas stations, to a cocktail party or reception where they are expected.

"And it's really ironic about some of these most difficult cases. The harder they are, the more you want to get them done. It's a challenge. But however I do it, I'm always very polite."

And Anne's most difficult challenge?

She thought for a moment. "Well, union officials and the very wealthy are usually quite hard to get to. They have all sorts of people around them to fend off outsiders. But probably the most difficult people to deal with generally are those who try to deny after the fact they have been served, because then you may have to show that you really have served them. For instance, one time, I had to take a picture while a colleague served the papers, so we could prove it, because these people had claimed several times before they weren't served. And then another time, I had some people who tried rolling up their windows as they drove away from a parking lot so I couldn't serve them. But I put it under their windshield wipers, and they tried to slip them off while turning on their wipers, and later, we found the papers in the street a few blocks away. But that counted as a valid serve. They knew what the papers were, and I recognized the people as the people to be served. After all, judges sometimes get very impatient with these people who try to elude being served. But then, at other times, if the judge thinks there wasn't proper service, even though the people got a notice to appear, he will require a service again. You just never know, so you have to be careful to know the laws and do it right, such as filing just the correct affidavit or declaration of due diligence to show you tried when you attempted four times to serve a company president at his office and finally leave the papers with a secretary on the fourth time around."

The interview was almost over, and we had one last question about the effect of this work on her personal life. Like many investigators, Anne described the problems with keeping her work life secret.

"People just have such funny ideas about private eyes, that I often avoid telling people what I do. It's easier to say I work for attorneys or do investigations for them. Because as soon as I say 'private

investigator,' everybody's first question is, 'Oh, do you carry a gun?'
People think you're licensed to go out there and shoot everybody up
like they do on TV. Everybody seems to have something to hide, so
they suddenly become very paranoid around you, especially men in
social situations. It's different when I'm with a cop—they understand
these things a little more. But for many other people, it's really
uncomfortable to feel they're with a private eye."

And perhaps her business may have contributed to Anne remaining single. And it certainly had an effect on many of the men she
dated.

"I sometimes think many of the men I date are intimidated by me.
They see I'm very independent, and I think that bothers them. They
like to feel in control of the relationship. And then, I think many of
them still hold to that tough-guy mystique, and think you must be
tough. Even when you tell them you don't carry a gun, they still
think you do. Or maybe they would like to believe it, because they
have this image of the beautiful blonde on the beach in Maui with
the .38 strapped to her bikini—the kind of *Charlie's Angels* look. So
it's like there's this real ambivalence in men about women in the
business. On the one hand, they'd like you to live up to this romantic image they see in the movies and on TV. But on the other,
they're deathly afraid of it. And the ironic thing is that the image
isn't true.

"Rather, this is a tough business. You have to be both good at
what you do and able to run a small business. And then you run into
all these people who don't understand or would prefer to see you
living this mystique, though they're afraid of it too. It's a real para-
dox," said Anne, and with that, the interview came to an end.

9

Gini Graham Scott: Being a Newcomer in the Business

After spending a few months with Sam Brown talking to private investigators about what they did, I felt I wanted to try again myself. I wondered what it was like to be a newcomer working as an investigator. Besides, this might help others considering entering the field, or becoming part-time investigators, which many people do.

The timing seemed perfect, too, since I was in my last year of law school, taking a course from investigator Hal Lipset. And I needed to investigate someone for the course. I decided to start my investigating with someone I was suing in small claims court. The person—I'll call him Carl Nelson—hadn't paid me for some GLASNOST games he bought for his store. And maybe, I thought, the investigation might help me win my suit!

Like any investigator, I started out with what I had to go on at the time—in this case, my original bill and receipt, which had Nelson's business number, home phone, former address, and his wife's work number. The last was a good thing to have, since Nelson had just been evicted from his former store for not paying the rent, and his own business phone had been turned off. I also had some information from a friend, Ann, who was also suing Nelson for not returning some furniture and dresses she lent him on consignment. The information included a driver's license, a copy of a check he had written to a friend, and a copy of the lease for the store from which he had just been evicted.

I hadn't really thought much about Nelson when I first met him, since my friend had referred him and I thought she had checked him out. He just struck me like the typical gung-ho sell-anything type of salesman. But now, gradually, a different picture began to emerge, as I began to piece together bits of evidence like a puzzle. For one thing, at twenty-nine, he seemed to be a man who moved a lot— three places in just one year—and he had recently gotten married and had a six-month-old baby. While he claimed he couldn't pay us—he owed me about $80 and about $500 to Ann—he lived in a luxury apartment building, plus he had signed a lease and put several thousand dollars down for several large fashion showrooms in an exclusive wholesale center soon going up. Then, too, while he told us for awhile that he was going to declare bankruptcy, he never did, and his promises to go job hunting never occurred. Rather, it seemed like he had just decided to relax and let his wife do the work so he could live off her.

While piecing together such information, through Ann's leads, I began to find other people who had similar experiences in giving Nelson merchandise. Repeatedly, they had called him about what they left on consignment. He never returned their items or they weren't paid. One woman had given him $50 worth of flowers she made to sell, but then she never heard from him again. People who did manage to get their money literally had to fight for it, such as one woman who appeared in Nelson's shop with her big burly husband, who held an inventory sheet showing what had been delivered and what they were picking up. He demanded payment, looking like he could turn Nelson into two pieces if he didn't.

I was amazed as this picture of Nelson as a kind of irresponsible, dishonest, conniving person emerged from this preliminary investigation. Before, I had thought that Nelson was a friend, and we all had trusted him and given him all sorts of things on consignment to help him get his business started. But now we all felt ripped off, especially since he continued to live in his luxury apartment, while claiming he couldn't pay.

"Well, that's the way it sometimes goes in this business," said Sam, when I described what I had discovered. "You're often not investigating the nicest people, and often you start seeing a hidden side of them."

And with that I went on to the next phase of the investigation—checking local public records. This is commonly the bedrock on which many investigations start. Then, what is drawn from these sources can lead you to more places for information, as well as people to interview.

The public records search took Ann and me all over San Francisco to various public buildings. There is no one place to go for everything. In addition, we had arranged for an interview with Nelson's previous landlord, whom Ann had located by driving out to the storefront where Nelson previously had his shop and by asking questions at neighboring stores.

We started off at City Hall in the tax collector's office to check out four addresses from Nelson's various checks, driver's license, order forms, and receipts, so that perhaps we might uncover the names of other landlords. After we gave the clerk the lot and block number, obtained from an hefty book of property records, he fed this information into a computer. In a few moments, it spat out the current owner's name and address, as well as the tax bill, showing whether it was paid. Then, at the tax assessor's office, we double checked on who owned what. It wasn't the most exciting work, doing all this checking, which is why some investigators do such work as a team, but it was necessary, and I was glad Ann was with me to help make the search go faster.

Then, on to the business tax collector, where I filled out a request form, and a few minutes later the clerk was back with information showing that Nelson did in fact have a license, which he had taken out with his wife about two years before. But this year they hadn't paid the bill—another sign of Nelson's failed business.

Next, a trip to the recorder's office, to check out whether Nelson actually owned the property he once bragged of owning. Ann rather doubted that he did, since he had lied to her about so much else. This would tell us for sure. The records were quick to check—three microfiche cards with recent property transfers—since 1990, since 1981, and transfers before then, listed by each individual grantee's or grantor's name, showing who sold the property (the grantor) and who bought it (the grantee). But nothing. Nelson's ownership of anything had, as Ann had suspected, all been a lie.

Then, on to the marriage records, also at the recorder's office. Again, we were provided the records on request, since they are public, and as they sped by on a film disc, we found Nelson's, which provided still more pieces of the puzzle. It showed that he had married his wife a few days before they got their business life together, and before his marriage, he had been just an ordinary office worker in an insurance company, with a few years of college. But then, after the marriage, he suddenly left his regular job to start the business. And very possibly, his wife, who was about ten years older and had a better job as a computer systems supervisor, was the one who contributed the money, or maybe her father did. The assorted bits of data that were filled in on the blanks of the marriage license, like the other bits of data we had obtained from other records, didn't say all this exactly. But they helped to fill in a picture of what might have happened and why. This is what some investigators do as they start to work on a case—gradually develop one or more theories and then continue to compare these with new facts to close in more and more on what is true.

In any case, the facts we had so far helped to create a picture of someone who was young, very ambitious, but naïve about business, and lied to build himself up and help his business grow. But then, when he realized he didn't know what he was doing, things started falling apart. If so, he probably wouldn't have had any serious civil or criminal problems in the past, and so that's what we checked next—the small claims court records, municipal court records, and superior court records, located in different sets of binders and on microfiche in three separate places. We wanted to see if he had been involved as a defendant or plaintiff in any court cases. And for each year we checked—we went back two years, since that's when Nelson had come to San Francisco—we had to look up his name as both a plaintiff and defendant.

It was a tedious process, and I could see how much of the work of an investigator could be this routine, careful fact-checking to pull together the pieces of a subject's life—not the flashy fast-cars image of excitement so often associated with the private eye. Also, I could see the reason why private investigators increasingly are going to computer databases where possible for this kind of routine information. The few minutes to check sure beats hours of trotting from office to office. And yet, despite the slowness and methodical nature of the process, I found it challenging, much like slowly and carefully fitting together the pieces of a jigsaw puzzle, as I wondered if this record or that might provide still another piece.

As it turned out, Nelson had no previous court record in other cases; at least no one else had sued him yet, nor had he sued anyone. My interviews with other people who had dealt with him in the past, though, suggested this situation could soon change. Maybe we were just the first of a long fallout from his business that failed.

Then, after a quick check of birth certificates at the Department of Health, just to be complete, we headed for the federal building to check on recent bankruptcy filings and district criminal court cases, to see if Nelson might perhaps be a defendant. But no, there was nothing there or at the Hall of Justice, which had the criminal records for municipal and superior court.

Meanwhile, as we checked, I felt an odd sense of power and discovery at being able, even though these were public records, to peer into people's past secrets and perhaps hidden parts of their lives. That struck me as a key part of the appeal of being a private eye. It was a little like the same sense of exploring the inner workings of society and people's lives that I felt when I did research as a sociologist or anthropologist, as I had done for many years. There the purpose was to create a kind of general picture of what really happened and why in people's lives to shape the pattern of life in a particular culture or arena of life. Here the focus was on a particular individual. But for me the feeling of curiosity and wonder in exploring was the same.

Then, Ann and I stopped briefly at the State Board of Equalization to see if Nelson had the resale license he was supposed to have for his business. Normally, our search might have taken a little longer, but because of our upcoming court hearing just a few days away, the supervisor intervened and checked the state's list of businesses himself by calling the state capital in Sacramento. A few minutes later, he was back with his report—yes, Nelson had taken out a license; it was back when Nelson opened his first showroom. But now, the supervisor reported, the license had been abandoned, because the business was defunct—which occurred when Nelson was evicted and closed his store. So this was one more bit of evidence that supported our emerging theory.

Then, we drove out to see Nelson's former landlord. On the way, we stopped at Nelson's now deserted storefront. His name was still lettered on the window and his store name was still printed on the blue awning. But inside, the one large room, with plain white walls and an unpainted wooden counter, was bare, except for some bits of left-over ribbon, newspapers, and wrapping paper still on the floor, like New Year's Day remnants. And there in the window was Nelson's eviction notice—both a stark reminder to anyone stopping by about what happened, and a lead to still more information about the case, since it included a court action and sheriff's file number, which would lead to detailed files about the case.

Then, we drove on to the grocery store, a few blocks away. One of the owner's sons who worked as a clerk led us through the store to a large upstairs office. When Mr. Devit, a tall distinguished Indian man of about fifty arrived about a half hour later, he was at first a little hesitant to talk, as people often are with an investigator they have just met. So we helped to set him at ease by describing our own cases. Finally, relaxing a little, he began to talk, though when I asked to take notes, he hesitated, as interviewees sometimes do, feeling uncomfortable having their words recorded. In this case, Mr. Devit seemed to be especially reticent. "I'm afraid of making an enemy of this man. He has hurt me already so much." So I put my notebook aside and concentrated on remembering everything I could, as Mr. Devit related his sad story, which was much like our own, but writ much larger, because Nelson had told him even bigger lies and he had lost much more.

"And he seemed so sincere and believable, in the beginning," Mr. Devit told us. "He claimed he was involved in some kind of manufacturing business and owned some property in the area. And he kept pleading with me about how much he wanted the place, so I finally agreed and turned down someone else. After all, he seemed like such an impressive young man. Someone who had done so much, and at such an early age. He even gave me a financial statement showing how well he was doing. But later I learned that none of this was true. He even made up the statement, and he didn't own the stocks, securities or properties he claimed. No wonder he seemed to be doing so well at his age—he made it all up."

Unfortunately, Mr. Devit had believed him at first, because Nelson's $5,000 checks for the first month's rent and security were good. But then, when the next month's payment came due, Nelson kept trying to postpone making it.

"He even claimed the earthquake had damaged some of his property, so wouldn't I be understanding," Mr. Devit said. "But then it turned out he didn't own any of this property."

At first, Mr. Devit went along, trusting Nelson's assurances. But after weeks and weeks of this, he finally gave up and filed for the eviction, letting his lawyer handle the matter.

"And even then he kept lying," Mr. Devit added. "And he acted so crazy. Which is why I am so afraid."

Mr. Devit explained. "Well, first, during the proceedings, he called the court to say he couldn't attend the hearing because there were threats against his life. And then a woman called, I think his wife, who asked me: 'Why are you threatening us?' But of course I wasn't, and I told her, 'Why should I do such a thing,' and hung up. But the call unnerved me.

"Then, at the court hearing, the bailiff said that Mr. Nelson had called to say he couldn't come because of the threats, and the judge told me Nelson had written him a letter in which he said he hadn't signed the lease and had given me the next month's rent, $2,100 in cash? But of course that wasn't true. I saw him sign the lease myself. And who would pay $2,100 in cash? So the judge did not believe him, and I won the eviction, plus past rent due.

"Yet, I still have collected none of it. And the place is still unrented. And I am quite afraid. He seems like such a dangerous man. I want nothing to do with him. So far, this has cost me so much, and I just want him out of my life."

Finally, the interview over, we asked Mr. Devit for a copy of his eviction notice, to help show Nelson's past pattern of failing to pay others in court. And then we said goodbye.

I felt sorry for him as we left. He seemed so defeated and bewildered by what had happened.

But later, when we stopped by Sam's office to report on the results of our investigation, Sam told me that it was important to avoid getting emotionally involved in these investigations.

"You'll sometimes meet a lot of hurt and pained people," he said. "It's a regular part of the work, because you're so often investigating because someone has caused someone else hurt or misery. But if you let it get to you, it can wear you down. It's like someone working in an emergency ward or a cop on the street. You've got to learn to shield your emotions and not pick up other people's pain. That helps to do the work."

Then, I described how we had spent hours going to so many places to check records. Sam then pointed out how such public records searches might be useful to get some of the latest information not yet on computer or some details not generally included in computerized records. However, we could have also saved a great deal of time by doing an on-line computer search, which is the growing trend in the industry for the first phase of an investigation. Still, there was a trade-off as Sam explained. For while the process might save time, it could be very costly, because on-line information is sometimes very expensive.

But in this case, the computer wouldn't have helped, because after we did the computer check, there was no public record for the categories we checked.

"Well, that sometimes happens," Sam observed. "Sometimes a computer can help, though at other times it can't, since every case is different, and the relevant information doesn't always get picked up in the computer files. So the computer is just one tool in an investigation."

And with that, the investigation was almost over. There were just a few last pieces I hoped to get—namely the phone numbers of the landlords at previous places Nelson had lived or of nearby neighbors who might have had some bad experiences with him not paying too. I tried using the phone directory and various criss-cross directories which list phone numbers by addresses. But none of the numbers were there, and Sam discouraged a computer search as being too difficult and expensive for a small claims case, because these were unlisted numbers, not in the usual directories.

I felt disappointed, since I had hoped this first investigation could be complete. But Sam consoled me, explaining:

"Look, you did just fine. What you found is the reality of a typical investigation. Not every investigation can be complete. An investigator doesn't always find everything, and there are often budget restrictions. You can only investigate as far as the budget goes, so you set priorities. You try to investigate what is most important and do as much as you can."

The investigation ended, we just had to prepare its results for court, as might an attorney who had hired an investigator. So I gathered together the assorted tax records, statements, eviction notice, and copies of other information into a logical sequence for presentation in court.

But unfortunately, when it came time to present my case, the judge only wanted to hear just the specifics related to my business arrangement with Nelson. He didn't care about the landlord who evicted Nelson or all the other witnesses who had been cheated, which I was hoping to use to increase the penalties and damages Nelson should pay. Since Nelson agreed he did owe me $80, that was all the judge thought he needed to hear, and on to the next case.

Eventually, as it turned out I did win my case—exactly the $80 that Nelson admitted in court, though I wondered about the usefulness of all the investigation we had done. Apart from my own interest in doing this just to experience what an investigator might do in a case, was all this effort worth it?

"Sure," Sam reassured me. "In any case, as an investigator, you want to do as complete a job as you can. And even if you weren't able to use this information in this case, you just never know till you come to court what the judge will do. Sometimes you can get the information in; sometimes you can't. Sometimes it will make a difference. Sometimes it won't. But since you never know, you want to be prepared.